DON'T BE A JERK

Also by Brad Warner

Hardcore Zen

Sex, Sin, and Zen

Sit Down and Shut Up

There Is No God and He Is Always with You

Zen Wrapped in Karma Dipped in Chocolate

DON'T BE A JERK

And Other Practical Advice from Dōgen, Japan's Greatest Zen Master

A Radical but Reverent Paraphrasing of Dōgen's
Treasury of the True Dharma Eye

BRAD WARNER

New World Library
Novato, California

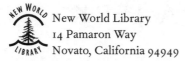 New World Library
14 Pamaron Way
Novato, California 94949

Text design by Tona Pearce Myers

Library of Congress Cataloging-in-Publication Data
Names: Warner, Brad, author.
Title: Don't be a jerk and other practical advice from Dogen, Japan's
  greatest Zen master : a radical but reverent paraphrasing of Dogen's
  Treasury of the true dharma eye / Brad Warner.
Description: Novato, CA : New World Library, 2016.
Identifiers: LCCN 2015050026 | ISBN 9781608683888
Subjects: LCSH: Sōtōshū—Doctrines. | Dōgen, 1200–1253. Shōbō genzō.
Classification: LCC BQ9449.D657 W37 2016 | DDC 294.3/85—dc23
LC record available at http://lccn.loc.gov/2015050026

First printing, April 2016
ISBN 978-1-60868-388-8
Ebook ISBN 978-1-60868-389-5
Printed in Canada on 100% postconsumer-waste recycled paper

 New World Library is proud to be a Gold Certified Environmentally Responsible Publisher. Publisher certification awarded by Green Press Initiative. www.greenpressinitiative.org

10   9   8   7   6   5   4   3

CONTENTS

INTRODUCTION

IT USED TO be that nobody outside the worlds of stuffy academics and nerdy Zen studies knew who Dōgen was. And while this thirteenth-century Japanese Zen master and writer is still not one of the best-known philosophers on the planet, he's well-known enough to have a character on the popular American TV series *Lost* named after him and to get referenced regularly in books and discussions of the world's most important philosophical thinkers.

Unfortunately, in spite of all this, Dōgen still tends to be presented either as an inscrutable Oriental speaking in riddles and rhymes or as an insufferable intellectual making clever allusions to books you're too dumb to have heard of. Nobody wants to read a guy like that.

You could argue that Dōgen really is these things. Sometimes. But he's a lot more than that. When you work with him for a while, you start to see that he's actually a pretty straightforward, no-nonsense guy. It's hard to see that, though, because his world and ours are so very different.

A few months ago, my friend Whitney and I were at Atomic City Comics in Philadelphia. There I found *The War That Time Forgot*, a collection of DC comics from the fifties about American soldiers who battle living dinosaurs on a tropical island during World War II, and

Whitney found a book called *God Is Disappointed in You*, by Mark Russell. The latter was far more influential in the formation of this book.

The publishers of that book, Top Shelf Publications, describe *God Is Disappointed in You* as being "for people who would like to read the Bible...if it would just cut to the chase." In this book, Russell has summarized the entire Christian Bible in his own words, skipping over repetitive passages and generally making each book far more concise and straightforward than any existing translation. He livens up his prose with a funny, irreverent attitude that is nonetheless respectful to its source material. If you want to know what's in the Bible but can't deal with actually reading the whole darned thing, it's a very good way to begin.

After she'd been reading *God Is Disappointed in You* for a while, Whitney showed it to me and suggested I try to do the same thing with *Shōbōgenzō: The Treasury of the True Dharma Eye*. This eight-hundred-year-old classic, written by the Japanese monk Eihei Dōgen, expounds on and explains the philosophical basis for one of the largest and most influential sects of Zen Buddhism. It's one of the great classics of philosophical literature, revered by people all over the world. However, like many revered philosophical classics, it's rarely read, even by those who claim to love it.

I immediately thought it was a cool idea to try to do this with *Shōbōgenzō*, but I didn't know if it would work. I've studied *Shōbōgenzō* for around thirty years, much of that time under the tutelage of Gudo Wafu Nishijima. Nishijima Roshi was my ordaining teacher, and he, along with his student Chodo Mike Cross, produced a highly respected English translation that was for many years the only full English translation available. I had already written one book about *Shōbōgenzō*, called *Sit Down and Shut Up* (New World Library, 2007), and had referenced *Shōbōgenzō* extensively in all five of my other books about Zen practice.

My attitude toward *Shōbōgenzō* is somewhat like Mark Russell's attitude toward the Bible. I deeply respect the book and its author, Dōgen. But I don't look at it the way a religious person regards a holy book. Zen Buddhism is not a religion, however much it sometimes looks like one. There are no holy books in Zen, especially the kind of Zen that Dōgen taught. In Dōgen's view everything is sacred, and to single out one specific thing, like a book or a city or a person, as being more sacred than anything else is a huge mistake. So the idea of rewriting Dōgen's masterwork didn't feel at all blasphemous or heretical to me.

But *Shōbōgenzō* presents a whole set of challenges Russell didn't face with the Bible. The biggest one is that the Bible is mainly a collection of narrative stories. What Russell did, for the most part, was to summarize those stories while skipping over much of the philosophizing that occurs within them. *Shōbōgenzō*, on the other hand, has just a few narrative storytelling sections, and these are usually very short. It's mostly philosophy. This meant that I'd have to deal extensively with the kind of material Russell generally skipped over.

Still, it was such an interesting idea that I figured I'd give it a try. My idea was to present the reader with everything important in *Shōbōgenzō*. I didn't summarize every single line. But I have tried to give a sense of every paragraph of the book without leaving anything significant out. While I'd caution you not to quote this book and attribute it to Dōgen, I have tried to produce a book wherein you could conceivably do so without too much fear of being told by someone, "That's not really what Dōgen said!" Obviously, if a line mentions Twinkies or zombies or beer, you'll know I've done a bit of liberal paraphrasing. I have noted these instances, though, so that shouldn't be too much of a problem.

In a sense, with this book I am following a time-honored tradition of misquoting Dōgen. When the first teachers of Soto Zen Buddhism showed up in America and Europe, there were not yet any translations of Dōgen in English or other European languages. So these teachers would just quote things from memory and translate them into English or French or whatever other foreign-to-them language they were attempting to communicate in on the fly.

Several well-known examples of this occur in the book *Zen Mind, Beginner's Mind* by Shunryu Suzuki. That book was compiled from transcripts of lectures Suzuki Roshi, who was then head of the San Francisco Zen Center, gave in the late 1960s. In it he quotes Dōgen a number of times, but most of these quotations are wrong.

For example, he has Dōgen saying, "Life is one continuous mistake." It's a great line, and lots of people — including me — have attributed it to Dōgen ever since. But when some folks at San Francisco Zen Center tried to trace that quote, nobody could find it. The nearest anyone has found is in the book *Eihei Koroku* (Dōgen's *Extensive Record*) in which Dōgen says, "There is the principle of the Way that we must make one mistake after another" and elsewhere he says, "Making mistakes, we make more mistakes."

As far as I'm concerned, though, Suzuki's Dōgen quotations are all close enough for rock and roll. He understood the meaning of Dōgen's words, even if he hadn't memorized them. Some people even say that Dōgen's own famous line, from his teacher Tendo Nyojo, about "dropping off body and mind" may be a misquote. Those words never appear in any of the existing transcripts of talks by Tendo Nyojo made by his Chinese disciples. However, this is perfectly fine. Buddhism is basically an oral tradition, not a religion based on a book. The meaning behind the words is far more important than the specific words used to convey that meaning. The way human beings tend to misremember what they've heard is actually part of the Zen tradition.

In any case, this is definitely *not* a new translation of *Shōbōgenzō*. We are lucky to be living in a time when several of those are available, with more on the way, so there's no reason for me to add to that pile. Instead, what I offer here is a sense of what I get when I read *Shōbōgenzō*.

The *Shōbōgenzō* proper consists of ninety-five chapters. Apparently Dōgen originally planned to write a hundred, but he died before he could write the final five. In this book I have paraphrased the first twenty-one chapters, although in two cases I combined chapters that are two-parters in the original into single chapters, so you end up getting nineteen paraphrased chapters, plus I give you "Fukanzazengi" as a bonus, which is often included in *Shōbōgenzō* translations as an appendix. These twenty-one chapters constitute volume one of the Nishijima/Cross translation. Nishijima and Cross followed the now-established tradition of organizing their *Shōbōgenzō* translation chronologically, with Dōgen's earliest dated writings first and his undated writings at the end. I haven't started work on volume 2 yet. This was a bear of a book to put together, and I want to see how it goes with this one before diving in again. That means volume 2 may be up to you, dear reader. If you like this one, let me know (especially by buying it!).

When I posted a few lines from this book on the Interwebs to see what sort of reaction they got, people immediately demanded to know what Dōgen "really" said, either in the form of a standard translation or in the original Japanese. So I anticipate that readers of this book will want the same. In many cases I have given alternate translations, or even Dōgen's actual Japanese. But if I did that for the whole book, the workload would've been too much, and the book itself would have been ginormous. Instead, I've put a bibliography at the end that includes the translations and Japanese versions I used. You'll have to look up the lines I haven't given alternate versions of for yourself, I'm afraid.

That being said, I really didn't want this to be a book full of those kinds of fake Buddha quotes people are constantly sending each other on Facebook, only to be told that Buddha never really said those things. So I've been pretty careful with my paraphrasing. I relied mainly on my teacher's translation of *Shōbōgenzō*. That edition is extremely useful because it has copious footnotes. Most lines, phrases, and words that could be translated very differently are noted, with the original Japanese. I also kept Kazuaki Tanahashi's translation at hand to double-check anything I had doubts about. If I still wasn't certain, I'd go to the original thirteenth-century Japanese text, which Nishijima Roshi provides in his twelve-volume translation of *Shōbōgenzō* into modern Japanese. Finally, I kept one eye on the Soto Zen Text Project's translation of *Shōbōgenzō*, which is currently incomplete and only available online, and another on the Shasta Abbey translation, which tends to be kind of florid in its language but doesn't stray too far from the original meaning. I also consulted the translation by Kōsen Nishiyama and John Stevens frequently, as well as the partial translations by Norman Waddell, Masao Abe, and Thomas Cleary; I consulted several other partial translations too.

As I said earlier, I studied and practiced the *Shōbōgenzō* in Japan with Gudo Wafu Nishijima for around two decades and before that did another decade of study and practice with an American teacher named Tim McCarthy. When I say, I "studied and practiced the *Shōbōgenzō*," I mean that I not only studied the text but also tried to put its lessons into practice in the traditional way.

I never entered a monastery as a full-time live-in monk, which many people consider the only way to practice what Dōgen preached. But this would ignore the fact that Dōgen taught a number of lay students throughout his life and, indeed, recommended zazen as a daily practice not only for those who live in monasteries but also to anyone interested in self-discovery. During those decades, I did zazen every day, attended a whole lot of Zen retreats, and read *Shōbōgenzō* numerous times by myself, besides listening to hundreds of Nishijima's lectures about it. I also read as much of the scholarship about Dōgen as I could handle, being a guy who is generally more drawn to works like *The War That Time Forgot*.

My teacher Nishijima Roshi was mostly a self-made scholar of *Shōbōgenzō*. He first came across the work in a used bookstore when he was in his teens. He said that it intrigued him because even though it was written in his own language, he couldn't understand it at all. And yet, like a lot of us, he could feel that although the book was opaque and hard to comprehend, it appeared to have a logic and power all its own. As weird as some of its passages are, it never seems like the ravings of a madman. Rather, it appears to be the work of someone who has touched a very profound truth and is struggling to put that truth into words that others can understand.

Later on Nishijima studied with Kodo Sawaki, the legendary "homeless monk" who never kept a temple of his own (until he was very old, anyway) and instead traveled all over Japan, leading retreats for interested laypeople. Sawaki was also a Dōgen scholar and professor at Komazawa University, which was founded by the Soto sect, the organization that traces their roots back to the temple Dōgen founded in the thirteenth century.

Nishijima devoted his life to studying *Shōbōgenzō*. The footnotes he added to his translations show the incredible breadth of his study. Every obscure old text Dōgen referenced, Nishijima looked up and read. Every name Dōgen mentions, Nishijima traces and gives you a brief history of the person. The translation he produced has yet to be equaled in its thorough scholarship, even though technically it's the work of an amateur, since he was never a professor of Dōgen studies or anything like that (he worked in finance most of his life).

For most readers, the biggest single obstacle in Dōgen's writing is his use of contradictions. He constantly tells you something is one way and then a few sentences or even a couple of words later tells you it's the exact opposite way. This violates one of the cardinal rules of logic. Aristotle said, "One cannot say of something that it is and that it is not in the same respect and at the same time." But Dōgen does that all over the place!

Nishijima Roshi's way of explaining this was to say that Dōgen adopted four points of view when talking about any given topic. These four points of view were (1) idealism/subjectivism, (2) materialism/objectivism, (3) action, and (4) realism, which synthesizes the other three. We can look at any topic through these four lenses, and it will appear quite different through each one. Often the same thing can look so different, depending on how you look at it, that it appears to be its own opposite.

Our Western philosophical tradition is generally confined to the first two of these points of view. Our religions are spiritual, which in most cases is a synonym for idealistic. Here I'm not using the word *idealistic* to mean that one has ideals in the sense of principles, morals, and ethics and sticks to them, or as in *idealism*, used almost like a synonym for *optimism*. I mean instead that religions take the stance that the spiritual side of our experience — the world of ideas and meanings and inner, subjective reality — is more real than the material side.

Science, on the other hand, is materialistic. It concerns itself only with physical matter and measurable energy and ignores or at least marginalizes the subjective world of ideas and spirituality. No matter what belief system you have, paper always burns at 425° F (218° C). No matter what religion you are, the speed of light as measured by a stationary observer is the same. More radical versions of materialism take the stance that our subjective/spiritual sense is negligible or even destructive. This can lead people to adopt the more common form of materialism, which says that the best way to live is to get as much money, social prestige, and power as possible: he who dies with the most toys wins.

In the nineteenth century, materialism became the dominant philosophical stance throughout the Western world. Sure, idealistic religions continued to exist. But science worked. It gave us more and better food, flush toilets in every home, lightbulbs, telephones, TVs, the Internet. But in the twentieth century it also gave us the atomic bomb, high-tech death camps, runaway pollution, and global climate change.

Some people urged a return to the spirituality of the past as a solution to all this. On September 11, 2001, a small group of religious fanatics tried to force us to turn back. But they failed miserably and at great cost. We know too much about the workings of the material world ever to deny what we have collectively learned. One of the great absurdities of our time is people denouncing science on the Internet. They might not be consciously aware of the irony of that, but subconsciously they know they're wrong and that scares them. People who are scared can be dangerous, and that's a serious problem. This is why Dōgen is so important today. Those who want us to return to spirituality are as dangerous as those who support a purely materialistic outlook.

Although Dōgen wrote *Shōbōgenzō* between 1227 and 1253 CE, it took hundreds of years before it became widely read. For almost six hundred years the book was all but forgotten. Even in Japanese monasteries that followed the Zen tradition he established, Dōgen's writings were rarely read. Yet his style of practice became hugely successful, even as his philosophical works lapsed into almost total obscurity. In the eighteenth century a few Japanese scholars began rediscovering his writings. But it wasn't until the twentieth century that Dōgen began to be widely read outside the scholarly community.

I once asked Nishijima Roshi why he thought that was. He said he believed it was because Dōgen was so far ahead of his time that very few people in his own day could understand him. For instance, he doesn't use modern psychological terminology, but anyone familiar with psychology can see clearly that he is talking about psychological concepts. To take just one example, he frequently writes of the subconscious, an idea that wouldn't be widely understood in Western society for centuries. Nishijima Roshi said that when we read Dōgen today we can follow his ideas in ways people of Dōgen's time were unable to.

We need Dōgen today — desperately. His philosophy offers us a way out of our continuing battles between the idealistic and the materialistic view. He offers us a Middle Way. We do not have to choose between science and religion. Dōgen offers us a sensible approach we can use to live with the inherent contradictions between these two outlooks. His philosophy is more relevant now than ever before.

I hope this book will make Dōgen accessible to people who aren't Zen nerds or scholars of ancient Buddhist philosophy. After all, Dōgen was not writing for an audience full of people with PhDs in Buddhist studies. He was writing for ordinary people like us. Dōgen himself was very scholarly, but his monks and the laypeople who attended his talks weren't a bunch of brainiac intellectuals. They were mostly rough-and-ready country folk who, though they were often bright and curious, were not very educated or worldly.

Unfortunately, up until very recently you had to have a vast education in classical Buddhism and ancient Asian languages to even read Dōgen at all. We owe a great debt to the scholars who did the hard work of making Dōgen accessible to Western people steeped in Buddhist lore. But I feel like the time is right to present Dōgen to everybody else.

I hope this is an enjoyable and interesting book that helps you look at things a little differently. I hope it gives you some laughs. I also hope a few of you take up meditation after reading it, because it's a really great thing to do.

Have fun!

1. DŌGEN'S ZEN FAQ
Bendowa
A Talk about Pursuing the Truth

MOST CONTEMPORARY EDITIONS of *Shōbōgenzō* begin with "Bendowa." The title consists of three Chinese characters that mean "endeavor," "way," and "talk." So a very direct and clunky translation would be "(A) Talk (on the) Endeavor (of the) Way." Kazuaki Tanahashi calls it "On the Endeavor of the Way," and Kosho Uchiyama calls it "The Wholehearted Way." My teacher Gudo Nishijima translates it as "A Talk about Practicing Zazen." When you read the piece it's clear that the *way* Dōgen is talking about *endeavoring* in here is the practice of zazen. So Nishijima Roshi took the liberty of just saying that outright, even though Dōgen was a bit cagey on the subject.

Some people with too much time on their hands debate whether "Bendowa" actually belongs in *Shōbōgenzō*. Since Dōgen himself died before he could compile a complete edition he was satisfied with, we'll never know. But we do know that he titled many of his pieces with the word *Shōbōgenzō* first and then the individual title of the fascicle (a fancy word for *chapter* — you knew that, but the first time I saw the word *fascicle* I thought it was the name of a naughty body part or something). However, "Bendowa" is not called "Shōbōgenzō Bendowa," so many experts say that "Bendowa" was meant as a separate piece.

On the other hand, it is stylistically very much like the other

1

Shōbōgenzō pieces and serves well as an introduction since it sets the stage for much of the rest of the book. That's why it was added to the edition published in the 1600s as chapter 1. It remains there in most editions today.

The chapter consists of a brief statement about how great zazen is, followed by a very short autobiography of Dōgen, followed by a section often called "Jijuyu Zanmai," or "the Samadhi of Receiving and Using the Self." It then concludes with a kind of FAQ (frequently asked questions) section about zazen, which is the longest part of the piece.

Regarding that second section, the word *samadhi* tends to be translated as a kind of trance or special state of consciousness. Even in Dōgen's day it was thought of that way. But Dōgen doesn't use the word like that. Here we get the first inklings of how he redefines the term. He tells us that zazen is our gateway to this state but makes it clear that the state is not something we achieve by doing zazen. Rather, zazen *is* this state itself, whether or not we know it.

We'll talk more at the end.

The Buddhas and Buddhist ancestors had a brilliant way of figuring out what the real deal was with the universe. They transmitted this method all the way down to our time. This method is the *samadhi* of receiving and using the self.

The truth is everywhere all around us, but if we don't practice, it doesn't show itself and we can't experience it. When we let go of reality our hands are filled with it and when we shut up about reality our mouths are filled with it. In zazen we practice the oneness of reality. But is all the stuff I just got done saying even relevant to such a state?

I started practicing Buddhism and doing zazen when I was about twelve years old. A few years later I met a master named Myozen at a temple called Kennin. Myozen was the only person who ever really understood what his teacher Eisai taught. Myozen and Eisai were part of the Rinzai lineage in Zen.

In my twenties, I traveled to China and studied with some really good teachers from a bunch of lineages. But finally I settled on a teacher named Tendo Nyojo (Ch. Tiantong Rujing, or sometimes Ju-ching, depending on who you consult, 1163–1228 CE). While I was with Tendo Nyojo I was able to complete the great task of Buddhist study.

I came back to Japan determined to tell folks about Buddhism and do the whole "save all beings" thing. This was 1227, when I was twenty-seven years old. But I felt like it was too much to deal with on my own, and that maybe Japan just wasn't ready for the kind of straight-up Bud-dhism I'd learned in China from Tendo Nyojo. So I figured I'd just kinda be a Zen hippie and wander around for a while, you know, like a cloud or whatever.

Then I thought about it some more. I figured that if there were just a few people who could get what I was saying it would be a shame for me not to make it available. So in order to do that I figured I'd compile a record of the teachings I'd heard and the customs I'd practiced at temples in China.

How about I start by giving you a brief outline of the history of Buddhism? Gautama Buddha became enlightened and transmitted the dharma to Maha Kashyapa. Many years later Bodhidharma brought Buddhism to China. Bodhidharma's disciple Taiso Eka (Ch. Dazu Huike, 487–593 CE) transmitted it to Daikan Eno (Ch. Daijan Huineng, 638–713 CE), who showed the Chinese that Buddhism wasn't about intellectual explanations but about real practice.

Daikan Eno had two really good students. These were Master Nan-gaku Ejo (Ch. Nanyue Huairang, 677–744 CE) and Master Seigen Gyoshi (Ch. Qingyuan Xingsi, 660–740 CE). Following Ejo and Gyoshi, Chinese Buddhism split into five lineages, which are the Hogen sect, the Igyo sect, the Unmon sect, the Soto sect, and the Rinzai sect. Of these only the Rinzai sect was widely influential in my time in China. Most of the temples I visited were part of this lineage.

Even though there are differences among these sects, they all rely on the one posture that carries the stamp of Gautama Buddha's mind. In other words, all these sects focus on sitting down and shutting up; they all practice zazen.

Until Bodhidharma came to China nobody there understood Bud-dhism. But after Bodhidharma showed them the practice of zazen, everything was clear. I hope the same thing will happen in Japan.

*Every Buddhist ancestor has practiced upright sitting in the midst of the *samadhi* of receiving and using the self. Every single person who followed the Way in India and China did this stuff. So that's what they taught people.

Real Buddhists all say that zazen is the best thing ever. From the first time you learn it from a teacher, you never need to burn incense, do prostrations, recite Buddha's name, or read sutras anymore. Just sit and get the state that's free of body and mind.

If one person sits zazen, being right in body, speech, and mind for just one moment, the whole universe enters this state. Every living thing becomes clear in body and mind at the same time, and they all experience the greatest freedom. It makes all Buddhas increase the joy surging up from the original source and renews their enlightenment. Every being everywhere together realizes themselves and experiences enlightenment.

Anyone who practices zazen enters directly into this state and receives the imperceptible mutual assistance of all things in the entire universe. Everybody shares in the benefits thus produced.

The perception of those individuals who practice zazen never interferes with the reality of zazen. It doesn't matter if you notice all this wonderfulness or not. This is because in the quietness, with nothing to accomplish, there is only direct experience. This realization takes place in the stillness of the self-receiving and self-using *samadhi* (in Japanese this is called *jijuyo zanmai*, hence the name of this section) and doesn't disturb so much as a single speck of dust.

If we were to divide zazen into two parts, practice and experience, we could consider each part separately. We could say that we practice in order to achieve enlightenment. But your perceptions cannot be the standard of enlightenment, because deluded human sentiment cannot reach the standard of enlightenment. Basically, you cannot know your own enlightenment because whatever you call enlightenment can't be enlightenment.

The experience of zazen is eternal. It's the same for everyone. We

---

* Here's where the section that some call "Jijuyu Zanmai" starts.

touch the deepest experience of all human beings throughout history when we allow ourselves to be truly quiet.

If all the countless Buddhas throughout space and time used all their infinite Buddha wisdom to try to calculate the merit of one person sitting zazen, they couldn't even come close.

Let's answer a few FAQs about Zen practice.

FAQ 1: I've told you all about how great zazen is, but maybe some doofus[*] might ask, "There are lots of ways to get into Buddhism; how come you're only talking about zazen?"

I say it's because zazen is the authentic way into Buddhist practice.

FAQ 2: "How come you say it's the authentic way?"

My answer is that Gautama Buddha himself taught zazen. Every other master after him in India and China got whatever realization they had from doing zazen. So I'm gonna promote zazen here in Japan.

FAQ 3: "It's too darned difficult for a regular guy like me to try to follow in the footsteps of Buddha! Chanting sutras and reciting the names of the Buddhas might naturally lead to enlightenment. But just sitting around not doing anything — how is that supposed to lead to enlightenment?"

It is super-ridiculous to imagine that reading sutras and chanting is going to lead to enlightenment if you don't actually meditate. You'd have to be in some kind of stoned stupor even to ask such a thing. People who only chant sutras are no better than frogs croaking in a pond. You should either get serious about meditation or just give up the game. Remember the story in the Lotus Sutra in which the Buddha tells a bunch of haters they should just go home instead of hanging around, causing his sincere students trouble? Get a clue from that.

Listen. How about you just set aside your doubts and check out some zazen for yourself?

––––––––––––––

[*] Dōgen really does characterize this question as coming from an ignorant or stupid person.

FAQ 4: "There are a lot of other kinds of Buddhism than yours, Dōgen! The guys over at the Shingon Temple say, 'The mind here and now is Buddha.' They say you don't need to meditate for a long time like you're telling us! In their school they say you can reach enlightenment right now! What's so cool about this process you're recommending? It sounds pretty wack to me!"

I don't want to cast aspersions on other forms of Buddhism, but we need to look at their practices and decide for ourselves if they're right. Lots of people get the truth in lots of ways. This is because the whole universal truth is present in every single speck of dust. It's everywhere.

Expressions like "the mind here and now is Buddha" are like reflections in a mirror, and we shouldn't get caught up in the words. The reason I recommend zazen is that it is the practice of immediate realization and direct experience of the truth. So take that, Shingon sect!

When we're looking for a teacher we should look for someone who has experienced the ultimate state, not some scholar who just counts words. That would be like the blind leading the blind. Whoever comes to me for instruction, even if it's someone who follows another religion, I'll teach that person zazen.

It's true that a core Buddhist teaching is that from the beginning we have never been without the supreme truth. But we get all caught up in the random secretions of our own brains and end up missing what's right in front of our faces.

Even though we can learn something about the insights of ancient masters by reading sutras about them, we only really need to just practice the method and the posture done by Gautama Buddha, and we can forget about everything else. If we do so we can leap beyond the bounds of delusion and enlightenment and stroll with leisure in the real world that exists outside any fixed criteria. There's no comparison between someone who has their own real experience and someone who just reads about the experiences of others.

FAQ 5: "There are loads of other Buddhist practices, Dōgen! Zazen is just one of them. So how come you say all of Buddha's teachings are contained in this one practice?"

You're only asking this because people have named the true

essential teachings of Buddhism the "Zen sect." This term was never used in ancient India. It was invented by the Chinese. This is because some dumbasses who encountered Bodhidharma and his followers thought he was a kind of Hindu who practiced a thing called zazen. Then they dropped the *za* part and started calling them the Zen sect. *Za* means "to sit" and *zen* is a Japanese pronunciation of the Chinese word *chan*, which is their pronunciation of the Sanskrit word *dhyana*, meaning "meditation."

But what the Buddha actually taught was zazen. This was transmitted to us by his authentic successors. Zazen is the complete path and the whole truth of Buddhism.

FAQ 6: "You can walk, you can stand, you can sit, and you can lie down. Isn't all that Buddhist practice too? Why are you so hung up on just sitting, Dōgen?"

Buddhists of the past have entered the state of experience in lots of ways. But we should remember that zazen is something all of them have done, even if they might have done other practices too. So we can conclude that sitting is the most reliable, stable, and enjoyable method.

FAQ 7: "Okay. Fine. Maybe some newbie can get something out of doing zazen. But what about someone who already has lots of experience? What are they gonna get out of it?"

Sigh! Even though we shouldn't tell our dreams to idiots or give oars to a mountaineer, nonetheless I will try my best to answer your dopey question.

First off, only non-Buddhists make a distinction between practice and experience. Because there is no such distinction, a newbie's zazen is exactly the same as that done by a person who's practiced for many years. This is why the ancient masters said not to expect any experience outside of practice. Experience is endless and beginningless.

I saw with my own eyes zazen halls in China that could seat hundreds or even thousands of people. These days China is the world's most advanced civilization, and Japan is a little backwater nation nobody much cares about.

When I asked my teacher Tendo Nyojo what the most important

Buddhist principle was, he said that it was the idea that practice and experience were one and the same. That is, you don't do zazen in order to achieve some result like enlightenment in the future. Zazen itself, he said, is enlightenment.

Master Nangaku Ejo said, "I do not deny that there is practice and experience, but they can never be divided." Even after we've attained the truth we still ought to keep practicing. So-called enlightenment experiences are not a finishing line.

FAQ 8: "Other guys before you have gone to China and brought Buddhist teachings back to Japan. How come they didn't say the same things as you?"

I say it's because the time was not yet right for those guys.

FAQ 9: "Okay, then, did those guys understand the universal teaching you claim to have received?"

Look. If they had understood it, they would have taught it. Right?

FAQ 10: "I once heard some kind of spiritual guy — maybe he was a Buddhist — say there's no reason to be scared of dying. All you gotta do, he said, is realize that the body is just a temporary material covering for your true eternal spiritual self. When your body dies, your true self gets reborn into another body. Once you understand this, after your body dies your spirit gets reborn in the spirit world, where it knows everything. So what use is it to sit and stare at walls? Isn't this what Buddha taught?"

This is not what the Buddha taught at all. Only a real dumbhead would think this idea is Buddhism. Buddhism teaches that body and mind are not separate things. The Buddhist schools that discuss eternity or permanence see all things as eternal and permanent, and the Buddhist schools that discuss emptiness or cessation see all things — both physical/material and mental/spiritual — as empty or temporary. None of the Buddhist schools ever divides the world into a permanent spiritual side and an impermanent material side.

You should understand that human daily life is, in itself, nirvana. If we think that Buddhism is about understanding that mind/spirit is eternal while body/matter is temporary and that Buddhist wisdom is separate from birth and death, even this thought is itself ephemeral and fleeting. Pretty ironic, eh?

Buddhism teaches that the nature of mind totally includes all forms. This means that nothing — not the material world or even nirvana — lacks the nature of mind. All entities can be considered together as just one undivided mind. This mind is not something separate from matter. So how could we perversely divide this oneness into body/matter on one side and mind/spirit on the other, or into life/death, as opposed to nirvana? Don't listen to the words of weirdos who spout baloney about the eternal spirit and the temporary body.

FAQ 11: "So does a person who practices zazen have to keep the moral precepts of Buddhism?"

Keeping the precepts and observing pure moral conduct is the habit of Buddhists. But even those who haven't formally received the precepts or have broken them can benefit from doing zazen.

FAQ 12: "Does it mess up your zazen practice if you also practice other stuff like chanting mantras or doing vipassana (analytical intro-spection)?"

My teachers in China told me they had never heard of any authentic master combining those kinds of practices with zazen. Unless you completely devote yourself to one practice, you'll never really master it.

FAQ 13: "I heard that only home-leavers (male and female Buddhist monks) should do zazen. What do you say to that, Dōgen?"

According to Gautama Buddha, men and women, nobles and commoners, are not distinguished from one another. Everybody can do zazen.

FAQ 14: "All right. That's cool. But monks have left the workaday world behind and have no hindrances in practice. How can a busy person like me with a real job and a family ever single-mindedly pursue Buddhist practice?"

Gautama Buddha left us a very wide and great gate of mercy in the practice of zazen, which allows literally everybody to enter. For example, there were several Chinese political officials who, in spite of the long hours they had to work, nonetheless also devoted a portion of each day to zazen practice.

In China people of military clans and civilian families still find time to practice zazen. The gods in heaven protect any country where people practice zazen and grant them a peaceful society, with a stable form of government.

When the Buddha was alive, even criminals and those who held mistaken views practiced with him and attained the truth. Among the later Buddhist patriarchs were woodcutters and huntsmen. So for now just seek the teaching of an authentic master.

FAQ 15: "But aren't we living in the Age of Decline predicted in the ancient sutras? How can we be expected to practice in such an awful time?"

Even though scholars of ancient texts talk about various ages in which the Buddha's teaching is supposed to flourish and then decline, I don't believe any of that stuff. Everyone can attain the Way through practice. We receive and use the treasure that is ourselves. A person who actually practices zazen can tell if they're in the state of real experience, just like you can tell if water is warm or cold by putting your hand in it.

FAQ 16: "If it's true that 'mind here and now is Buddha,' as the sutras say, then even if we don't read sutras, or chant, or practice zazen we can have confidence that our Buddhism lacks nothing. We're all enlightened anyway, right? So why should we waste time meditating?"

This is a pretty dumb thing to say. If we could attain the truth just by being told we're already Buddhas, then why hasn't everyone who ever heard such a thing been enlightened? Gautama Buddha wouldn't have taken the trouble to expound his teachings if it were that easy. Here's a story to illustrate this point.

Once a monk named Soku (Ch. Xuanze, dates unknown) was leaving the temple when Master Hogen Bun-eki (Ch. Fayan Wenyi, 885—958 CE) asked him, "How long have you been my student?"

The monk said, "Three years."

The master said, "You're a new guy here. How come you never ask me any questions?"

The monk said, "I won't lie. Before I came here I was at another temple, and while I was there I attained enlightenment."

The master asked, "With what words did you enter this state?"

The monk said, "I asked my teacher just what is this monk that I call myself. He said, 'The brothers of fire come looking for fire.'"

The master said, "Nice words. But I don't think you really got it."

The monk said, "I understood that he meant I was looking for myself when I already was myself."

The master said, "Now I'm sure you didn't get it! If it was like that there wouldn't be any Buddhism at all!"

The monk got all mad and flustered and immediately left the monastery. But on his way out he thought, "This master is well respected all over the country. Maybe he's got a point." He went back to the master and asked, "Just what is this monk I call myself?"

The master said, "The brothers of fire come looking for fire."

Upon hearing these words the monk understood the Buddhist teachings perfectly.

If the intellectual idea that we ourselves are already Buddhas were the teachings of Buddhism, the master wouldn't have admonished the monk. So, from our very first meeting with a master we should single-mindedly do zazen. Then our practice will not be a waste of time. Which would be good, since it takes so long.

FAQ 17: "I've heard a lot of stories about how different Buddhist masters got enlightened. Like, Buddha was supposedly enlightened when he saw the morning star. Another guy got enlightened when he heard a pebble hit a bamboo stalk, and another guy got enlightened looking at some flowers. Some people got enlightened just by hearing a single word or sentence. Did those people all do zazen?"

You should know that these people had no divided consciousness when these things happened and no intellectual doubts about pursuing the truth. It wasn't these external triggers that somehow produced their enlightenment.

FAQ 18: "China is the center of civilization. Over there everyone understands Buddhism really quickly. But here in Japan our whole country is just a bunch of stupid barbarians. How can a bunch of dim-witted apes like us ever hope to understand Buddhism, much less practice zazen?"

I agree that Japan is a pretty backward country. But even in advanced countries there are backward people, and vice versa. A lot of supposedly stupid people in the past were nevertheless able to attain enlightenment.

Buddhism has been around only for about two thousand years now. It has traveled into many countries, some of which were just as much rural backwaters as Japan. But the teachings of Buddhism are already damned good to begin with. So when the time comes it will spread, even in backward countries. All human beings have the seeds of deep wisdom. It's just that in Japan only a few of us have been struck by the experience of profound truth.

That ends the FAQ section. It is my intention to lay out the teachings I heard in China on paper as well as the various rules and practices I observed in the temples over there for Japanese people who are interested.

We Japanese are fortunate that some people brought Buddhist teachings over from China a few hundred years ago. But we're still confused about what it all means. Even though this is so, we can practice zazen in our country. If people want to learn how to do zazen I have already written a handy guide called *The Universal Guide to Zazen*.

Maybe it'd be more proper if I waited for some kind of official decree or royal permission to teach Buddhism, but I just can't hang on that long.* It's not always a good thing to wait for favorable circumstances, since you never know when or even if those will come. Shall we just consider today to be the starting point?

To this end I have written this piece so that true students who want to experience Buddhism in practice will have a guide.

— Composed August 15, 1231, by the monk Dōgen,
who received the dharma in China

* I've dealt with Japanese bureaucracy myself, and I can tell you he's right!

This is one of the most popular pieces of Dōgen's writing. There are a lot of translations, and there are whole books devoted to explaining it. Let's talk about a little of it, shall we?

In the autobiography section Dōgen mentions Eisai, the first Zen teacher he encountered. In his other writings Dōgen says that what impressed him about Eisai was his realistic attitude. When Dōgen was fourteen, he became troubled by the insistence of the teachers of the Tendai sect, with whom he was studying Buddhism, that everyone and everything is perfect as they are. Why then, he asked, do we need to practice at all? Nobody could answer him. Later he heard that a master named Eisai had said, "I don't know about Buddhas of the past or future. But I know that cats and cows exist." I understand that probably just sounds kind of weird. But what it means is that Eisai wasn't interested in abstract philosophy but in practical, real-world matters.

Unfortunately Eisai probably died before Dōgen could actually meet him. Dōgen's writings are unclear on this point. Some scholars today think it's possible that teenage Dōgen might have attended a lecture or two of Esai's. But it's fairly certain that they never really talked to each other since Dōgen was just a kid when Eisai died.

However, Dōgen did study with Eisai's successor, Myozen. He considered Myozen to be the only one of Eisai's students who ever really understood Eisai. Myozen and Dōgen traveled together to China. But Myozen died during that trip, and it became Dōgen's sad duty to transport his teacher's remains back home.

After this autobiographical stuff we get to one of the most important sections of "Bendowa." The "Jijuyu Zanmai," or "The Samadhi of Receiving and Using the Self," section is not actually set off in the original text. I added a footnote there to let you know where it was because these days lots of people do treat it as a separate piece.

This bit of "Bendowa" is chanted in many Zen temples during sesshins, which are periods of zazen lasting several days to a week. It actually ought to be pronounced "Jijuyo," but in most Japanese Soto temples these days they insist on mispronouncing this as Jijuyu Zanmai.

If you look at the Chinese characters used to spell it out you can see for yourself it's 自受用三昧 (*jijuyō ʒanmai*). The characters break down to "self," "receive," "use," and "samadhi."

The last character is always pronounced *yō*, except in this special case and maybe a small handful of others. I asked a number of people why this was, but nobody knew the answer. My friend Yuto, abbot of Yuuin-ji Temple, said it's like the way Americans say "way da go" instead of "way to go."

In the sentence that I've rendered as, "In the authentic transmission of Buddhism it is said that zazen is the best thing ever," the word *ʒaʒen* doesn't occur in the original. Dōgen actually says 仏法 (*buppo*), which means "Buddhist dharma" or "Buddhist method." I think it's clear in context that he means zazen, so that's the word I used.

Dōgen says, "From the first time you learn (zazen) from a teacher, you never need to burn incense, do prostrations, recite Buddha's name, or read sutras anymore. Just sit and get the state that's free of body and mind." But check out chapter 25 of this volume, and you'll find Dōgen's detailed instructions about burning incense, doing prostrations, and chanting sutras. I'll talk about this more extensively in that chapter. But suffice it to say, in spite of what he writes here, Dōgen did these ceremonial things in the temples that he founded. So he is not saying that you shouldn't do this stuff at all. He's just saying that zazen is the supreme form of practice and that the other things are quite different matters altogether.

Part of what he's probably doing with this line is trying to counter a couple of very popular movements that were just getting off the ground in Japan back then. One was started by his contemporary Shinran (1173–1263 CE) who founded the Jodo Shinshu movement. This movement said that people in the so-called Degenerate Age of Buddhism, which supposedly started around 1000 or 1500 CE, couldn't possibly attain enlightenment. However, if they chanted the name of Amida Buddha, then after they died they'd be reborn in the Pure Land in the Western Heavens, which Amida had prepared for them. There, in that much more favorable environment, they could get enlightened. Nichiren (1222–1282 CE), another contemporary of Dōgen, founded a similar movement in which his followers chanted "Homage to the Lotus Sutra" (*namu yoho renge kyō*) for similar reasons.

We don't know for certain that Dōgen had these particular movements in mind, specifically since they were so new. However, this kind of thinking was becoming trendy in Japanese Buddhism. Many people were searching for easier ways to realization than the tedium and difficulty of sitting and facing yourself for long stretches of time, as the Buddha and his followers did. Lots of people today propose the same thing, including one famous American Zen master who claims to have discovered a special process that'll give you a true enlightenment experience in about an hour. There's also an app for your iPhone that its makers claim can give you an hour's worth of meditation in just twelve minutes. But Dōgen called BS on that kind of crap.

The bit that says, "The perception of those individuals who practice zazen never interferes with the reality of zazen. It doesn't matter if you notice all this wonderfulness or not" is most often translated as something like, "But that which is associated with perceptions cannot be the standard of enlightenment because deluded human sentiment cannot reach the standard of enlightenment." This part always makes me smile, but not because of the text itself. When I was sitting a sesshin at a temple in the forests of southern Minnesota we chanted "Jijuyu Zanmai" every day in the usual Japanese style, a kind of robotic monotone. Whenever we got to the line I just quoted I had to stop myself from laughing because when we all chanted "de-lu-ded hu-man sen-ti-ment" in a robotic monotone it sounded like the Daleks from *Doctor Who*.

By the way, Dōgen's praise for the wonders of zazen in this section goes on waaaayyy longer than what I've given you here. It's really beautiful and there are quite a few very good translations available in a number of books and online. I encourage you to check them out.

It's interesting to me how similar Dōgen's eight-hundred-year-old

FAQ is to the kinds of questions I receive via email and at talks all the time here in the twenty-first century. It's particularly striking that the Japanese people of Dōgen's time complained of their supposed natural inability to meditate, as compared to the Chinese and Indians. This is exactly the same kind of nonsense Westerners today complain about when they say that as non-Asians they can't possibly meditate the way the Japanese can. It's such a good excuse for not making the effort that it's lasted for centuries and even crossed continents! The excuse of being too busy has lasted for hundreds of years too.

Also in this chapter you start to get a feel for how snarky Dōgen could be. He really doesn't pull any punches and even gets kind of nasty. All the parts where I have Dōgen calling his hypothetical interviewer's questions stupid or where I have him even belittling her/him for asking such dopey things are right there in the original text. I didn't add them myself to try to be funny or punk. Dōgen really wrote it that way.

It's frankly a somewhat off-putting approach, and in later writings Dōgen generally tones down some of this aggressive stuff. Though he also gets even meaner in a few of his later pieces. So watch out!

I tend to think of this as coming from youthful overenthusiasm and the sense of urgency he must have felt about getting his message across. After all, he was just thirty-one when he composed "Bendowa" and was writing about a grand adventure he'd had when he was in his teens and twenties. He'd had some very profound experiences in his meditation, revelations of the deepest truths of the universe. But he was still a young man with strong convictions and a burning need to convey them.

In his history of Buddhism, Dōgen mentions Maha Kashyapa and Bodhidharma. Both are almost definitely based on historical people. But these days scholars doubt a lot of what has been traditionally said about them. Stephen Batchelor, in his book *Confessions of a Buddhist Atheist*, posits that Maha Kashyapa may have been more of a savvy organizer who managed to hold the group together after Buddha died than the deeply enlightened master the tradition portrays him as. We'll probably never know the real story.

As for Bodhidharma, it appears there might have been more than one Buddhist teacher with that name and more than one teacher who brought Buddhism to China. The stories of all these individuals appear to have been combined into a single narrative later on. Dōgen doesn't say anything about this. Either he didn't know or he didn't consider it important. Given how well-read he was about Buddhism, I tend to think he knew or at least suspected this but just didn't care. The traditional story works well enough for most uses, so why complicate it?

The philosophical position Dōgen takes in much of this piece is somewhat like the Yogacara school of Buddhism, which Western scholars sometimes call the "Mind Only School." But Western scholars, as well as a number of Asian scholars, misunderstand Yogacara as espousing some kind of what they call "radical idealism." They think it's saying that all things are *in the mind*, that the material world doesn't exist, that only the mental/spiritual world is real, but that's not what he's saying at all.

Dōgen talks about this in other chapters. The short version is that this idea of all things having the nature of mind means that mind/spirit and body/matter are undivided. The separation we believe exists between the two is an illusion. All things are alive and have mind, including what we call inanimate objects. In *The Power of Myth* Joseph Campbell says, "There is a plant consciousness, there is an animal consciousness, and we share all of these things. I begin to feel more and more that the whole world is conscious..... When you live in the woods, as I did as a kid, you can see all these different consciousness[es] at work with themselves...the whole planet [is] an organism. And if you think of ourselves as coming out of the earth, rather than have being thrown in here from somewhere else, we are the Earth, we are the consciousness of the Earth. These are the eyes of the Earth. And this is the voice of the Earth. What else?" Same idea.

This is not the same thing as the idealistic or spiritual view that says mind or spirit or consciousness is either the only reality or at least the most important and fundamental aspect of reality. Rather, he is saying that mind is an aspect of all things. We can't divide the universe into a spiritual or mental realm on one side and a physical, material realm on the other. Mind and matter are an undivided unity.

Philosophers and religious thinkers in the West and the East have struggled with the so-called mind-body problem for as long as philosophies and religions have existed. Although Eastern philosophy is often referred to as monist in contrast to dualistic Western philosophy, dualistic and materialistic philosophies have always been a part of Eastern thought.

There is a massive amount of literature on this subject, but it is not the purpose of this book is to provide a detailed twenty-first-century argument to convince contemporary readers that Dōgen is correct. I want only to present what Dōgen said as clearly as I can. These days one could attempt to test this view by doing complicated high-tech experiments on the human brain. Lots of people are working on this sort of thing. In Dōgen's time, such research was impossible. But that doesn't mean that Dōgen's view is based on mere speculation. He did do research — on himself, using the zendo as his laboratory. People who haven't engaged in the practice tend to imagine that this is pretty much the same thing as speculating. It isn't.

Since he talks so much about zazen in this chapter, let's take the next chapter to look at what zazen is, according to Dōgen's definition.

2. HOW TO SIT DOWN AND SHUT UP
Fukanzazengi
The Universal Guide to the Standard Method of Zazen

LIKE "BENDOWA," "FUKANZAZENGI," or "The Universal Guide to the Standard Method of Zazen," isn't really part of *Shōbōgenzō*. But it's so much like the other parts of *Shōbōgenzō* that many editions these days include it as an appendix.

Carl Bielefeldt wrote a book called *Dōgen's Manuals of Zen Meditation* all about "Fukanzazengi" and its origins and history. If you want to know that stuff in tremendous detail, I highly recommend it. In that book Bielefeldt says that "Fukanzazengi" first appeared as part of certain editions of *Dōgen's Extensive Record* (*Eihei Kōroku*). Then after people had gotten used to that version, a different, apparently earlier version of "Fukanzazengi" was discovered in the twentieth century.

Dōgen seems to have written "Fukanzazengi" at the request of certain Japanese students of his who lamented that no brief instruction manual on zazen existed in Japanese at the time. This traditional assumption is based on the reference Dōgen makes to "Fukanzazengi" at the end of "Bendowa," as well as to another little note in Dōgen's handwriting saying he composed a work with that title at the request of his students.

In spite of the fact that "Fukanzazengi" doesn't even belong in *Shōbōgenzō*, I'm making it chapter 2 of this book because it contains a lot of information that is significant to the rest of *Shōbōgenzō*. Specifically, it contains Dōgen's instructions for how to practice zazen. Since the entire book is ultimately about practicing zazen, you really need to know what he's talking about right from the outset, or you're going to be lost later on.

One of the most important messages of this chapter is that zazen is a physical practice as much as it a mental one. He calls it the "vigorous road of getting the body out." I'll talk a bit more about that particular line later. It seems that in Dōgen's time, just like in ours, people thought meditation was something that happened in the mind and that what you did with your body while meditating was arbitrary or unimportant.

But Dōgen spends most of this chapter describing in detail the physical practice of zazen and comparatively little describing what to do mentally. When I teach zazen I often tell people that it's kind of like a yoga class where there is only one posture and you hold it for a very long time. Let's see how Dōgen puts it.

When you investigate it, the truth is everywhere, so why do we need to rely on practicing meditation and experiencing realization? The dharma vehicle is sitting in our driveway all gassed up and ready to go; why should we make a big effort? The whole body is fresh out of a nice hot shower; why would anyone need to scrub or shampoo? We never stray from the right path, so why even bother training?

Yet even if there is the slightest discrepancy we lose our minds in confusion. If we think we're totally enlightened, that's just evidence that we're stuck in our own heads and have lost the vigorous method of getting the body out.

Gautama Buddha and Bodhidharma did zazen, as did all the great masters of our tradition. Why should we think we can do without it? We should stop chasing words, take a step backward, and turn our light inward. This will cause body and mind to drop away so that our original face can appear. If you want to attain *it* then just start doing *it*.

A quiet room is best for zazen. We shouldn't eat or drink too much, or too little. Put aside everything else. Don't think of good or bad. Don't judge your practice. Stop ruminating and deliberating about stuff. Don't try to become a Buddha.

Put a thick mat (called a *zabuton* in Japanese) on the floor and a round cushion (called a *zafu* in Japanese) on top of that.

Full lotus postition

Sit in the lotus or half-lotus posture. For the full-lotus, put your right foot on your left thigh and your left foot on your right thigh. For the half-lotus just press your left foot into your right thigh. Put your right hand over your left foot, facing palm-up, and place the left hand on the right palm. Your thumbs should meet and form a little circle near your belly button.*

Sit up straight, not leaning to the right or left or inclining forward or backward. Your ears should be in line with your shoulders and your nose with your belly button. In other words, make your spine straight. Keep your mouth shut and your eyes open.

Breathe softly through the nose. Once you've settled into your posture, sway a little to the left and right to find your balance point. After you've got that, think the thought of not-thinking. This is totally not the same as thinking. Try it and see! This is the essential secret of zazen.

Zazen is not meditation or concentration. Zazen is the peaceful and joyful gate to the dharma. The whole universe opens up to you. If you do it this way you'll be like a geek at a comic book convention or like Luke Skywalker when he hit the thermal exhaust port. Then the dharma will manifest before you and darkness and distraction will vanish like the Death Star blowing up.

Stand up slowly after you get done with your zazen.

Some Zen masters in the past have attained enlightenment upon hearing a flagpole fall down or upon hearing someone shouting at

---

* I think it's easier to look at a drawing, so I've provided one. Other arrangements of the legs are acceptable, but if you can manage the full- or half-lotus or at least the Burmese posture, it makes the rest of the practice easier. I'll talk about that later too.

them, and others attained it in different circumstances. We can't really understand these events intellectually. They are standards of action that exist prior to recognition.

It doesn't matter if you're smart or dumb. Anyone can pursue this way, regardless of intelligence.

Every master before us has done this practice. So even though those masters may be different from us, we can certainly do it too. Why should we wander aimlessly through dusty foreign lands (as did the son of the king who forgot he was a prince in the story told in the Lotus Sutra) when the truth is right here?

It is very difficult to attain a human body.* We should use this rare opportunity to concentrate on what's most important. We shouldn't waste time with fleeting pleasures like watching reruns of *The Flintstones*.** Life is short, snuffed out in an instant, over in a flash. Get to work now.

There is an old story about a guy who collected Godzilla action figures, but when the real Godzilla came to visit him he ran away. We shouldn't be like that, just reading stories about other people who've done zazen but not doing it ourselves.

If we practice long enough the treasure house will open naturally and we'll be able to use its contents as we like.

I don't really want to add anything to "Fukanzazengi." I like it just the way it is. Dōgen says all there is to say. But here goes anyhow.

Of course Dōgen didn't really say that the dharma vehicle was all gassed up. But he did say the essential vehicle (宗乗 *shōjō*) is self-existent (自在 *jizai*), so why do we need spiritual improvement (功夫 *kufū*)? Those last two characters are also the same Chinese characters for kung fu, but I'm pretty sure he didn't mean, "Why do we need kung fu?" Nor did he say anything about hot showers or shampoo. But he

---

* It was thought that it was better to be born as a human than even to be born as a god or deva because gods and devas had it so good they never had the will to pursue the truth.

** See explanation on the facing page.

did say that the body (全体 *zentai*) is free from dust and dirt (塵埃 *jin-nai*) and that sweeping and polishing (払拭 *fusshiki*) were unnecessary.

And of course Dōgen did not say anything about watching reruns of *The Flintstones*. What he did say is usually translated as, "Who would take wasteful delight in the spark from a flint stone?" But I have never once been able to read or chant that without thinking of Fred and Barney. Now you won't be able to either. I guess people in his day thought that watching sparks fly off flint stones was a cool thing to do. They had not yet invented *World of Warcraft*.

The thing about geeks and comic conventions and Luke and the thermal exhaust port was originally a dragon finding water and a tiger in its mountain stronghold — basically examples of animals/people/things and the places where they live/belong/are comfortable. Luke hitting the thermal exhaust port is an image implying a bit more of a "woooo-hoooo!" vibe than I wanted, but I couldn't resist it. Thanks to Joseph Naeem and James Hansen for those examples, by the way.

The Nishijima/Cross translation of the last line in the opening section concludes, "What use are the tiptoes of training?" This has always mystified me since the Nishijima/Cross version is so close to the original, yet all the other translations have something different here — different both from Nishijima/Cross and from each other. I can only assume that *tiptoes* must be Nishijima and Cross's translation of 脚頭 (*ashi-atama*), which literally means "foot-head." Many other translators take this odd character combination to mean something like "wandering around." It's a combination not used in modern Japanese, in which つま先 (*tsumasaki*) is the word for "tiptoes," or Chinese, in which 脚尖 *jiaojin* (literally "foot-point') is the word for "tiptoes." Everyone seems to be just guessing what Dōgen's weird character combination means.

Another place the Nishijima/Cross translation differs from all the others I've seen is the line I've paraphrased as "we're stuck in our own heads and have lost the vigorous road of getting the body out." The thing about "getting the body out" is the Nishijima/Cross translation of the word 出身 (*shushin*) that appears in this line. In modern Japanese this word means "birthplace." But it literally means "depart-body." Most other translators take it to mean something like "total emancipation" (as in Waddell/Abe and the Stanford Soto Zen Text Project) or "absolute way" (as in Yokoi/Victoria) or "living way to salvation" (as in Masunaga Reiho). Only Nishijima/Cross takes it as a reference to the body. And yet I think they're right. For one thing the character for *body* is right there. Also much of the rest of the piece deals with the physical practice of zazen and very little with the kind of enlightenment experiences that phrases like *total emancipation* suggest.

Dōgen talks a bit in the piece about *zafus* and *zabutons*. These days you can find all sorts of meditation supplies online or at your local Zen center or yoga shop. But if you don't want to pay for that stuff you can just make do with things around the house. When I started practicing I was a poor college student who played in punk-rock bands. I couldn't afford no fancy-schmancy meditation cushions! I sat on rolled-up towels and couch cushions for a long time before I invested in an official *zafu*. I still don't have a *zabuton*.

I've noticed that Americans get particularly upset about the part of the instructions where he talks about the full- and half-lotus postures. We have very strong ideas about equality, and we hate anything that excludes somebody because of things they can't help, like tight muscles that won't allow them to get their knees down to the floor or perhaps debilitating physical conditions that make these postures impossible.

In my travels, I've found that people who actually have such conditions but who really want to practice in spite of them can always find a work-around. I've never met anyone who needed such a work-around who got very upset about Dōgen's failure to write about such work-arounds. The ones who get most upset are always those who don't really need them but would like to see themselves as advocates of those who do. They're never advocating for anyone specific, by the way, just hypothetical people. When I hear from people like this I tend to think it might be more effective just to concern oneself with one's own practice instead.

Moving right along, what are we to make of all that "dropping off body and mind" business? According to a story that was probably made up by a later biographer, Dōgen's own awakening was triggered by hearing his teacher Tendo Nyojo tell another student to drop off body and mind. Dōgen himself never says it happened quite like this. But it's clear from his writing that this phrase, which he attributes to Tendo Nyojo, was really important to him. My teacher Nishijima Roshi liked to explain dropping off body and mind as the process of entering a state that is neither too spiritual nor too materialistic, neither too sharply focused nor too fuzzy and lazy.

A little bit after talking about dropping body and mind, Dōgen says, "Zazen is not learning meditation or concentration." The word he uses is 習禅 (shū-ʒen), which means something like "learning meditation." In other parts of this book, I've sometimes chosen to use the word *meditation* as a synonym for ʒaʒen. That makes the prose flow a bit easier and makes use of a term most folks are more familiar with than ʒaʒen. But it's not quite right. Meditation generally has an object, a goal. Zazen does not. That's what Dōgen means here. His zazen is to be done completely without a goal.

Whenever the subject of goalless practice comes up, there's always some smart-ass in the room who says, "If your goal is to have no goal then you still have a goal! HA!" This sounds like a reasonable argument, but actually it's not. If you really, concretely work with the goal of having no goal, you'll see for yourself that it's very different in practice from working toward a goal in the more common way.

Then there's that bit about thinking the thought of not-thinking. This is one of those parts some people like to discuss endlessly. It comes from a dialogue between Master Yakusan Igen (Ch. Yaoshan Weiyan, 745–827 CE) and an unknown disciple. Yakusan tells the disciple to think the thought of not-thinking. The disciple asks him what that means and Yakusan says, "It's utterly different from thinking."

Dōgen then quickly moves on without elaborating further. I believe that's significant. If he'd wanted to explain it more thoroughly, he would have, as he often did explain such things. I believe he wanted his readers — us — to work the meaning out for ourselves in actual practice.

But in terms of linguistics, when Yakusan talks to his student he first uses a word he made up: *fushiryo* (不思料). The *shiryo* part of this word is better translated as "consideration" than "thinking." The kind of thought he's referring to is the deliberate pondering of things and not the kind of random stream of images that comes into our heads for no clear reason. So you're not trying to make your mind a complete blank. You're just trying not to play with your thought the way your mom probably told you not to play with your down-there bits. The *fu* part is a denial, like the prefix *non* in English.

When the disciple asks what that means, Yakusan uses another made-up word, *hishiryo* (非思料). The *hi* prefix (pronounced like "he" as in "he and she," not like "hi" as in "hi there") is a stronger denial. It's kind of like the *il* in illegal or the *im* in immoral. It has a stronger negative feel to it. But that's just linguistics.

"Thinking not-thinking" is kind of like having the goal of being goalless. Semantically you can say the goal of being goalless is still a goal and the thought of not-thinking is still a thought. But in actual practice you make your goal not to have a goal, and it works. Same with thinking of not-thinking. You just kind of set your mind on not pondering or considering your thoughts. You don't actually have to work all that hard. You don't have to battle your own thoughts and try to tame them.

When thoughts come, don't try to stop or suppress them. Just allow them to pass away naturally. Some take longer to fade than others, but all thoughts will always fade given enough time, especially if you can learn to avoid the temptation to feed into them or play with them.

For me, thinking the thought of not-thinking means to aim for a state that transcends thought. Transcending thought is not as hard as it might sound. Each time I get caught up in thought, I adjust my posture. I have never once found myself caught up in thought and not had my posture go subtly (or sometimes not so subtly) wrong. The body follows the mind.

Once I've adjusted my posture, I continue until the next time I get caught in a thought. And then I do it again. And again. And again. You get the idea.

When I was in Munich, Germany, a little while ago, my friend Annette, who was hosting me there, took me to a river called Eisbach, which means "Ice Brook." There's a bridge over the river under which there is a standing wave, owing to some kind of concrete thing under the water. People like to surf that wave. As I stood there watching the surfers stay on for a little while and then fall off, I thought about Dōgen's advice about thinking the thought of not-thinking.

No matter how good those surfers were, nobody could stay on that wave for more than about a minute. Even though it was about as predictable as a wave could possibly be, it was still a vibrant, living thing. When those surfers crashed after a minute or so, they didn't waste a lot of time beating themselves up for not staying on for five or ten minutes. Everyone knows that simply can't be done. They crash and then they get right back on the wave again.

For me, zazen is kind of the same. I ride my nonthought for as long as I can, then I crash and get right back on it again. How long I stay there depends on factors beyond my control. It depends on what's been going on for me that day or that week, how much I've eaten, how much sleep I've gotten, what the person next to me smells like, and an endless list of other factors I can't do anything about. In zazen we are not trying to establish control of our thoughts. That's an illusion anyway. Just stay upright as long as you can, crash as you inevitably must, and get back on again.

Dōgen then says not to think good or bad. In other words, don't judge your practice. Our judgments about our meditation are no more valid than any other random thought that drifts through our brains.

People always get worried about whether they're doing zazen right. But basically if you're doing it at all, you're probably doing it right — even if your thoughts won't stop, even if you're sleepy or irritable, even if it just feels boring.

After a while you get better at this. But I don't think anyone ever perfects it so much that they never get caught in thought sometimes. Even Gautama Buddha spoke of the "temptations of Mara" right up till the end of his life. Mara is a Satan-like figure from early Buddhism who supposedly appeared to Buddha on the night of his enlightenment and offered him all kinds of cool stuff, if he'd just give up meditating. It's very similar to the story of Christ's temptation in the desert. I don't think Buddha was being tempted by demons. He was talking about how his own mind could still lead him astray sometimes, in spite of his enlightenment.

Dōgen describes this process as "taking the backward step and turning our light inward." So it's an introspective practice. We are shining a light into ourselves to see what's in there. Let's talk about that a little.

One funny thing about zazen is that, unlike most other forms of meditation, we keep our eyes open. This is a way of acknowledging the outside world as part of our practice and as a part of us. If we close our eyes and shut out the outside world, we get a little unbalanced. We can start to believe that what we are is limited to that which is enveloped in what Dōgen likes to call our "skin bag." Or, conversely, the lack of visual input leads us deeper into the world of our own fantasies and abstractions. By opening our eyes, we are letting in that light that Dōgen says we should shine inward. So although we are shining our light inward, we also accept that there is no hard line that divides ourselves from the outside world, or the rest of the universe.

Still, rather than trying to search for answers from outside in the form of words in books or instructions from teachers, in zazen we strive to see the answers we already possess. So we sit and quietly observe the most boring thing imaginable, a blank wall. It is exactly like watching paint dry. We do this without any expectation. We just accept whatever we encounter.

My best advice for "Fukanzazengi" is just to read it and then try doing what it says. It can't hurt. If you start doing it, I guarantee you'll have a much easier time with this book. You can still enjoy the book even if you don't do zazen. But you'll get more out of it if you do.

As Dōgen says, "If we practice long enough the treasure house will open naturally and we'll be able to use its contents as we like." We'll understand that the world we live in already is better than anything we could possibly imagine.

3. DŌGEN EXPLAINS THE HEART SUTRA
Maka Hannya Haramitsu; Prajña Paramita
The Heart of Great Perfect Wisdom Sutra

THE GREAT HEART of Perfect Wisdom Sutra is probably the single most important Buddhist sutra, aside from the collected words of Buddha himself. In fact, for some forms of Buddhism, particularly Zen Buddhism, the Heart Sutra is arguably more important than Buddha's own words.

We don't know precisely when the sutra was written. It's in the style of the earliest Buddhist sutras and refers both to Buddha and Shariputra, but it was definitely composed long after both men were dead. Current scholars estimate that it was written somewhere between 350 CE and the seventh century CE. Some maintain it's older than that. But few would place it any earlier than the second century CE, some six hundred years after Buddha's death.

It belongs to a group of sutras known collectively as the Mahayana, or Great Vehicle, sutras. These sutras appeared centuries after Buddha died and were part of a movement to popularize Buddhism outside the monastic communities that had dominated it for the first centuries of its existence. They often espoused the bodhisattva ideal, the idea that one should seek to save all beings before saving oneself.

We don't get too much of the bodhisattva ideal in the Heart Sutra. Instead, it is about *prajña*. Nishijima Roshi describes *prajña*, which is usually translated as "wisdom," as "a kind of intuitive ability that occurs in our body and mind, when our body and mind are in the state of balance and harmony." So it is not intellectual wisdom, but a wisdom that includes both the physical and the mental and at the same time transcends the categories of either physical or mental. It is not spiritual, and yet it is not materialistic, either.

Zen temples both in the West and in Japan chant this sutra in what is known as Sino-Sanskrit. Often when English speakers hear this sutra they assume that the chanting is in Japanese and that those who understand Japanese understand what's being chanted, but that's not true. It's actually Sanskrit translated into Chinese and then chanted using the Japanese pronunciations of the Chinese characters. So it makes only slightly more sense to Japanese speakers than it does to those who don't speak Japanese.

For that reason, in the beginning of this chapter Dōgen explains to his Japanese audience what the Chinese characters of the sutra actually mean by translating some of them into colloquial Japanese. But he goes beyond this, adding his own insights and referencing other sutras and stories.

Since the Heart Sutra is so short, I've put the whole thing below before my paraphrase of Dōgen's commentary. That way you'll be familiar with it, just like Dōgen's original audience was. This is a tricky chapter, full of lots of weird poetic statements that are tough to understand. If you find these parts difficult, just read through them without trying too hard to understand them intellectually. That's what I always do.

観 自 在 菩 薩 行 深 般 若 波 羅 蜜 多 時
kan-ji-ʐai-bo-satsu-gyō-jin-han-nya-ha-ra-mi-ta-ji
Avalokiteshvara Bodhisattva, when deeply practicing *prajña paramita*

照 見 五 蘊 皆 空 度 一 切 苦 厄
shō-ken-go-on-kai-kū-do-is-sai-ku-yaku
clearly saw that all five aggregates are empty
and thus relieved all suffering

舍 利 子 色 不 異 空
sha-ri-shi-shiki-fu-i-kū
Shariputra, form does not differ from emptiness

空 不 異 色
kū-fu-i-shiki
emptiness does not differ from form

色 即 是 空
shiki-soku-ʒe-kū
Form itself is emptiness

空 即 是 色
kū-soku-ʒe-shiki
emptiness itself form

受 想 行 識 亦 復 如 是
jū-sō-gyō-shiki-yaku-bu-nyo-ʒe
Sensations, perceptions, formations, and consciousness
are also like this

舍 利 子 是 諸 法 空 相
sha-ri-shi-ʒe-sho-hō-kū-sō
Shariputra, all dharmas are marked by emptiness

不 生 不 滅
fu-shō-fu-metsu
they neither arise nor cease,

不 垢 不 浄
fu-ku-fu-jō
are neither defiled nor pure

不 増 不 減

fu-ʒō-fu-gen

neither increase nor decrease

是 故 空 中 無 色

ʒe-ko-kū-chū-mu-shiki

Therefore, given emptiness, there is no form

無 受 想 行 識

mu-jū-sō-gyō-shiki

no sensation, no perception, no formation, no consciousness

無 眼 耳 鼻 舌 身 意

mu-gen-ni-bi-ʒes-shin-i

no eyes, no ears, no nose, no tongue, no body, no mind

無 色 声 香 味 触 法

mu-shiki-shō-kō-mi-soku-hō

no sight, no sound, no smell, no taste, no touch,
no object of mind

無 眼 界 乃 無 意 識 識 界

mu-gen-kai-nai-shi-mu-i-shiki-kai

no realm of sight...no realm of mind consciousness

無 無 明 亦 無 無 明 尽

mu-mu-myō-yaku-mu-mu-myō-jin

There is neither ignorance nor extinction of ignorance...

乃 至 無 老 死 亦 無 老 死 尽

nai-shi-mu- rō -shi-yaku-mu-rō-shi-jin

neither old age and death, nor extinction of old age and death

無 苦 集 滅 道
mu-ku-shū-metsu-dou
no suffering, no cause, no cessation, no path

無 智 亦 無 得
mu-chi-yaku-mu-toku
no knowledge and no attainment

以 無 所 得 故
i-mu-sho-tok-ko
With nothing to attain

菩 提 薩 捶 依 般 若 波 羅 蜜 多 故
bo-dai-sat-ta-e-han-nya-ha-ra-mi-ta-ko
a bodhisattva relies on *prajña paramita*

心 無 罣 礙
shin-mu-ke-ge
and thus the mind is without hindrance

無 罣 礙 故 無 有恐怖
mu-ke-ge-ko-mu-u-ku-fu
Without hindrance, there is no fear

遠 離 一切 顛 倒 夢 想
on-ri-is-sai-ten-dō-mu-sō
Far beyond all inverted views,

究 竟 涅 槃
ku-gyō-ne-han
one realizes nirvana

三 世 諸 仏

san-ze-shō-sbutsu

All Buddhas of past, present, and future

依 般 若 波 羅 蜜 多 故

e-han-nya-ha-ra-mi-ta-ko

rely on *prajña paramita*

得 阿 耨 多 羅 三 貘 三 菩 提

toku-a-noku-ta-ra-san-myaku-san-bo-dai

and thereby attain unsurpassed, complete, perfect enlightenment

故 知 般 若 波 羅 蜜 多

ko-chi-han-nya-ha-ra-mi-ta

Therefore, know the *prajña paramita*

是 大 神 咒

ze-dai-jin-shu

as the great miraculous mantra,

是 大 明 咒

ze-dai-myō-shu

the great bright mantra,

是 無 上 咒

ze-mu-jō-shu

the supreme mantra,

是 無 等 等 咒

ze-mu-tō-dō-shu

the incomparable mantra,

能 除 一切 苦 真 実 不虚
nō-jo-is-sai-ku-shin-jitsu-fu-ko
which removes all suffering and is true, not false

故 説 般 若 波 羅 蜜 多 咒
ko-setsu-han-nya-ha-ra-mi-ta-shu
Therefore proclaim the *prajña paramita* mantra,

即 説 咒 日
soku-setsu-shu-watsu
the mantra that says:

揭 帝 揭 帝 波 羅 揭 帝
gya-te-gya-te-ha-ra-gya-te
(gone, gone, gone beyond)

波 羅 僧 揭 帝菩 提僧 莎 訶
ha-ra-sō-gya-te-bo-ji-so-wa-ka
(gone beyond beyond, Bodhi Svaha!)

When Avalokitesvara, the bodhisattva who embodies compassion (also called Kwan Yin in Chinese or Kannon in Japanese), practiced the deepest intuitive wisdom he found that all five aggregates were empty and got over all suffering and distress.

The five aggregates are form, feeling, perceptions, impulses to action, and consciousness.

When you really get this, that's *prajña* (wisdom) itself. When you understand this, then "form is emptiness, emptiness is form." Furthermore form is form, and emptiness is emptiness. Every concrete thing is like that.

Prajña is also the twelve classes of perception, which are the six sense organs and their objects.*

---

* The first five senses in Buddhism are the usual ones: sight, sound, taste, touch, and smell, while the sixth is the mind as a synthesis of those five.

There are eighteen kinds of *prajña* in the form of eyes, ears, nose, tongue, body/skin mind; the *prajñas* of sight, sound, smell, taste, touch, objects of mind; and the *prajñas* of the consciousness of these six.

Prajña is also the Four Noble Truths Buddha spoke of in his very first sermon, which are suffering, accumulation (or craving), dissolution (or freedom from suffering and craving), and the path that leads to dissolution.

There are also the six kinds of *prajña*, which include generosity or free giving, observance of the moral precepts, patience, perseverance, meditation, and *prajña* itself.

Prajña also includes insight into the nature of the present moment.

Plus there are the three kinds of *prajña* realized as past, present, and future. *Prajña* is also the six elements of earth, water, fire, wind, space, and consciousness. *Prajña* is the four classes of action, namely, walking, standing, sitting, and lying down.

There's an old Chinese story that relates to this. A Buddhist monk vows to worship the profound pinnacle of *prajña* wisdom. The monk then rattles off all the various things that *prajña* is supposed to include, saying that each one of these things individually can be grasped. The Buddha hears him saying this and says, "That's right! The profound *prajña* wisdom is tricky and hard to understand."

Nothing appears or disappears. This is what we as Buddhists worship. This is reality itself. At the moment of true worship all the various explanations of *prajña* can be understood. This *prajña* is called "emptiness."

Here's another story. The Hindu god Indra asks the monk Subhuti how a bodhisattva should study the most profound *prajña*. Subhuti says they should study it as empty space. This means that "studying *prajña*" and "empty space" are the same thing.

Then Indra turns to the Buddha and asks him how good men and women who receive, recite, and proclaim about this highest *prajña* should guard it. Subhuti jumps back in here and asks Indra if he can see this thing he's asking about guarding. Indra says he can't.

Subhuti says that when good men and women dwell in this profound wisdom they are guarding it. Even if every human and every non-human being tried to harm them, Subhuti says it would be impossible. So guarding those who dwell in *prajña* is like guarding empty space.

My teacher Tendo Nyojo wrote a poem that goes:

The whole body's like a mouth hanging in space
Not asking where the wind blows it's ringy thing
It announces *prajña* all over the place
Ring-a-ling, ding-a-ling, ching-a-ling, dingy-ding!

This ringing of *prajña* is the whole body, the whole self, and the whole wide world.

The Buddha said that the Buddhas and honored ones are identical to the highest *prajña* wisdom, and vice versa, because they have totally relied on *prajña* to come into being, and because all virtuous conduct and physical/mental states realized in zazen rely on *prajña* wisdom in order to come into being.

All these manifestations of *prajña* are emptiness and don't appear or disappear, aren't tainted or pure, and don't increase or decrease. The realization of *prajña* is the realization of the Buddhas and honored ones. To serve and revere *prajña* is the same as serving and revering the Buddhas and honored ones.

— First preached during the summer retreat of 1233
and then copied on March 21, 1244

I've never been quite sure what to make of this chapter. It's partially a translation of the Heart Sutra into colloquial Japanese and partially a commentary on it. But it never really settles into one or the other.

Since Dōgen held on to it for nine years after he preached it and then included it in his masterwork, he must have been pretty satisfied with it. I just sometimes feel like he could have done a little better. But maybe it's one of those pieces that's of its time and place. Maybe it meant a lot more to the people he originally preached it to than it does to me, eight hundred years in Dōgen's future on a continent he didn't even know existed. That's not to say I don't like it. I just feel like, in comparison to how detailed he gets with other less significant Buddhist works, it's weird that he says so little about the Heart Sutra.

The Heart Sutra is extremely popular with people who like to explain Buddhist sutras. You can find lots of books about it. Even my own first book, *Hardcore Zen* (Wisdom Publications, 2003), contains a chapter in which I try to explain the meaning of the Heart Sutra. And I spent a lot more pages on it than Dōgen did. Just sayin'. Among the many other books that do the same thing, my personal favorite is Red Pine's book *The Heart Sutra* (Counterpoint Press, 2005). It's very short and concise, and Red Pine refrains from some of the more speculative stuff other commentators get into. Kazuaki Tanahashi also wrote an excellent book called *The Heart Sutra: A Comprehensive Guide to the Classic of Mahayana Buddhism* (Shambhala, 2015).

But let's take a look at what Dōgen had to say.

In classical Buddhism it is said that human beings do not have souls but that we are composed of five aggregates, or *skandha*s, in Sanskrit. The word *skandha* is also sometimes translated as "heap." The five heaps are form, feelings, perceptions, formations, and consciousness. *Skandha* number four is the odd one out. I'll get to it in a minute.

I like how consciousness is only one of these aggregates. In many idealistic religions and Eastern-influenced new age philosophies, consciousness is considered paramount. We are "pure consciousness," it is often said. Deepak Chopra is a real champion of this notion. Several Captain Kirk–era *Star Trek* episodes are based on this idea too. Kirk is always getting his consciousness transferred into another body or meeting aliens who are pure consciousness or whatever. But Buddhism doesn't accept this idea. Consciousness is just part of what we are, and not even the most significant part. Form (or matter) is equally important, as are the other *skandha*s.

I think most of the *skandha*s, apart from number four, are easy to understand and tend to be translated consistently. The fourth *skandha* gets translated dozens of ways. The Chinese character used to indicate it is 行 (*gyō*). In common usage this just means "to go." The Sanskrit word is *samskara*. I'm using the English word *formations* because that's the most commonly used translation. My first teacher's teacher used the word *impulses* instead. The fourth *skandha* is generally understood to be the impulses toward action that precede action itself, as well as those actions. So our actions are part of who we are. It's not that we are inert things who do stuff. Rather, the stuff we *do* and who we *are* are inextricably woven together.

The main point of the piece is an explanation of *prajña* wisdom as emptiness. Emptiness in Buddhist terms doesn't mean nothingness. It means that every single thing we encounter — including ourselves — goes beyond our ability to conceive of it. We call it emptiness because nothing can ever explain it. Reality itself is emptiness because we can't possibly fit it into our minds.

So *prajña* wisdom is intuitive understanding of this emptiness. It isn't wisdom in terms of knowledge. It's the "wisdom that knows at a glance," to quote a line from "Bendowa." It's beyond thought and perception. Dōgen likens it to empty space.

Current physics says that empty space is a very powerful thing, maybe the most powerful thing of all. Some physicists have speculated that empty space gave rise to the whole universe just by being empty. Perhaps Dōgen understood this even way back then. But since I don't understand the mathematics behind this scientific conclusion, I think I should avoid commenting on it. I just find it interesting.

Dōgen here says that real *prajña* includes everything. So for him the whole universe is a kind of wisdom. It's not that wisdom is something we possess and that we use to make judgments about other things. Wisdom is self-existent. We perceive and make use of it. But we don't make it. A wise person isn't necessarily smart in terms of how much knowledge he or she possesses. A wise person is someone who is in tune with the wisdom that already exists all around. We guard this wisdom by allowing it to be as it is.

Dōgen's teacher Tendo Nyojo says that the body is like a wind chime ringing wisdom for anyone who wants to hear. When Zen people say the "body" they generally mean the entire physical world by extension. So even real wind chimes proclaim wisdom when they ring. They do so because they are real.

Near the end of the piece Dōgen says, "The Buddha said that the Buddhas and honored ones are identical to the highest *prajñā* wisdom, and vice versa." So it's not that Buddhas are wise or possess wisdom. Wisdom is Buddha and Buddha is wisdom. This means that a Buddha is not a person in the usual sense, and wisdom may also be different from what we imagine it to be.

Let me attempt to explain what I think this means by using a somewhat difficult example. Recently there was a big scandal involving the late Joshu Sasaki Roshi, a Zen teacher who ran centers in California, Arizona, and several other places. He's alleged to have groped numerous female students over the course of decades. Yet even many of those who were wronged by him say that Sasaki was capable of deep wisdom and insight. He's far from the first person who did nasty things but who is still acknowledged to have been capable of great wisdom.

These scandals left people wondering, Were these guys insightful teachers or just sleazy human beings? In some people's minds it was a clear either/or choice. For example, lots of people seem ready to completely disregard everything Sasaki said in light of the allegations against him.

Now, I grant you that if you were not already a student or fan of Sasaki there's probably no compelling reason to become one now, especially since he's dead. But what if you were a student or follower? What if you got a lot out of the things he taught you? Do these new allegations mean all that was some sort of a scam? Does it mean that everything you learned was bogus?

I think Dōgen would say no. A person is a Buddha when she acts like a Buddha, when she manifests wisdom. When she fails to do so, she's not a Buddha. Thus a person can be a Buddha one minute and a jackass three minutes later. You don't just become a Buddha at the moment of your first enlightenment experience and then stay a Buddha forever.

I want to be very clear here. I do not offer this as an excuse or rationalization for Sasaki's behavior. If the allegations against him are true, and it appears that most of them are, then he did some really reprehensible things.

Nope. What I'm saying is the exact opposite of excusing behavior like Sasaki Roshi's. You do not become a Buddha by having some magical, mystical experience that confers Buddhahood on you, after which you can just slack off for the rest of your life. Buddhahood is something fragile and precious that must be cared for and maintained. It's not automatic, and it's not easy.

Rather than revering supposedly special people for being Buddhas, we should revere the Buddha present in all people, whenever and wherever it manifests. Dōgen talks about learning from anyone, no matter what their station in life, if that person says or does something wise.

Dōgen concludes this essay on the Heart Sutra by saying, "To serve and revere *prajña* is the same as serving and revering the Buddhas and honored ones." So we don't need to worship special people or special books. We revere wisdom itself. That makes a whole lot more sense.

4. NOTE TO SELF: THERE IS NO SELF

THERE PROBABLY IS not one teaching in the entire Buddhist canon that causes more confusion than the teaching of no-self. The existence of a self is taken as a given by pretty much every religion and philosophy, apart from Buddhism. In fact, the idea of no-self is so difficult that there are even sects of Buddhism that find work-arounds to redefine self and try to sneak it in through the back door somehow.

When I first encountered this idea of no-self, I conceived of it the way most people do when they first come across it. First off, it seemed completely absurd. It was the denial of something that I could clearly see for myself was true.

You can deny the existence of the Loch Ness Monster or Bigfoot. You can tell me there's no Santa Claus or Easter Bunny. But the existence of self? Come on! That's obvious. René Descartes proved the existence of self with a simple five-word formula: "I think, therefore I am." End of argument. Self must exist because here I myself am, thinking of things and writing them down, and here you yourself are reading them. Who else could be doing these things if it wasn't my self and your self? How could anyone with any common sense at all deny that?

But okay. I was game to try. I respected my first Zen teacher, and I didn't think he would tell me lies. He believed there was no self, and it seemed like this belief made his life better. My life was not going that great and I wanted some of whatever it was that seemed to make his work. Besides that, the rest of what he said about Buddhist philosophy and practice made sense. Or, when it didn't make sense, at least it usually didn't feel like it was denying something I could clearly see was true. So I started working with the idea of no-self.

My initial forays went something like this. I figured I had a self but that it was my job to eradicate it in order to feel happier and more peaceful. My understanding of self was that it included my personal jumble of likes and dislikes, attitudes, ideals, personal history, beliefs, habits, hobbies, and so on. I figured I had to somehow get rid of all that and become a clean, blank slate. If I could whitewash everything I considered to be "me," I would be rid of self and then maybe I'd stop being such a wreck all the time. So I went about trying to do that.

But as I was doing that, I started to realize that my first teacher, Tim, didn't appear to have erased his personality. He liked certain things and disliked others. Just like me, he adored *Star Trek* but thought *Lost in Space* was pretty dull. He had very specific opinions on politics. He had some rather peculiar habits that he didn't seem keen to eradicate. He was, in fact, a very strong personality, a very strong self, if that's how *self* was defined. This was one of the things I liked about him. So what was I doing trying to erase my personality?

Tim really liked a book called *Zen Mind, Beginner's Mind* by Shunryu Suzuki, which I've already mentioned, so I read that through a few times. In the chapter titled "Emptiness" Suzuki says, "When you study Buddhism, you should have a general house cleaning of your mind. You must take everything out of your room and clean it thoroughly. If it is necessary, you may bring everything back in again. You may want many things, so one by one you can bring them back. But if they are not necessary, there is no need to keep them."

That actually kind of scared me. For one thing, I'm a fairly messy person. I didn't like cleaning my room at all in those days. There are a few photos of rooms I lived in when I was younger that make me cringe when I see them now. And even today I'm probably not most people's image of the ideal housekeeper. But that isn't what really put me off. What made me truly scared was the idea that I'd have to do a house cleaning *of my mind*.

Nowadays, having lived in Japan for eleven years, I know precisely the type of house cleaning Suzuki was thinking of when he said this. In Japan there's a tradition of doing something called *osoji* at least once a year. *Osoji* literally translates as something like "big cleaning." It's like what we call spring cleaning, but more extensive than what most Americans do when they spring clean. In Japan, during *osoji* time, you take everything out of the house. And I do mean everything! The books, the knickknacks, the dishes, the bookshelves, the furniture — everything that's not nailed down gets taken outside. Sometimes even the stuff that *is* nailed down gets taken apart and moved outside. Then you clean up the house thoroughly, after which you clean up all the stuff you took out, and then you start putting it back inside. It's a pretty massive task. When you're putting stuff back in, you get to see how much useless junk you've accumulated since the last *osoji* and you always end up throwing a lot of it away.

Osoji usually takes place around New Year's Day, a time during which most businesses are closed for five days, although the tradition of remaining closed for five days is slowly starting to erode. So not only is this tough work, but it's usually cold as hell outside when you're doing all that scrubbing. When I first encountered this tradition it seemed like madness. But once you're done, your house feels great!

I didn't know anything about *osoji* when I first read Suzuki's book, but now that I do I get an even clearer picture of what he was saying. If I'd known then what I know now, I'm sure I would have found the prospect even scarier.

What he's talking about is metaphorically taking everything that you think of as your self out of your head and looking at it carefully and critically to see if it's really necessary. He does say you can bring some of it back inside. But read between the lines, and you can see that he's implying that there's a lot of stuff in there you won't want to bring back.

This idea scared me because it wasn't just paperback novels I'd finished reading or broken guitar effects boxes I finally had to admit I'd never get around to fixing that he was telling me to throw away. He was telling me to throw away pieces of *me*! That is a much scarier prospect. It wasn't just scary. It sounded utterly impossible.

For me this was especially tough because I prided myself on being a true individualist. I got through high school knowing that even if I was just a nerd boy that the pretty girls ignored, at least I was truer to myself than the jocks and preppies who liked what everybody else liked and dressed the way everybody else dressed. I dared to be different and I was, I thought, justifiably conceited about it! I had to be! It was all I had going for me!

Now here I was just a couple years out of that mess, being told to clear all that stuff out. What would I have left if I did? Would I become a mindless vegetable? Would I turn into one of those culties who just stares blankly off into space all the time? Or worse, would I become just like the jocks and preppies I hated, accepting everything the mainstream media told me because I had no self and therefore no opinions of my own? Or would I be opening myself up to being brainwashed by my teachers? Would I be just like the pod people from *Invasion of the Body Snatchers*? The prospects were not attractive!

But the idea of no-self isn't like that at all. It's not that we have a self and we are being asked to get rid of it. There is something real that we call "self" and that we ascribe certain characteristics to. It's just that once we call that thing "self" we are already on the wrong track, and anything else we say about it will be mistaken.

It would be ridiculous to insist that the aspects of our experience indicating that we are autonomous individuals with our unique history, personality, and point of view simply do not exist. I have my own credit cards and driver's license, which you cannot use. I know the password to my Wi-Fi at home, and you do not. I remember things that happened in my life that I could not possibly convey to you, even if I tried my hardest. I have opinions that you do not and probably a few you couldn't even comprehend, the same way I cannot fathom why some people hold the opinions they hold. All this and more applies to you as well and to every human being or animal who has ever lived.

When Buddhists talk about no-self they are not saying all the foregoing is false, nor are they saying it's all true but that we have to utterly destroy these aspects of who we are. Rather, they are saying that applying the idea of self to this real stuff is a mistake.

The word used in early Buddhist writings for the concept of self is *atman*. Atman was an idea propagated by many Indian philosophers and is similar to the Christian idea of the soul. It starts from the sense of "I am" that all of us experience. This "I am" feeling is taken as evidence that there is a permanent abiding something in us that remains stable and constant throughout the changes we experience. Thus the soul you had as a four-year-old child is the same soul you have today. This soul is different from the body because even though the body clearly changes, the soul does not. Many philosophers further extrapolate that the soul survives the death of the body. This makes sense if we accept the basic idea of the soul. If you believe that the soul remains unchanged while the body ages, it follows that the soul is not the body and it therefore follows that the soul could go on even after the body decays and dies.

The Buddha completely rejected this idea. First of all, he noticed that what we refer to as the soul or the atman *does* change. Our personalities do not remain static throughout our lives. We mature internally as well as externally. The Buddha did not accept the idea that body and mind were two different kinds of substance.

Yet *something* experiences the world uniquely in the case of each one of us. You are reading this book. Somehow my thoughts about self are being conveyed to you across time and space. My thoughts are not exactly the same as yours, or you wouldn't have bought this book. You are not me, and I am not you. What are we to do with that except say that you have a self, and so do I? Even if we don't accept the idea of the immortality of the soul or the idea that mind is made of some kind of ethereal substance that is different from matter, we have to accept that your mind and my mind are not the same mind. Otherwise we wouldn't need to have conversations or read books or watch movies or listen to music in order to access each other's thoughts and feelings.

Most of us only ever experience that way of looking at things. No, that's not exactly right. Most of us are taught that looking at things this way is the only correct way of understanding the world. I think everyone experiences the other side of the equation at some point in their lives. As children, our sense of self is much more fluid than it becomes later. We also have moments of transcendence when the barriers between ourselves and others fade away. Sometimes this happens during sex. Sometimes it happens in large public gatherings like concerts or sporting events. Sometimes it happens in religious services and ceremonies. We all know about this other side of human experience, but we are conditioned to disregard it. Or we imagine that it only happens at rare, special times and places. We miss the fact that this transcendence is actually continuously happening throughout every moment of every day.

Meditation practice helps make this clearer. Moments of transcendence and oneness no longer seem like anomalies. You start to notice that your individual identity and the identity of the universe itself are not two separate things.

Certain Indian philosophers who meditated took this as evidence that the individual atman was part of a supreme atman that was basically the soul of the entire universe. They called this super-atman "Brahman." And just to confuse those of us outside India, they also called certain people who preached this idea Brahmin and named their chief god Brahma. Be that as it may, this Brahman is said to be *sat-chitananda*, or "being, consciousness, and bliss."

Yet, like the atman, Brahman is supposed to be something apart from the material universe. The Buddha could see no reason to believe in the existence of something beyond the material universe. It's not that he thought matter was the only thing there was. Rather, he saw that matter and the immaterial were different aspects of the same unified reality. Form is emptiness, emptiness is form.

The idea of no-self means that we do not interrupt this oneness with our individuality. In the January/February 1985 issue of *Matter* magazine, my all-time favorite singer-songwriter, Robyn Hitchcock, told an interviewer, "Inasmuch as a mind can discuss itself — it's a bit like a mirror looking at itself, only I don't know how much truth there is in that. You put two mirrors up against each other, and there's infinity, but you can never see it, 'cause your head blocks it off." This is a remarkably astute metaphor for the problems inherent in looking at the true nature of what we call self.

We are both individuals and expressions of the universe. These are not mutually exclusive. Dōgen talks about this a lot throughout *Shōbōgenzō* because it was as difficult an idea for him and his students as it is for us. The next chapter contains some of his best lines on the subject of no-self. Let's take a look!

5. YOU ARE NOT YOURSELF
Genjo Koan
The Realized Universe

"Genjo Koan" is without a doubt the most important chapter in *Shōbōgenzō*. It may, in fact, be the most significant philosophical piece Dōgen ever wrote.

It was originally written in 1233 as a letter to a lay student named Koshu Yō. All we really know about Mr. Koshu is that he lived in Kyushu, which is the southernmost of Japan's main islands and a long way from where Dōgen set up shop in central Honshu. It's been speculated that Mr. Koshu may have been a government official, but nobody's really sure.

But what a letter! It has been the subject of hundreds of commentaries and many full-length books. Right now, as I write this, there are two books in print in English just about "Genjo Koan," and both are excellent and worth seeking out: *Realizing Genjokoan* by Shohaku Okumura (Wisdom Publications, 2010) and *Dōgen's Genjo Koan: Three Commentaries*, edited by Mel Weitsman, Michael Wenger, and Shohaku Okumura (Counterpoint Press, 2013). I devoted a chapter of my book *Sit Down and Shut Up* to a discussion of it, and there must be a thousand websites, blogs, and other pieces about it on the Interwebs.

For all the attention it gets, most English translations of "Genjo Koan" take up about three and a half pages. My teacher Gudo Nishijima's version takes up six, but only because he added twenty-four footnotes, some of which are very long, as well as an introduction and some notes about the meaning of the word *koan* and the use of koans in Zen practice.

Shohaku Okumura defines *genjo* as "reality actually and presently taking place" and *koan* as "absolute truth that embraces relative truth." The Chinese characters Dōgen uses for *genjo* are 現 (*gen*), which means "to appear" and 成 (*jō*), which means "to become." Okumura's definition is pretty much the standard one, although a lot of people just translate it as "realized." But don't look up *realized* in your Japanese-English dictionary and expect to find *genjo* as a translation. It's Dōgen's own word.

Let's talk about koans for a sec. Once a guy came up to me after a talk and asked about these "rones" he'd heard of in Zen. "You know, rones!" he said, as if repeating the word more loudly would explain it. After a minute or so of discussion he said they were weird questions you were supposed to meditate on. That's when I figured out he meant koans. There is, needless to say, a lot of confusion about the word.

Koans are the one thing that people who know nothing about Zen seem to know about. Usually they're described as illogical questions intended to drive a meditator to break through the bonds of intellect and have a mystical experience. The one everybody knows is, "What is the sound of one hand clapping?"

The word *koan* is actually an abbreviation of the phrase 公府之案牘 (pronounced *ko-fu no an-toku* in Japanese), which in ancient Chinese means a "public case." Koans are stories about Zen teachers and their students, generally recorded in the form of a conversation. They are often contradictory and appear to be illogical. But they're not. They have a logic of their own: the logic of contradiction.

Although Aristotle said that contradictions were the antithesis of logic, in the real world there are always contradictions. Things are often one way and another at the same time. Love is pleasurable and painful. Happiness can make you sad sometimes. Chinese food can be sweet and sour. Newspapers are black and white and re(a)d all over. In this piece Dōgen pushes the idea of contradiction as the most realistic way to understand what life actually is.

Let's get to the text, and then we'll talk about it after.

When all things are Buddha-dharma there's understanding and mis-understanding, there's training and results, there's life and death, and there are Buddhas and just plain folks. When the zillions of things and phenomena are seen as having no self, there is no misunderstanding or enlightenment, no Buddhas or just plain folks, no life, and no death. The Buddha-dharma is originally beyond having lots and having little, and so there is life and death, delusion and realization, just plain folks and Buddhas. But although this is true, flowers, though we love them, still die, and weeds, though we hate them, still grow all over the place.

Pushing ourselves to practice and experience stuff is delusion. When stuff actively practices and experiences us, that's realization. Those who understand misunderstanding are Buddhas. But to have misunderstandings about understanding makes you just a regular person. Some folks attain realization based on realization, and some just get delusional about delusion. Buddhas don't need to recognize themselves as Buddhas, but when they practice the state of Buddha they go on experiencing the state of Buddha.

Even if we use our entire body/mind to look at forms and hear sounds, perceiving them directly, our perception isn't like the reflection of the moon in water. When we look at one side, the other is dark.

To study the self is to forget the self; to forget the self is to be experienced by the zillions of things; when experienced by the zillions of things our own body and mind drop away. Then we can forget about realization and allow that forgotten realization to continue forever.

When you first look for the dharma you're far away from it. But when the dharma is transmitted authentically you are immediately your original self.

If you're in a boat and you look at the shore, you might think the shore is moving. But if you look at the boat, you know it's the boat that's moving. Likewise, when you look at stuff with a muddled-up body/

mind you get the idea that you have a permanent self. But if you look at things clearly you see that nothing has a permanent self.

Firewood becomes ash and doesn't go back to being firewood again. But we shouldn't think of firewood as its past and ash as its future. Both firewood and ash have their own position in time and space. The past and future are cut off. Firewood and ash each have their own past and their own future. Just as ash doesn't go back to being firewood, human beings, when they die, don't come back to life again.

We Buddhists don't say that life turns into death or that death turns into life. Instead we talk about "no appearance" and "no disappearance" (he's quoting the Heart Sutra here). Life is what happens while we're alive, and death is what happens when we die. We don't say that winter becomes spring, or that spring becomes summer.

Realization is like the moon reflected in water. The moon doesn't get wet, and the water isn't broken. The entire moon and sky can be reflected in a dewdrop on a blade of grass. Realization doesn't break an individual, just like the moon doesn't break the water. And an individual doesn't hinder realization, just like a dewdrop doesn't get in the way of the sky. The depth of realization is like the height of the moon.

When the dharma hasn't completely filled your body/mind, you feel like you're totally full of it. But when it does fill you, you feel there's something missing. For example, if you sailed way out into the ocean and looked around you'd think the ocean was circular, but it's not. It's got all kinds of little corners and shapes and all that. When fish see the ocean it's like a palace; when gods see it, it's like a string of pearls. But we humans just see it as round. Everything's like that.

There are all kinds of situations in the world, but we can't really understand them. If you want to understand them, you have to remember that oceans and mountains have all sorts of characteristics you can't see. Even you, just as you are right here and now, have a whole lot of aspects you're completely unaware of. Just bear that in mind. Okay?

When fish swim there's no end to the water, and when birds fly there is no end to the sky. The more water or sky fish or birds use, the more use they can make of it. The less they use, the less they need. Each one covers the whole of water or the entire sky. So water and sky are life itself. Practice/enlightenment is just like this.

If a fish or bird tries to understand the water or sky apart from swimming or flying in it, it can't do so. When you find the place you actually are, you actualize the fundamental point. This Way and *this place* exist as reality because they're not big or tiny. Nor are they related to us or to the external world. They don't exist already or appear spontaneously. Likewise, if you just penetrate one thing completely, you understand everything in the moment of real action.

This, right now, just this — just reading this book or whatever it is you're doing — this is the place where reality exists. And that's why we can't realize it! Because we can't step outside of what is and look back at it. We're part of it. Even when you realize everything, don't imagine that you'll intellectually understand it or even notice it. It's beyond your knowledge.

Once Zen master Mayoku Hotetsu (Ch. Magu Baoche, dates unknown, student of Baso Doitsu, Ch. Mazu Daoi, 709–788 CE) was fanning himself on a hot day. His student came up to him and asked, "Since air is all over the place and goes everywhere, why are you using a fan?"

The master said, "You only know the abstract principle that air is all over the place. You don't know that it goes everywhere."

The monk said, "Okay, then, what's the fact of it going everywhere?"

In answer to this, the master just kept fanning himself.

This is the authentic Buddha-dharma. Somebody who says air is all over the place so why use a fan doesn't know why people use fans. The behavior of Buddhists makes the Earth manifest itself as god and ripens the Milky Way into delightful cheese. And everybody likes cheese, right? Except vegans. And even most of them like it. They just don't like how it's produced. Which I respect.[*]

— Written on August 15, 1233,
for Koshu Yō of Kyushu and edited in 1252

It's hard to know where to begin. As I said in the introduction to this chapter, there are already a lot of good books just about "Genjo Koan,"

---

[*]   Dōgen really does end by saying words to the effect of "it ripens the Milky Way into delightful cheese," but he doesn't say anything about vegans. I just felt like it needed that for contemporary readers.

and now I've gone and written about it as well. Since there are already some extensive interpretations of "Genjo Koan," I'm going to keep my notes on this chapter short and save my longer explanations for chapters about which less has been written.

I used to use the last line in the first paragraph of "Genjo Koan" as a way to quickly judge whether a particular *Shōbōgenzō* translation was worth checking out. In Japanese it's 華は愛惜にちり、 艸は棄嫌にお ふるのみない (*hana wa aijaku nichiri, kusa wa kiken ni ofuru nomi nari*). Nishijima/Cross translate this as "flowers, while loved, fall; and weeds, while hated, flourish." Nishiyama/Stevens have, "People hate to see flowers fall and do not like weeds to grow."

It's a fairly straightforward line. Yet some translators do strange things to it. For example, the usually reliable Kazuaki Tanahashi translation (in this chapter his collaborator was Robert Aitken) has, "Yet in attachment blossoms fall, and in aversion weeds spread." Norman Waddell and Masao Abe have, "Flowers fall amid our regret and yearning, and hated weeds grow apace." Jiyu-Kennett translated it as, "Whilst we adore flowers they wither; weeds grow strong whilst we long for their destruction." Taizan Maezumi translated it as, "Flowers fall just giving rise to attachment, and weeds spring up arousing antipathy."

I figured that line was a kind of benchmark. If the translated version was simple and direct, the way the original Japanese is, then the rest of the translation could be expected to be simple and direct. If the translator made that line convoluted or mystical sounding, I would expect the rest of the translation to follow suit. Of course that's a highly simplistic idea. It's not really true overall. But when I was a young, eager Buddhist student who didn't know poop from Shinola, I decided that would be my way to make a quick assessment.

The major point in this piece is the idea of nonself. As I said in the previous chapter, lots of people imagine that the Buddhist idea of nonself means that you somehow have to make your self or your personality disappear. It's not like that. It's not like the real something you call your "self" suddenly vanishes upon enlightenment or needs to be destroyed before enlightenment can happen. It doesn't go anywhere. There's nowhere for it to go. It's just that you understand that "self" is far too limiting of an image to contain it.

This is what Dōgen means by all that stuff about realization not breaking an individual any more than the reflection of the moon breaks a dewdrop. You're still just as much you as you ever were. My first Zen teacher, Tim McCarthy, had a great way of putting this. He said, "It's more you than you could ever be." In this case "it" is the great unnamable something, the universe itself.

Except you don't notice this. Not really. You can't stand apart from it and notice it the way you can stand in front of a box of cookies and notice it's a box of cookies. You can't because you're one of the cookies. It also doesn't fit into what you label as "you." And yet some kind of awareness of it will be established by pretty much anyone who continues the practice long enough and sincerely enough.

The more standard translations of "Genjo Koan" have Dōgen saying, "To study the Buddha Way is to study the self. To study the self is to forget the self. To forget the self is to be actualized by myriad things. When actualized by myriad things, your body and mind as well as the bodies and minds of others drop away. No trace of enlightenment remains, and this no-trace continues endlessly." Let's look at that line by line.

The first sentence is, "To study the Buddha Way is to study the self." Sometimes translators say "Buddhism" instead of "the Buddha Way." There really isn't a word in Japanese that corresponds exactly to the English word *Buddhism*. The word *Buddhism* was created by British people researching the cultures they encountered in Asia and trying to define them in British terms. They figured that the temples dedicated to Buddha were like churches and that what went on inside them was like Christianity. They figured these people worshipped a god they called Buddha.

They weren't that far off, really. A lot of Buddhism has degenerated into something very much like the worship of a god who happens to be called Buddha. Much of Asian Buddhism is full of superstition and belief in the supernatural. Much of it involves fear of what amounts to punishment and damnation by Buddha if one fails to live in accord with his teachings or fails to venerate him properly. There have been cases like that guy who was deported from Sri Lanka for insulting Buddha by having his face tattooed on his body. Never mind that the standard face of Buddha probably no more resembles what the man himself actually looked like than the blond-haired, blue-eyed Jesus of contemporary Sunday school books looks like a Palestinian Jew of two thousand years ago.

But Dōgen is clearly differentiating what he's teaching from all that stuff. "To study the Buddha Way," he says, "is to study the self." It's not about memorizing ancient Buddhist sutras. It's not about venerating the image of Buddha. It's not about all the costuming and ceremony. None of that stuff can really be called studying the Buddha Way. It's all about studying the self.

To do this, you forget the self. This means you leave behind all your preconceptions about what the self is. You're not trying to eradicate a self that already exists. You're trying to see what this existing thing you've called "self" actually is rather than what you imagine it to be.

When you do this you are "actualized by myriad things" or "by everything," if we want to stop using words that only Buddha-nerds use, like *myriads*. You see that what you call "self" is the manifestation of everything. You reflect and refract the universe around you in a unique way, and that unique way is commonly called "self." But it does not belong to anyone — certainly not to you!

When you understand this, your mind and body drop away, as do the mind and body of everything else. You stop conceiving of things in terms of mind and body, or spirit and matter. You see that nothing in the universe is purely mind/spirit and nothing is purely body/matter. These designations are far too limiting. Reality itself is beyond any such definition. But it's not beyond them in terms of being very far away. This immediate existence, right here and right now, is already beyond mind/spirit or body/matter.

I hope that explanation made at least a little sense. Dōgen will return to this point over and over. So don't worry if you don't get it just yet.

I'm really fond of the line about when you haven't experienced realization you think you're fully realized but when you really experience it, you feel as if something's missing. This relates to what Tim called the balance of doubt and faith. He said you need to have an equal degree of doubt and faith to really understand Zen. Too much doubt, and you're sunk. But too much faith also gets in the way.

The many self-described "self-realized masters" in our midst these days never really get it. They just have a little taste of it and think they have the whole thing. Those who are actually fully realized always feel like something's not quite finished, because that's the actual truth of the matter. The universe/you is both complete and self-sufficient and at the same time incomplete and fully dependent on everything else. It's one of those Zen contradictions. It may not make intellectual sense in terms of Aristotelian logic. But look around at real life, and you'll see that's the way it is.

All that stuff about birds and fishes and sky and water is just saying that you can't step outside the universe — which is identical to your "self" — and view it objectively. As Robyn Hitchcock says, "your head keeps blocking it off." Yet you can realize the entirety of the universe *as* yourself. You are intimately a part of everything. Absolutely every element of your body/mind right now was present at the very moment of creation and long before (if a word like *before* even pertains to such a thing) and will be here forever. Everything you are is connected intimately to the entire universe, near and far, past, present, and future. Just by being yourself, you are everything.

But Dōgen then tells us that story about the master with the fan. Just because we are everything doesn't mean we can just sit back and it'll all be groovy. We have to do something. We have to practice. We have to take action. This very action is how we activate our realization. Whether or not we know it makes no difference at all. Gudo Nishijima puts it like this: "The experience of the ultimate state is realized at once. At the same time, its mysterious existence is not necessarily a manifest realization. Realization is the state of ambiguity itself."

The last bit about the Milky Way turning into cheese is kind of funny to me. Why cheese? The actual piece says the "long river" (長河 *nagakawa*), which is a name for what we call the Milky Way, ripens (参熟 *sanjuku*) into 酥酪 (*soraku*), which is something more like "curds and whey" than cheese. It implies transformation.

In that book of commentaries on "Genjo Koan" I mentioned earlier, Shunryu Suzuki commented on this line, saying, "Only by your practice, when you practice zazen in this way, aiming at this kind of goal, will you have a chance to attain true enlightenment." This might seem to be the antithesis of goalless practice. Notice, though, that he says, "*aiming* at this *kind of* goal." Suzuki was not a native English speaker. But you can see that he is trying hard to get his point across that it's not the specific goal we care about so much as aiming toward something like it.

This is a theme that Dōgen beats nearly to death throughout *Shōbōgenzō*. We are exactly the truth of what we are — what the universe is — right here and now. Yet we need to do some work to truly become what we already are. This is the meaning of his metaphor about the wind being ever-present and our need to use a fan to cool ourselves on a hot day.

Another theme he brings up here is one he also brought up in "Bendowa," the rejection of the idea of reincarnation, or at least of the standard new age bookstore idea of reincarnation. It's evidently a big enough deal to Dōgen that he brings it up twice. But it's not big enough for him to spend a whole lot of ink explaining.

For people interested in Buddhism in the West in the twenty-first century, though, reincarnation is a huge deal. Some people these days get into Buddhism mainly because they're interested in reincarnation. Since that's the case, I thought I'd devote a chapter to that idea alone.

6. DID DŌGEN TEACH REINCARNATION, AND DOES IT EVEN MATTER IF HE DID?

KURT VONNEGUT ONCE said he never put a love story into any of his novels because as soon as there was a love story readers would latch on to that and forget everything else in the book. I feel the same about talking about reincarnation or rebirth. But here goes anyway.

We just looked at "Genjo Koan," in which Dōgen makes one of several critical comments about the matter of reincarnation. He also does this in "Bendowa," and he'll do it again in an essay called "Mind Here and Now Is Buddha." Yet whenever I say, as my teacher Gudo Nishijima Roshi also said, that Dōgen denied the belief in reincarnation, I get a lot of flack from Dōgen scholars and other people who are, for whatever reason, really fond of the idea of reincarnation.

I got an email a while back from a Dōgen scholar who said in part:

I was checking out some of your videos and came across one on reincarnation in which I appreciate what you say about how we can't know what happens after death, and therefore Zen doesn't emphasize that teaching. However you also say that Dōgen "was very adamant that there is no reincarnation, that the idea of reincarnation is a non-Buddhist idea that was grafted onto Buddhism later on and isn't originally part of Buddhism." Wow. I am concerned that others will actually think that is Dōgen's and

Buddha's view. As you probably know, there are many, many early Pali Suttas in which the Buddha talks about rebirth (I don't like to use the word *reincarnation* which seems to imply there is some kind of 'self' which reincarnates), including his description of his own night of awakening in which two of the three knowledges he realized involve seeing into rebirth (of course no atman is involved in Buddha's view, and like karma and everything else for that matter, rebirth is only conventionally true). And Dōgen, though it's true he doesn't emphasize the teaching, clearly teaches rebirth in the *Shōbōgenzō* fascicles "Sanjigo," "Shinjin Inga," and especially "Doshin." Statements such as "death does not turn into birth" in "Genjo Koan" are just talking about abiding in a dharma position, like 'winter doesn't become spring.' I was wondering where you got the idea about Dōgen's adamant view that there is no reincarnation.

In response, I said that I got my ideas about Dōgen's views on reincarnation mainly from "Bendowa," which we have looked at. Here's the Nishijima/Cross translation of what Dōgen says there: "According to that non-Buddhist view, there is one spiritual intelligence existing within our body. When this body dies, however, the spirit casts off the skin and is reborn on the other side; so even though it seems to die here it lives on there. Therefore we call it immortal and eternal. But if we learn this view as the Buddha's Dharma the delusion would be too shameful for comparison." This Dōgen calls the Heresy of Senika. Senika was an Indian philosopher who popularized this idea.

In "Genjo Koan," Dōgen says, "Firewood, after becoming ash, does not again become firewood. Similarly, human beings, after death, do not live again." Although there are lots of variations in the English translations of *Shōbōgenzō*, every translation I'm aware of says pretty much the same thing at this point. Tanahashi says, "You do not return to birth after death." Nishiyama/Stevens say, "When human beings die, they cannot return to life." Thomas Cleary says, "After dying a person does not become alive again." Shasta Abbey's translation says, "After someone dies, he does not come back to life again." In case you want to know what he says in Japanese it's 人のしぬるのちさらに生 とならず (*hito no shinuru no chisara ni iki to narazu*).

Dōgen follows this by saying, "At the same time, it is an established custom in the Buddha-Dharma not to say that life turns into death. This is why we speak of 'no appearance.' And it is the Buddha's preaching established in [the turning of] the Dharma wheel that death does not turn into life. This is why we speak of 'no disappearance.' Life is an instantaneous situation, and death is also an instantaneous situation." This is the Nishijima/Cross translation. But again, the other translations of this part are all pretty much the same

Lots of people are obsessed with life after death. It's understandable. Death is a scary prospect to most of us. In the novel *John Dies at the End*, by David Wong, a character says, "You're going to die, Arnie. Someday, you will face that moment. Regardless of what you believe, at that moment you will either face complete nonexistence, which is something you can't possibly imagine, or you will face something even stranger that you also can't possibly imagine. On an actual day in the future, you will be in the unimaginable, Arnie. Set your mind on that."

Lots of curiosity seekers who proclaim themselves as being "into Buddhism" these days often appear to be motivated mostly by a desire to replace the unimaginable with something imaginable. They want to be told by someone who they think holds some kind of mystical enlightened knowledge that they will live forever. People love to be told they will live forever by someone who supposedly knows. That's why the book *Heaven Is for Real*, the story of a little kid who supposedly came back from the dead, sold a truckload of copies.

My Dōgen scholar friend said he prefers the word *rebirth* to *reincarnation*, yet he uses the two as synonyms later on in his email. Everybody does. What most audiences I encounter conceive of when they hear the word *rebirth* is precisely Senika's view. For example, the current Dalai Lama is said to have become the Dalai Lama because the previous person who held that title supposedly left clues as to where he would next be reborn. Following his death, certain learned priests in his lineage followed those clues and found a baby. They showed that baby some objects and checked his reaction to them. When they were satisfied that the baby in question had reacted correctly to these items, they declared the baby to be the reincarnation of the dead Dalai Lama. This is a traditional custom, going back centuries.

When most Western audiences — and Eastern ones too, for that matter — hear stories like this, they imagine that the Dalai Lama died, left his body, and entered another one. That's certainly how I understood it the first time I heard it. Later on I read a couple of books on the subject and encountered a more nuanced view of the Buddhist concept of rebirth. One metaphorical explanation I encountered said that it was like lighting a candle with another candle and then blowing out the first candle. The flame on the second candle isn't the same flame, and yet it depends on that first flame for its existence. Another explanation was that it was like bubbles on a river. Bubbles form on the surface of a river due to disturbances to the water. When these bubbles burst, the water from which they were formed doesn't disappear. It reenters the river. Later on, other bubbles will be formed out of the same water.

I heard those explanations, tried to work out what they meant, and came up with my own interpretation of the teaching. The only problem was that my interpretation of that more nuanced view of Buddhist rebirth added up to something like, "You die and get reborn; you just don't have a soul."

One of the problems for contemporary Western people is that Buddha's attitude toward rebirth is entirely different from ours. We want to live forever. Buddha and his followers did not. To him and to the audience he spoke to, rebirth was not a good thing.

Take, for example, this excerpt from a short book (which can be found online) called *The Truth of Rebirth* by Thanissaro Bhikkhu. "When any of the Buddha's fully awakened disciples passed away, he would state that one of the amazing features of their passing was that their consciousness could no longer be found in the cosmos....One of his own amazing attainments as Buddha, he said, was that after the end of this life, the world would see him no more."

In absolute contrast to this, when most Western people hear about rebirth and reincarnation, they think it sounds really great. As Oasis said, "I wanna live I don't wanna die...you and I we're gonna live forever." Yet here we see Buddha saying that one of his "amazing attainments" was that once he was dead he was going to stay dead for eternity. That's supposed to be good?

In any case, in spite of what the guy who wrote me that email says, Dōgen never does anything I would call "teaching rebirth." I'm aware that he says things that seem to hint at his belief of what we might call rebirth, especially in the ones my friend who wrote the email mentioned. These are "Shin Jin Inga" ("Deep Belief in Cause and Effect"), "Sanji no Go" ("Karma in the Three Times"), and "Doshin" ("The Will to the Truth"). But these passages could be interpreted very differently. There's a more important question: Why does it matter what Dōgen believed about rebirth, anyway? I'll get to that in a bit, but I want you to keep it in mind. Let's talk about what Dōgen wrote first.

In "Deep Belief in Cause and Effect," Dōgen references the famous koan story of Hyakujo's Fox. In this story we hear about a man who claims to have been reborn as a fox for five hundred lifetimes because of an incorrect statement he made about the nature of cause and effect. To read the story of Hyakujo's Fox as a teaching about rebirth is the same as insisting that the biblical story of Adam and Eve in the Garden of Eden is historically accurate. Focusing on the myth used to illustrate a point and interpreting that myth as factually true is a mistake Joseph Campbell harshly criticizes in *The Power of Myth*.

The actual point of the story is about believing deeply in cause and effect and not accepting superstitious ideas about miracles or other events that violate cause and effect. He is using the myth of rebirth to make a point about the Buddha's teaching, not to teach that we get reborn after we die.

In parts of the chapter "Karma in the Three Times" it sounds significantly more like Dōgen is teaching rebirth. But there are other ways of looking at it. This chapter begins with Dōgen citing an ancient Buddhist story. It goes like this:

> The nineteenth patriarch, Venerable Kumaralabdha, arrives at a country in central India, [where] a saint called Gayata asks, "In my family, father and mother have always believed in the Three Treasures yet they have been beset by ill health and, in general, are disappointed in all their undertakings. My neighbor's family has long done the work of caṇḍalas [so-called untouchables in the Hindu caste system], yet their bodies are always in sound health and their doings harmoniously combine. What is their good fortune? And what is our guilt?"
>
> The Venerable One [Kumaralabdha] says, "Retribution for good and bad has three times. Generally, people...do not know that shadow and sound accord with [their sources], not differing by a thousandth or a hundredth and — even with the passing of a hundred thousand myriad kalpas — never wearing away."

Dōgen goes on to explain this, saying, "These words 'Retribution for good and bad has three times' mean (1) retribution is received in the immediate present; (2) it is received in one's next life; (3) it is received latterly."

Then he says, "If people have committed in this life the five actions [leading to] incessant [hell]*, they will inevitably fall into hell in their next life. 'The next life' means the life following this life."

Dōgen goes even further, saying, "If people, having committed in this life either good or bad, feel the effect of good or bad karma in a third life or in a fourth life or even after hundred thousands of lives,

---

* Just in case you're wondering, the five sins in question are (1) to kill one's father, (2) to kill one's mother, (3) to kill an *arhat*, which is a sort of Buddhist saint, (4) to cause the Buddha's body to bleed, and (5) to disrupt the sangha.

this is called 'karma that receives [retribution] latterly.' " Here Dōgen appears to be saying, "Watch what you do because even if you do bad stuff and then die at a ripe old age, having lived a prosperous and comfortable life, you're going to get reborn and have to pay for all the bad stuff you did in a subsequent life." It's very hard to argue that there is any other interpretation than that.

It really does seem to me that Dōgen is talking about actual rebirth here. Still, the chapter is not really about rebirth specifically. It's about karma or the law of cause and effect. The myth of rebirth is used to illustrate something about the nature of cause and effect. So I would argue that Dōgen is not "teaching rebirth" in this chapter. Here's why.

Dōgen is not saying, "Hey, kids! Here's what happens after we die!" He is trying to emphasize the importance of our action in the present moment and how what we do has effects that reverberate for a very long time. His intended audience believed in rebirth, and so he used that belief as a way to stress how important it is to behave morally. He is not saying anything like that kid who supposedly wrote *Heaven Is for Real*. He is not claiming to have special knowledge of what lies beyond death. He is using assumptions already held by his audience to emphasize his point about the importance of moral action in the present.

The one place I know of where Dōgen seems to really be doing something like teaching rebirth occurs in another of the chapters my Dōgen scholar friend mentioned. It's called "Doshin" or "The Will to the Truth." The section goes like this:

Even between abandoning this life and being born in a next life, in which period there is said to be a middle existence whose length is seven days, even during that period, we should intend to chant the Three Treasures without ever lulling the voice. After seven days we [are said to] die in the middle existence, and then to receive another body in the middle existence, for seven days. At the longest [this body] lasts seven days. At this time we can see and hear anything without restriction, as if with the supernatural eye. At such a time, spurring the mind, we should chant the Three Treasures; we should chant without pause, not forgetting to recite namu-kie-butsu, namu-kie-hō, namu-kie-so [homage to the Buddha, homage to dharma, homage to sangha]. When, having passed out of the middle existence we are drawing close to a father and mother, we should steel ourselves and even when, due to the presence of right wisdom, we are in the womb-store [world] that will commit us to the womb we should chant the Three Treasures. We might not neglect to chant even while being born. (from the Nishijima/Cross translation)

I would argue that even in this most blatant and specific of all Dōgen's references to rebirth, he isn't really "teaching rebirth." He is again using the myth of rebirth to emphasize a different point. He is more concerned with how important it is to revere the Three Treasures — Buddha, dharma, and sangha — than he is in explaining what happens after we die. He does get into some of the supposed mechanisms of rebirth, like those bodies that last seven days each, but he doesn't dwell on them. If he were "teaching rebirth" his emphasis would be on the mechanism of rebirth, not on the importance of revering the Three Treasures.

As I said, one might ask if Dōgen himself believed in rebirth. It sure sounds like he did when we read these passages. But then we have to return to what he says in chapters like "Bendowa," "Genjo Koan," and "Mind Here and Now Is Buddha." The only times I'm aware of in which Dōgen squarely looks into the notion of rebirth, he very clearly denies it.

Those who cling to the idea that Dōgen believed in rebirth will usually say that what Dōgen denies in these chapters is a false idea about rebirth — the idea that a person's real essence is a soul that leaves the body and gets reborn in another body. But then we come to a passage in "Genjo Kōan" in which he says, "Just as firewood does not become

firewood again after it is ash, you do not return to birth after death."
You can't get much clearer than that!

The aforementioned person who wrote the email said, "Statements
such as 'death does not turn into birth' in 'Genjo Kōan' are just talking about abiding in a dharma position, like 'winter doesn't become
spring.' " I'm afraid I don't really get it when people start using phrases
like "abiding in a dharma position." I've always found phrases like that
extremely opaque.

I think what he's getting at is the concept that there is an absolute
kind of truth and a relative kind. There's an idea in Buddhist circles
that Buddhism speaks of two truths, one absolute and one relative.
Many believe that Buddhism talks about one set of ordinary truths that
apply to our regular lives and about a different set of truths that transcend our ordinary reality.

I've always been very uncomfortable with the idea of dividing
Buddhism into absolute truths and relative truths. I don't ever read
Dōgen as espousing one set of truths for some imaginary absolute real-
ity and a completely different set of truths for our day-to-day existence.
I feel like he's always talking about our day-to-day existence. He just
understands ordinary existence better than most of us.

So did Dōgen believe in rebirth? You've just read all the most direct
statements he ever wrote on the subject. So now you know as much as
I do, and as much as any Dōgen scholar out there does, about Dōgen's
personal belief in reincarnation/rebirth or lack thereof. So I might as
well ask you. Did Dōgen believe in rebirth?

Which brings me to what I think is a much more crucial point than
whether or not Dōgen believed in rebirth, which is, even if he did, so
what? Why is it important whether or not Dōgen believed in rebirth?

For me, as an admirer of Dōgen, it does have some significance. I'll
try to explain why.

I have read and reread *Shōbōgenzō* and Dōgen's other writings more
times than I can count. I had a teacher who was a legitimate Dōgen
scholar. In my zazen practice I've often found that the things Dōgen

said which at one point seemed incomprehensible have later, after a lot of sitting, been confirmed.

Because of this I've come to trust Dōgen. He seems to have had deep insights into the nature of things. So if he believed in something like rebirth, it seems sensible to me to think he had some good reasons for believing in it. Perhaps his own experiences in zazen, which must have been far deeper than mine, led him to this belief. Maybe he could recall his past lives. He never claims he could, but who knows? Furthermore, I'd certainly very much *like* to believe in rebirth. Everybody wants to imagine they'll live forever, at least if they're not ancient Indians.

Here's my conclusion. I feel that Dōgen most likely did believe in something we might call rebirth. Yet even if he did, he clearly did not think that belief was very important. However, he clearly *did* think it was important that his students should reject the idea that they will live forever, transmigrating from one body to another. To me, this is far more significant. Why does he consider that idea to be detrimental to practice? And if we take this idea that he thought was so problematic and frame it in different words, does that make it better?

To me, Dōgen seems to be saying again and again and again, "Focus on this life. Live this actual day. Pay attention to just this very moment. This is where it's all happening, not in some future lifetime, not in your next birth or your 'middle existence' between incarnations. Just here. Just now."

So, in spite of what a lot of Dōgen scholars will tell you, I'm telling you that Dōgen never once "teaches rebirth." There is not a single instance anywhere in his writings or in his recorded talks where he lays out exactly what he believes about what happens after a person dies and where he encourages his students to have faith that this is what will become of them as well. While one might argue that there is tangential evidence in his works to suggest that he appears to hold some of the standard ideas most Buddhists have about this, he clearly does not consider them to be of any real significance to the main message he is trying to convey. Even when he denies the so-called Heresy of Senika regarding what happens after we die, he does not then advocate a different view about life after death. Instead he urges his students — us — to focus on the here and now.

Even if there is life after death, we still should not miss the significance of this lifetime. If you cultivate a habit of always looking toward the future or past for validation, then even if you do wind up going to heaven or being reborn into a cooler place than you live now, you'll just spend your whole time wherever you end up looking for the next thing.

In the book The *The Zen Teaching of Homeless Kodo* (Wisdom Publications, 2014), Kodo Sawaki, one of my teacher's teachers, said it best: "It's very unskillful to use this body of five feet only as a five-foot body. It's foolish to live merely using up fifty, eighty, or one hundred years of longevity. To practice the buddha way is to become a person who will never die, who is not at all different from the buddha pervading the entire universe forever." We live forever by practicing the Buddha Way right now. If we wind up being reborn after we pass from this life, that's fine. If not, that's okay too.

7. WON'T GET FOOLED AGAIN
Ikka No Myoju
One Bright Pearl

THIS SERMON OF Dōgen's, preached in 1238, contains one of my favorite stories in all of Zen. It's about a guy who realizes he can't be deceived by others. I'll save my comments about the story for the end, though. I think it's better to let you read it without filling you up with my ideas about what it means beforehand.

The title is pretty straightforward. *Ikka No Myoju* unambiguously means "One Bright Pearl." There are no fancy made-up words or reinterpretations of existing terms, as was the case in "Genjo Koan."

The central story in the piece concerns how the guy who said he couldn't be deceived also said that the whole universe was one bright pearl. It's a beautiful and optimistic image, so what's not to like? The fact that the incident that eventually led him to this conclusion was stubbing his toe really bad on a rock makes it even better.

Before he was a Zen master, Gensa Shibi (Ch. Xuansha Shibei, 835-907 CE) was a fisherman. But when he was thirty years old he decided to leave fishing behind and go off to the mountains to find the truth.

He climbed up Mount Seppo and became a disciple of Master Seppo Gisan (Ch. Xuefeng Yicun, 822-907 CE). There Gensa became known for his hard practice and almost stubborn dedication.

But after a period of studying with Seppo, Gensa figured it was time to go meet some other teachers so that he could get a more well-rounded education. He packed his bags and started walking toward the temple gate.

Just then he stubbed his toe on a big rock. There was blood all over the place, and his toe hurt like nobody's business. Gensa thought, "Some say the physical body doesn't exist, so where, then, is this pain coming from?" He returned to the temple.

Seppo, his teacher, saw him and asked, "What's up, Mr. Hard Practice?"

Gensa said, "My trouble is I can't be fooled."

Seppo said, "Who doesn't know this deep down? But who else besides you can say it out loud?" After waiting a beat, Seppo said, "So how come you decided not to leave this temple and further your education?"

Gensa replied, "Bodhidharma didn't come to China. The Second Patriarch (Huike, Bodhidharma's successor) didn't go to India."*

Seppo liked Gensa's answer and told him so.

Gensa, being an uneducated fisherman, never read a Buddhist sutra in his life. He just dedicated himself to practice. Gensa had only one robe, which he patched up whenever part of it wore out, and he wore underwear made out of paper and grass. He really took the impoverished monk thing seriously. He never left Seppo and eventually became Seppo's successor.

Years later Gensa was preaching and told the audience that the whole universe was one bright pearl. One of his monks asked him how we should understand that phrase. Gensa said, "The whole universe is one bright pearl. What are you gonna do with your understanding?"

A couple of days later Gensa said to the monk, "The whole universe is one bright pearl. How do you understand this?"

The monk said, "The whole universe is one bright pearl. What am I gonna do with my understanding?"

---

* Historically speaking, Bodhidharma did go to China. He is regarded as the first Indian Zen teacher to do so. His successor, Huike, however, did not go to India.

Gensa said, "I see you are struggling to get inside a demon's cave in a black mountain."

Gensa was the first to call the whole universe one bright pearl. That means it's not big or small, not square or round, not active, not obvious. It's not life and death in terms of coming and going, so it is real life and real death in terms of coming and going. The past has left and the present has arrived. Who can see it as moment following moment, and who can see it as solid and stable?

The whole universe causes things to accord with ourselves and ourselves to accord with things. Emotions and intellect separate us from the real universe. But even those things are kind of like turning your head or making a face. They make us feel separation, but even they are part of reality.

Someday everybody will understand this phrase "one bright pearl." The body and mind of the present moment are one bright pearl. It isn't that there are, or are not, miscellaneous things in the universe. It's just that they're all one bright pearl.

Even though it seems like that monk who said, "How should we understand it?" was just being intellectual, the question was a manifestation of the workings of the universe. To express the truth that things are just what they are, Gensa asked, "What are you gonna do with your understanding?"

If we try to run away from the reality that things are exactly as they are, even our running away is part of that reality.

A couple of days later, when Gensa asked the monk the same question the monk had asked him, Gensa was saying that yesterday he preached a general rule but today he's talking about the exception that makes the rule. He's laughing about turning yesterday's teaching upside down.

The monk says, "The universe is one bright pearl, what am I gonna do with my understanding?" We should do zazen for ourselves, turning our own light inward, and think about how often understanding things is actually useful. It's like milk cakes and veggie crackers. Theory and practice are the same thing, expressed in two different ways.

Gensa said, "I see you're struggling to get into a demon's cave in a black mountain."

The sun is always the sun and the moon is always the moon. The whole universe is one eyeball of the true dharma eye.* The whole world is just brightness, and the whole world is just the whole world.

All Buddhas manifest their bodies and preach the dharma because of this one bright pearl.

Sometimes the one bright pearl is concealed, like in the old story of the guy who sewed a pearl into the clothes of his drunken friend so that he'd find it later and be able to use it to get a cab ride home. We're like that because we possess the truth, only we're in such a stupor we don't realize it.

Even when the universe shows us different faces — sometimes things are going great and sometimes things really suck — it's still one bright pearl. The moment we recognize that the bright pearl exists is also the bright pearl itself.

Even if we think we can't possibly be the bright pearl, that's just the bright pearl doing the thinking. Basing our action on fleeting thoughts is just brought about by our limited understanding.

How could we not love the infinite colors of the one bright pearl? Don't worry about being caught up in the world of cause and effect. When the universe becomes thoroughly right, the bright pearl is its eyes.

Neither you nor I know what the bright pearl is or is not. But we can just rely on Gensa and trust that the universe is one bright pearl.

Our minds are not our own, so why worry about whether or not the universe is a bright pearl? Who is it that has those concerns? Ask yourself that!

No action or image has ever been realized except by relying on the one bright pearl.

So stepping forward or stepping backward into the demon's dark mountain cave is the bright pearl itself.

— First preached at Kannon-dori-kosho-horin-ji Temple
on April 18, 1238, and then copied at Kippo Temple
on July 23, 1243, by Ejo, Dōgen's assistant

---

* This is a pun on the word *Shōbōgenzō*, "Treasury of the True Dharma Eye."

In my book *Sit Down and Shut Up* I wrote a lot about the phrase "I can't be fooled." As I said, this was very meaningful to me in my study and practice of Buddhism.

Buddhism is about cutting through delusion. I think most of us imagine that delusion is caused by forces outside our control. We're "educated" by a society that doesn't even understand itself. So how can we help but be deluded? Or we're "born into a world we never made," as Howard the Duck said. So delusion or deception, we think, comes from outside.

But when Gensa stubbed his toe, he saw through that. He understood how he had created his own delusions and therefore had the power to end them, right there and then. His teacher said that everybody knows this, but only Gensa had the guts to say it out loud.

These days lots of people say they understand that they themselves are the only real source of their own delusions and deceptions. But when you really push them you see that they'd still like to put the blame on somebody else. I know I'm like that. Even after a few so-called enlightenment experiences, you can still fall back on the idea that delusion comes from someplace other than your own silly self. We all do it. Even Dōgen admits he does it sometimes too when he says that neither you nor I know what the bright pearl is or isn't.

I like the idea that Gensa expresses a bit of regret at the realization that he can't be deceived. People tend to think that Buddhist enlightenment must be all happiness and bliss. But actually one tends to also feel a kind of regret. To really know for absolute certain that you could never blame anyone else for anything is difficult. It requires that you take full responsibility for absolutely everything. I can see why Gensa would feel a bit regretful about that. First, he would regret having caused so much difficulty for himself and others. Second, he would regret no longer having anyone else to point the finger at. I'm going to talk more in detail about this line in the next chapter.

When Gensa's teacher asked why he didn't follow through on his plans to leave the temple, Gensa replied, "Bodhidharma didn't come to

China. The Second Patriarch (Huike, Bodhidharma's successor) didn't go to India." As you already know, if you read the preceding section, Bodhidharma actually did go to China in the traditional story. Almost certainly at least one of the people on whom the Bodhidharma legend is based — if not all of them — did go to China. But Huike didn't go to India, where Bodhidharma came from. The standard interpretation of this saying is that these guys did what they did without any specific conscious intention. Bodhidharma didn't decide he ought to go to China. He just did what felt right. Huike didn't decide not to go to India. He also just did what felt right. They just followed their intuition. Gensa is saying that his intuition is that he should stay with Seppo.

The other key point in this piece is something Dōgen comes back to again and again. It's that even our mistakes are part of the perfection of the universe.

This is good to keep in mind when doing zazen practice. Often people think they're doing it wrong because nothing freaky happens to them. They don't see visions of five-hundred-foot-tall multiarmed Vishnus hanging in the air in front of them, or they don't watch their bodies merge into the center of the cosmos, or experience whatever fantasy they've cooked up about how "enlightenment" ought to be.

But even what you think of as "bad zazen" is still the working through of universal karma. Everything is enlightenment — even delusion!

Still, as Dōgen also says, we try to penetrate the mystery. We fan ourselves even though air is ever-present, to paraphrase "Genjo Koan."

The phrase "I see you are struggling to get inside a demon's cave in a black mountain" is a linguistic conundrum. My paraphrase is based on the Nishijima/Cross translation. However, Kazuaki Tanahashi has Gensa saying, "I see you have worked out a way to get through the demon's cave on the black mountain." The Nishiyama/Stevens translation is, "You now know that even in the Black Mountain Cave of Demons there is complete freedom." Shasta Abbey's translation says, "It is indeed clear to me that, even though you are blindly looking into the demon's cave within the pitch black mountains of ignorance, you are doing your training." A. Charles Muller, of Tokyo University, who has translated several *Shōbōgenzō* chapters and made them available online, has this line as, "You know, you are living in the depths of a devil's cave in the black mountain."

It looks as if Nishijima/Cross's and Muller's translations have Gensa telling the monk he's wrong, while the others have Gensa affirming that the monk is on the right track, at least to some degree.

What is actually written in Chinese is 知汝向黒山鬼窟裏作活計. Breaking down each character, we get the following: 知 (*zhī*, "know"), 汝 (*rǔ*, "you"), 向 (*xiàng*, "facing"), 黒山 (*hēishān*, "black mountain"), 鬼 (*guǐ*, "demon/ghost"), 窟 (*Kū*, "cavern"), 裏 (*lǔ*, "inside/bottom"), 作 (*zuò*, "work"), 活計 (*huójì*, "manual labor" in Chinese and "livelihood" in Japanese). Dōgen's notes in the margins would make the Japanese 知りぬ汝は黒山鬼窟裏に向かって活作スコト計ヲ. This means, "I understand that you are working facing deep into a demon's cave in a black mountain."

There's still some ambiguity in Dōgen's Japanese about whether Gensa is acknowledging that the monk is doing his training or whether he's just saying the monk is wasting his time. I think Dōgen is saying the monk is confused. Let me tell you why.

Throughout *Shōbōgenzō*, whenever a monk just repeats the words of his or her teacher back at the teacher, the monk is usually characterized as being stuck in the area of the intellect. So I think it's fair to assume that is what's going on here as well. There's no better example of this than the story of Gutei's finger.

Whenever someone asked him a question about Zen, Master Gutei just raised his index finger. One of Gutei's monks was asked something about Zen and raised his index finger in response. Gutei heard about this and called the monk to him. He asked the monk a question about Zen, the monk raised his index finger, then Gutei whipped out a knife and cut off his finger. The monk was crying in pain and Gutei called his name. When the monk looked up, Gutei raised his finger. The monk was instantly enlightened.

I tend to believe this story was exaggerated. The real Gutei probably just twisted the monk's finger or something like that. Having him cut it off with a knife made a better story. But the point is the same. If you just parrot back an answer, even if it's the right answer, it's meaningless unless you know it for yourself. So I think that's what's happening in this story.

My favorite piece of this chapter is what I have paraphrased as, "Even when the universe shows us different faces — sometimes things are going great and sometimes things really suck — it's still one bright pearl. The moment we recognize that the bright pearl exists is also the bright pearl itself. Even if we think we can't possibly be the bright pearl, that's just the bright pearl doing the thinking. Basing our action on fleeting thoughts is just brought about by our limited understanding."

This is a pretty liberal interpretation of what Dōgen actually says. He goes on much longer than this, citing a couple of old Chinese stories. I tried to squash a lot of what he says here into a short paragraph without so many literary allusions, and I may have done Dōgen a bit of a disservice in doing so. I hope you'll be inspired to seek out and read what Dōgen actually wrote in one of the full or partial translations I've listed in the bibliography.

Speaking of difficult translations, I'd like to spend the next chapter explaining why it's so hard to translate Dōgen into English and what sort of compromises one has to make when doing so.

8. YOU CAN'T SAY "I MISS YOU" IN JAPANESE

YOU REALLY CAN'T. There is no equivalent in Japanese to the word *miss* in the sense of "I miss you." The best you can do is to rephrase "I miss you" into something that translates back to "When you're not around I'm lonely" or "When you're not around I'm sad."

That's pretty close to what we generally mean most of the time when we say, "I miss you." But it's not exactly the same thing.

For example, try saying something like "I miss living in Japan" — which I tried to do the other day in an email to a friend back there — or "I miss the rains down in Africa" in Japanese and you're stuck. You're not lonely because you don't live in Japan anymore. Or maybe that's part of it, but that's not what you really mean. You're not sad because you can't see the rains in Africa these days. Or maybe you are, but that's not really what you wanted to say. Not exactly, anyhow.

Now imagine trying to deal with phrases like that, only they're in eight-hundred-year-old Japanese. Maybe you understand Japanese, but nobody talks like that anymore. You understand the words but they don't add up to anything. Or they add up to something really ambiguous so you're not sure which way out of dozens you should take them. Now imagine the writer you're translating also speaks fluent Chinese and likes to throw in phrases in that language too. And he is fond of making up his own words or making weird puns out of Chinese phrases that date back hundreds of years even before his time. Translating Dōgen is tough!

Luckily these days there are some really top-notch English translations of Dōgen. Even so, in writing this book, I still frequently double-checked the original Japanese, as well as my teacher's modern Japanese rendition of *Shōbōgenzō*. I have even tried my hand at directly translating bits of Dōgen into English. When I wrote *Sit Down and Shut Up* I decided that I would never quote Dōgen unless I knew exactly what he said in Japanese. I wouldn't just quote him out of an English translation, even if I knew it was a reliable one. This is one of the reasons it took me five years to write that book!

Since we're talking about the problem of translating Dōgen, now is a good time to go into how I feel about the major English translations of Dōgen's *Shōbōgenzō*. Here's my rundown.

There are currently four complete English translations of *Shōbōgenzō* that I know of. I believe only two of these are still in print on paper as of this writing, though another (Shasta Abbey's) is available online. In order of my own preference, here is the list. (They go by author, since they're all called *Shōbōgenzō*):

1. Gudo Nishijima and Chodo Cross. This is the one done by my ordaining teacher and his student Mike Cross (Chodo is his dharma name).

2. Kazuaki Tanahashi and the San Francisco Zen Center. Kaz Tanahashi is a friend of mine. He translated *Shōbōgenzō*, with a group of teachers from San Francisco Zen Center acting as cotranslators. Someone different helped with each chapter.

3. Kōsen Nishiyama and John Stevens. This was the standard English edition for a long time but has since gone out of print and can be hard to find.

4. Shasta Abbey. This was translated by the Reverend Master

Hubert Nearman of Shasta Abbey, which was founded by the
Reverend Master Jiyu-Kennett.

A fifth complete version is being worked on at Stanford University
under the auspices of the Soto-shu of Japan, the organization that claims
to be directly descended from the sangha Dōgen founded. The Stanford
edition has been in progress for a number of years now; I'm starting to
wonder if it will ever come out. The sections I've seen look really good,
though. So I hope they eventually get around to publishing it.

One issue with the Stanford version, though, is that it is being done
under the auspices of the Soto-shu of Japan. The Soto-shu is a very
large religious institution, much like the Holy Roman Catholic Church
or the Church of Jesus Christ of Latter-day Saints. They have a lot
invested in producing an edition that adheres to their version of the
"authoritative" — to use their own word — interpretation of Dōgen.
Their history in this area is not particularly inspiring. In the 1700s, for
example, they convinced the Japanese government to ban the publication of *Shōbōgenzō* so that interpretations counter to theirs could not be
produced. We'll talk about that later.

A number of partial translations also exist. Norman Waddell and
Masao Abe put out a book called *The Heart of Dōgen's Shōbōgenzō*, which
contains nine chapters. Thomas Cleary translated thirteen chapters and
called this collection *Shōbōgenzō: Zen Essays by Dōgen*. Taizan Maezumi
and Francis Dojun Cook published a book called *How to Raise an Ox:
Zen Practice as Taught in Master Dōgen's Shōbōgenzō*, which contains ten
translated chapters of *Shōbōgenzō*, along with other material. A few others are out there online, and there are probably some Dōgen translations that I haven't even come across yet.

In terms of writers of books about Dōgen (as distinguished from
translators of Dōgen), Taigen Dan Leighton is really good, and so are
Steven Heine, Carl Bielefeldt, and William Bodiford. Hee-Jin Kim
is highly regarded too, although I'm less familiar with his work. The
scholarly stuff they produce is pretty dense to me and generally hard to

get through. I consult it when I need a reference. But you're not likely to see me sitting at a bus stop with a scholarly treatise on Dōgen.

As you have probably figured out, I am very much biased toward the Nishijima/Cross translation. I know firsthand about the process by which they arrived at this translation. Mike Cross is a very precise person in everything he does. What Gudo Nishijima and he created is the closest thing you'll ever get to being able to put on a pair of magical glasses that allows you to read the actual Japanese.

Yet what it benefits from in terms of precision it sacrifices in terms of poetry. Dōgen was a poet and a master of prose. His writing is flowing and beautiful. The Nishijima/Cross translation often gets fairly clunky. In order to get the meaning just right, Nishijima and Cross had to forgo making it smooth and poetic.

My second favorite translation is Kaz Tanahashi's. Kaz brings back the poetry that Nishijima and Cross lost. Many of his cotranslators at San Francisco Zen Center are accomplished writers. Tanahashi's version is pretty accurate too.

However, there are no footnotes, as there are in the Nishijima/Cross translation, though there is an extensive glossary. Mostly, though, you just have to trust the translators and either skip over Dōgen's obscure references or look them up yourself. Still, it's not a bad version, and it is much more pleasurable to just sit and read than my teacher's translation.

The only thing that really bugs me about the Tanahashi translation is that it is the San Francisco Zen Center's take on *Shōbōgenzō*, and that means certain things. It appears to have been translated with an eye on making it as inoffensive as possible to the sensibilities of ultrasensitive folks from the Bay Area.

For example, the phrase "sit upright like a king of (or under) the Bodhi tree" (覚樹王に端坐 *kakuju-oh ni tanza*) in "Bendowa" is rendered as "sit upright beneath the glorious Bodhi tree" so as not to be sexist by using the word *king*. Where Dōgen refers to the full-lotus posture (結跏趺坐 *kekka fuza*) in the original, Tanahashi has him saying "sitting in meditation" so as not to offend anyone with tight hamstrings.

In a section I was just working on, the gender-neutral word 親 (*oya*), meaning "parent," is translated as "mother" so as to make Dōgen seem more gender inclusive. The list goes on.

The text is peppered with this kind of thing, to its detriment. If they were trying to paraphrase, as I'm doing, it wouldn't matter. But if you're presenting the book as a translation, you need to leave things like that alone. Even so, I still highly recommend the Tanahashi translation. Overall it's really, really good.

Kōsen Nishiyama and John Stevens call their edition of *Shōbōgenzō* "a combination of translation, commentary and paraphrase." They say, "Even a semi-literal [translation] produces a mutant brand of English that alternately confounds and amuses the reader." So their version is actually closer to the kind of paraphrasings you're getting in this book than it is to the other translations. (Except there are no references to zombies and Doritos.) It's okay for what it is, but it's not that much closer to Dōgen's actual words than this book is.

The Shasta Abbey translation is its own sort of beast. As you might guess from the fact that it's credited to the *Reverend Master* Hubert Nearman, the folks at Shasta Abbey are fond of Catholic-style titles. I'm told they're also fond of Catholic-style rituals and have remade the standard Zen service into something much closer to what one might find at one's local Catholic parish.

As such, their version of *Shōbōgenzō* reads sort of like the King James Bible. There aren't any *thou*s and *begat*s and suchlike, but there is a tendency toward flowery, religious-sounding language. Important words are Capitalized just like in the Bible and This can make it Kind of Strange to Read (see what I mean?). Dōgen generally wrote in a fairly colloquial style for his time, so I'm not sure why the folks at Shasta Abbey rewrote it the way they did. Maybe they just wanted something that sounded better when quoted from the pulpit?

Still, for all that, it's a reliable translation. It has footnotes too. Not as many as the Nishijima/Cross version, but at least it's got some, and that's useful. Plus, you can download it for free, so that's nice.

Let's take a specific example to show what you're up against when trying to make *Shōbōgenzō* readable in English. The key phrase in the early part of "One Bright Pearl," which we just looked at, is the one I've translated as, "In the end my problem is I can't be fooled."

Gensa's answer in the original is not in Japanese but Chinese. It is 終不敢誑於人. The first character, 終 (*zhōng*), means "after all." The second, 不 (*bù*), means "not." The third, 敢 (*gǎn*), means "dare" in contemporary Chinese, but it also means "sad" or "pitiful" in more ancient usage. The fourth, 誑 (*kuáng*), means "cheat." The fifth, 於 (*wū*), means "alas." And the final character, 人 (*rén*), means "people."

Nishijima/Cross translate this sentence as, "In the end I just can't be deceived by others." Tanahashi's translation has, "No one can be deceived." Nishiyama/Stevens have Gensa saying to his master, "Please don't kid me!" The exclamation point is theirs. Thomas Cleary's version has, "I never dare fool people." The Shasta Abbey translation has Gensa saying, "I have never dared to deceive anyone about that!" Again, the exclamation point is theirs. When I asked a friend who is a native Chinese speaker what she made of the phrase, she had to consult an online source dedicated to Buddhist language usage and finally came up with, "I am myself, no matter what other people say; they can't change who I am."

In Nishijima Roshi's translation of *Shōbōgenzō* into contemporary Japanese, this same sentence is rendered into modern Japanese as 他人様のいうことではなかなか納得しない困った奴です (*taninsama no iu koto de wa naka-naka nattoku shinai komatta yatsu desu*). This means something like, "My problem is I am someone who just can't be convinced by what others say." Just translating this into English gave me some headaches, owing to its use of certain Japanese idioms that don't have good direct translations.

For my paraphrase, I finally decided to go with a version that's similar to Nishijima's contemporary Japanese because that's what the Chinese seems to me to infer and because it makes the most sense to me. This just goes to show you what one has to deal with when working with this text. Everyone has troubles.

Dōgen scholar Carl Bielefeldt, who was one of the main people involved in the Stanford University translation project, wrote an essay called "Translating Dōgen: Thoughts on the Soto Zen Text Project." In it he says of their work, "We want to it to be accurate. But what does that mean? True to the letter of the original? True to the meaning? True to the spirit? True to Dōgen's intention in writing it? True to the varied Sōtō traditions of interpretation? ... [A] translation that we put by our bedside or stuff in our back pack when we go camping [?]" These are all very good questions.

He continues, "If you do too much *Shōbōgenzō*, you begin having dreams in which you're in a book store with Dōgen, and he's interpreting the titles. *Understanding Investment*. For students of the Dow, this should be 'investment in understanding'; it should be 'divestment of under-standing.' It should be not only 'under-standing' but 'over-standing'; not only 'under-standing' but 'under-sitting.' We should walk, stand, sit, and recline in our vestments as the Dow; we should take up our vestments as our body and mind, slough off our vestments as our body and mind. Etc., etc."

I've tended to pass over a lot of these difficult-to-translate passages in my paraphrasing since they're so hard to come to terms with. But *Shōbōgenzō* is chock-full of them. You can come away from reading an essay like Bielefeldt's thinking that there's no way anyone can ever convey what Dōgen actually wanted to say!

In fact, most Japanese people find Dōgen's prose almost as confounding as we do. Pretty much the only significant difference is they don't have to decode the Chinese and Japanese characters it's written in. As Nishijima Roshi said, what first fascinated him about *Shōbōgenzō* was that it was a book that was written in his own language but that he could not understand at all. Most Japanese people interested in *Shōbō-genzō* turn to the various modern Japanese translations now available and rarely attempt to read the original.

Let me try explaining the problem in a different way. I'm kind of a dinosaur nut in my spare time. There are almost as many books about dinosaurs on my shelves as there are about Buddhism. What we know about dinosaurs we know only from the fossils they left behind. No one has ever seen a living dinosaur, and unless we end up creating time machines or being able to do *Jurassic Park*–style DNA reconstructions, no one ever will. All paleontologists can do is make educated guesses based on a lot of very degraded data.

In a sense that's what you get when you try to read Dōgen. You're looking at the fossils he left behind. But we have an advantage that paleontologists don't: Dōgen actually taught his understanding face-to-face to real people, who then taught it to others, and so on. We have a connection to the understanding behind the fossilized words. And that face-to-face understanding is what Dōgen's written words were meant to convey in the first place.

Because of this, much of the best literature out there about *Shōbō-genzō* is not in the form of translation. In fact, some of it barely even mentions *Shōbōgenzō*, or it even gets parts of it wrong in terms of pure linguistics. Among these books, my personal favorite is, once again, Shunryu Suzuki's *Zen Mind, Beginner's Mind*. This book isn't really about Dōgen per se. But it is totally informed by Dōgen's work, as are all of Dainin Katagiri's books. I've already mentioned Kosho Uchiyama's *Understanding Genjo Koan*. That one's really great, as are his other books. There are many others too.

But books are not all we have. We also have flesh-and-blood human beings who embody Dōgen's understanding. It would be impossible for me to make a comprehensive list of these folks. But later on I'll be talking about three who were significant to me personally. Some of the people who embody Dōgen's understanding are authorized lineage holders, and some are not. I can't tell you how to find one for yourself. But I can assure you that they do exist. If you come across one such person, consider yourself very lucky. He or she is a treasure and not someone ever to take lightly.

Now let's get back to looking at the fossils Dōgen left behind.

9. A LIST OF RULES
Ju-undo Shiki
Rules for the Hall of the Accumulated Cloud

THE SATURDAY-AFTERNOON LECTURES by Nishijima Roshi that I attended for more than ten years always followed the same format. First we'd do thirty minutes of zazen. Then we'd move to another room, and Nishijima would start reading a chapter of *Shōbōgenzō*. Sometimes he'd stop and comment on something. But mostly he just read the English translation he was working on with Mike Cross straight through. After about thirty minutes of this he'd ask if anyone had questions, and a discussion would follow. After about thirty more minutes of talking we'd adjourn. He started at the beginning of *Shōbōgenzō* and went through every chapter week by week till the final one. Then the following week he started over again.

For most of the time I went to these lectures he was actively working on his English translation. So we were listening to a work in progress, although by the time I joined the group most of the major work was done.

Most of the chapters in *Shōbōgenzō* are deeply philosophical. But a few are very dry, technical pieces about proper etiquette in a Zen monastery. Whenever Nishijima got to one of Dōgen's nuts-and-bolts pieces like the one we're about to look at or the one a few chapters later about washing, I always hoped he would just skip it. He never did. He always said that Dōgen's was a "philosophy of action." It wasn't just a philosophy of thoughts and concepts; it was a philosophy you actually did. Chapters like this one, he said, give us a glimpse into how Dōgen carried out his philosophy on a day-to-day basis.

This chapter is basically a list of rules for how monks ought to behave in the meditation hall. The specifics of the rules don't really matter that much for anyone who doesn't plan on opening their own Japanese-style meditation center. In fact, most contemporary meditation centers, even in Dōgen's tradition, don't really follow all these rules to the letter anymore.

It's the attitude that these rules express that's important. If you can find the attitude that lies behind them, you can come up with your own completely valid tradition for whatever you do in life. It can inform how you treat your desk and your cubicle, or the room with your guitars and amplifiers, or the studio where you keep your paints and brushes, or whatever you spend your day doing.

People who have a will to the truth and who throw away fame and profit may enter the zazen hall. Don't let insincere people in. If you let somebody in by mistake then, after consideration, kick them out. Nicely.

Remember that not too many people have the will to the truth or the guts to throw away fame and gain. The efforts we make right here and now will become the source of Buddha's way for future generations. Feeling compassion for the future, we need to value the present.

Everyone in the hall should harmonize like milk and water. We should all promote each other's moral behavior. For now we are students and teachers, but in the future we will be Buddhist patriarchs.

Our practice is tough, so don't forget your honest intention. We've all left our homes and families. Now we rely on clouds and rivers, on nature itself. Taking care of each other's health and promoting each other's practice is worth even more than anything our parents did for us. Our parents are only parents between birth and death, but the members of this hall are friends forever.

We shouldn't go out a lot. If necessary you can go out once a month. Our predecessors lived way up in the mountains and never saw anybody else. We should remember how they shut themselves away from the world and covered their tracks.

Now is the time to act, just as if your head was on fire. How could we not regret wasting this time on secular pursuits? Our life is like a dewdrop on a blade of grass. We don't know when we'll lose it. To waste it would be pitiful.

Even though there are books about Zen, don't read them in the meditation hall. Go somewhere else if you want to read. Don't waste any time.

Let the leader of the hall know where you're going, no matter what time it is. Don't wander around willy-nilly. That messes up stuff for everybody. You don't know when you're gonna die, so don't risk dying while you're just out farting around.

Don't smack people for making mistakes. Don't hate other people's mistakes. An old master said that if you don't pay attention to other people's errors or to your own correctness, everyone will respect you. But don't learn other people's bad habits, either. Practice your own virtue. Buddha stopped people from doing wrong, but he never hated them.

Whenever you want to do something, whether it's a big deal or a small one, let the leader of the hall know. People who do stuff without letting the leader know should be expelled. If formalities between students and leaders are disrupted it gets hard to tell right from wrong.

Don't gossip in or around the hall.

Don't practice ceremonial walking in the hall.

Don't bring counting beads into the hall, and don't walk around with your hands hanging down.

Don't recite sutras in the hall unless a donor requests it and everybody recites together.

Don't blow your nose loudly in the hall, and don't hack or spit. That's gross. Work on your behavior as if you were a fish in a stream that was drying out.

Don't wear clothes made of brocade in the hall. Wear clothes made out of paper and cotton and the like. Since ancient times people who clarified the truth did it that way.

Don't come in the hall drunk or high. If you do so by accident, then prostrate yourself and apologize. Don't come in smelling of leeks and onions.*

If people argue they should be sent back to their rooms. People arguing messes things up for everybody. People who see an argument coming but don't do anything about it are equally at fault.

Anyone who ignores the rules of the hall should be expelled. Anyone who is in cahoots with such a person is also at fault.

Don't annoy everybody by bringing visitors into the hall. If you have to talk to visitors near the hall, be quiet about it. Don't brag to visitors about your training, hoping they'll give you a present. If a visitor really wants to come in and walk around the hall, you can bring them in. But tell the hall leader about it first.

Remember, we monks live in this hall, we eat and sleep here as well as meditate. So don't be lazy about the rest of your duties, like going to lectures and stuff.

If someone drops their silverware or chopsticks while eating they have to pay a penalty from their oil ration. So be careful with that stuff.

Follow the Buddhist precepts. Those precepts should be engraved on your bones and etched into your brain.**

We should pray that our whole life will be peaceful and undisturbed so that we can pursue the truth naturally.

These few rules are the body and mind of the eternal Buddha. We should revere and follow them.

— Written by Dōgen, the founder of
Kannon-dori-kosho-horin-ji Temple, on April 25, 1238

----

* There are two ways of interpreting what Dōgen wrote here. It could also mean, "Don't come in all red-faced and drunk." The "leeks and onions" version is the more common interpretation in Japan, but the one about being drunk makes more sense in context. Still, the "leeks and onions" version is something you'll probably hear if you hang out with Zen people.

** The precepts are: observe the rules of society and the rules of the universe; work for the salvation of all; don't kill; don't steal; don't desire too much; don't lie; don't live by selling intoxicants; don't criticize monks or laypeople; don't berate others; don't be stingy; don't get angry; and don't abuse the three treasures, Buddha, dharma, and sangha. We'll take these up later.

Those rules are pretty straightforward. Buddhist temples both now and in the past tend to have big, long lists of very specific rules. But Dōgen's rules are all pretty basic and general. Later in life he did produce longer lists of rules, but they all derived from this simple set.

When you get right down to it, all these rules can pretty much be summed up as, "Don't be a jerk in the meditation hall." It's all about respecting others and letting them get on with what they came into the hall for in the first place: to be monks and meditate together. If you can just do that consistently, you really don't need any other rules.

All the Zen places I've visited in my travels as a teacher and writer have had some version of these rules. When you go to Tassajara during the summer as a student, they make you sign a piece of paper saying you understand and intend to abide by their rules, which are just a variation of these.

You no longer have to pay a penalty in oil for dropping your chopsticks at most Zen temples. The folks at Tassajara are actually pretty tolerant about that kind of thing since they get so many newcomers. But you're still not allowed to come in drunk. Nose blowing, while grudgingly allowed in most Zen places I've been to, tends to be discouraged. If you blow your nose once in most contemporary Zen places, nobody will say anything, but if you do it several times they might ask you to step outside.

In the old days, monks ate and slept in the meditation hall. These days there are still temples that hold formal meals in the meditation hall. The monks eat in a style called *oryoki*, which is intended to allow you to kinda sorta keep meditating even while you eat. In an *oryoki* meal service, you stay at your cushion and someone brings your food to you in a very ritualized way. Serving is usually done on a kind of rotation so that everyone gets an opportunity to be a server.

After the food is served you chant several verses of thanks to those who made the food and to the food itself. After all, even if you're the strictest vegan in the world, something died so that you could live, even if it's just a carrot or a mouse that got in the way of the harvester. You also chant a vow to use the energy you derive from your food to continue your practice. Only then are you allowed to eat, and the eating itself is done in a highly controlled manner. It's a beautiful practice and it's also super-annoying — often in equal measures.

You don't find too many places where they still sleep in the meditation hall except in the really austere temples in Japan. In those temples you can't bring any more stuff with you than can fit in a little box by your meditation cushion. So you have to leave your electric guitar and your PlayStation2 at home.

Whenever I come to that line about hacking and spitting it reminds me that the temple these rules were written for was mostly filled with young dudes. In those days male and female training centers were separate. For the most part they still are in Asia. These guys were often in their early teens when they joined. Dōgen, for example, was twelve when he became a monk, and that was not unprecedented. Instead of envisioning ancient temples filled with stereotypical serene monks straight out of Central Casting, it may be more useful to envision them full of hormonally charged teenagers with little formal education and lots of issues such as depression, social anxiety, problems with their parents, maybe a little post-traumatic stress, and plenty of other baggage.

You get a different kind of clientele at most Zen centers in the West these days. People at Zen centers are generally pretty well educated and tend to be older. The Zen temples I go to in the States generally seem to be full of graying middle-agers. In Dōgen's day most of the monks were farmhands, country boys. So probably a lot of them didn't have very good manners to begin with, just in general. It must have been a steep learning curve for some of them to enter a temple, and I'm sure a lot of them were sent home because they just couldn't hack it. (I mean, with all their hacking and such.)

Which is not to say that Zen temples these days aren't still full of people with issues. You don't generally take such a drastic step as moving into a meditation center unless you are aware that something is very wrong in your life and that you need help. In some ways contemporary

Zen centers resemble halfway houses for people who are seeking ways to get by in the world without falling to pieces.

Of course not everybody is an emotional mess. And since the practice really does help with these issues, you'll find lots of people who are handling things very well in spite of whatever issues they were battling when they first arrived. Also, there tends to be a strong sense of comradery among those who know how hard life was before they entered monastic life and how hard monastic life can be, as well as why monastic living helps.

Among the specific rules Dōgen cites here, the thing about walking around with your arms hanging down is an especially irksome point for me. When you're inside a Zen meditation hall you're supposed to walk around with your hands held in front of your chest in a gesture called *shashu*. That's a way of showing respect to the space itself and to the people in it. Whenever I go to Zen places in America and Europe there are always a few people who either didn't get the instruction about that or who figure it doesn't apply to them. They look like a bunch of low-class gorillas to me when they walk around with their arms hanging down and swinging around.

Anyway, as I said at the beginning, to me this chapter is all about attitude. It's about being respectful and the importance of disciplined practice. But don't fret too much. If you find yourself in a Zen place somewhere and you've forgotten the rules, just look around and see what everyone else is doing. It's not all that choreographed. You'll be fine!

10. YOU'RE ALREADY ENLIGHTENED, EXCEPT YOU'RE NOT

Soku Shin Ze Butsu

Mind Here and Now Is Buddha

ONE OF THE great joys of doing this project is that I'm starting to understand and see things about *Shōbōgenzō* that I managed to miss over the past twenty-odd years of studying it.

The first time I read it I did so because I'd been listening to Nishijima Roshi's lectures for a year or more, and he always talked about *Shōbōgenzō*. I knew he was pouring all his energy into translating the complete text into English. He was not the first person to do this. But his version was only the second complete translation into English ever done. At the time it was published, the previous complete edition was out of print, so his was really the only English version you could get with every chapter included.

The first complete version by Kōsen Nishiyama and John Stevens was, even in those days, nearly impossible to find and has become even harder to get in recent years. When I started this project I did a search on Amazon and someone had volume three of that edition, going for $28,729.14. You also needed to kick in $3.99 because at that price they couldn't possibly throw in free shipping. A few weeks later I spotted a full set of all four volumes for $100, which I bought right away for my research, since I'd never owned the full set before. That's about the best price you can expect to find.

Be that as it may, since Nishijima was involved in such a monumental undertaking and since I knew him personally, I figured the least I could do was read the darn thing. So I dug in. I didn't concern myself with understanding what I was reading. My goal was simply to turn the pages, scan my eyes across the words, and take in whatever I could.

Eventually I read the four volumes all the way through, three times. I also reread the parts I particularly liked God only knows how many more times. Dozens, I'm sure. Since then I've lectured on *Shōbōgenzō* and written books about it. But I'm still finding new things.

For example, while preparing this book I noticed that Dōgen mentions the phrase "mind here and now is Buddha" a number of times in his early pieces and then later on gives us an entire chapter just about that phrase. For the first time I saw how he was engaging in an ongoing dialogue with his audience.

In some ways, Dōgen was sort of like an ancient Buddhist blogger. He wrote these pieces and then delivered most of them as sermons in his temple. Afterward there must have been questions from the monks. I don't think they did Q&A sessions after Dōgen's talks, although there's no way of knowing. But Dōgen and his monks lived together in a tiny temple in the middle of nowhere (or at least on the outskirts of Kyoto, if we're talking about his first temple). The monks must have taken Dōgen aside from time to time and asked about the things he said. In reading these pieces I'm starting to view them as the fruits of these discussions.

Or perhaps it's more accurate to say that these pieces were the dregs of the discussions, the fossils, the little bits that were left over after the good stuff was gone. Buddhism being an oral tradition, face-to-face conversation always beats anything that can be written down. Remember that.

In his introduction to this piece Nishijima Roshi says, "The principle 'mind here and now is Buddha' must be understood not from the standpoint of the intellect, but from the standpoint of practice. In other words, the principle does not mean belief in something spiritual called 'mind' but it affirms the time 'now' and the place 'here' as reality itself."

We'll take this up and more after looking at the piece itself. See you there!

Every Buddha and every patriarch maintained the principle that mind here and now is Buddha. However, this phrase was not heard in India. It was first spoken in China.

When dumb people hear "mind here and now is Buddha" they think it means that the intellect and sense perception of people who've never established the truth is Buddha. That's because they don't have decent teachers.

A guy called Senika was a good example of someone who thought he understood Buddhism and wrote a lot about it but never got it at all. Here's what he says.

> The great truth exists in our body here and now, so it's easy to recognize. The everlasting soul can differentiate between cold and heat and pain and pleasure, and can recognize aches or itches. Things come and go, but the soul remains unchanged. This spiritual intelligence pervades all things without distinguishing ordinary from sacred.
>
> Even though we may encounter illusory things, they're all just like flowers floating in the sky. Once we develop the right kind of wisdom, all that stuff vanishes. The soul alone remains. When you die, your soul comes out of your body like a guy running out of a burning house.
>
> This everlasting, all-pervading soul is what we call "Buddha" or "enlightenment." Or we call it the "true self" or "original essence."
>
> After you recognize what you really are, you no longer have to transmigrate through birth and death, and you don't get reincarnated again. There is no reality other than that of the all-pervading soul.

That's what the non-Buddhist Senika says.

Master Nan'yo Echu (Ch. Nanyang Huizhong, c. 675–775 CE) asks a monk, "Where are you from?"

The monk says, "I'm from way down south."

Master Echu says, "Are there good teachers down there?"

The monk says, "Sure. Lots!"

Master Echu says, "What do they teach?"

The monk says, "Down south they say 'mind here and now is Buddha.' Buddha is consciousness itself. The body appears and disappears but the true, all-pervading spiritual essence is eternal. Like a snake shedding its skin or a guy moving out of a crummy apartment, the eternal spirit moves on when the body dies."

Master Echu says, "If that's so, all they're teaching you is the non-Buddhist philosophy of Senika."

Master Echu says he's heard a lot of teachers say crap like this and they're always hugely popular. But, Master Echu says, "If seeing, hearing, awareness, and recognition are the same as Buddha-nature, why would Vimalakirti (a layman of Buddha's time who understood Buddha's philosophy clearly and engaged in a lot of dialogues with him that formed a book called the Vimalakirti Sutra) say, 'The dharma is transcendent over seeing, hearing, awareness and recognition?'"

Master Echu was a really great Zen teacher, so we should listen to him and not to Senika. The immediate universe is not waiting for realization. This concrete world doesn't recede or appear. It's not just mind. Mind exists as fences and walls. It doesn't get muddy or wet. It's never artificial.

We realize in practice that mind here and now is Buddha. The mind which is Buddha is here and now, the Buddha here and now is mind, mind and Buddha are here and now, and Buddha-mind is here and now.

Realization in practice is just *mind here and now is Buddha*. That's why Master Chorei Shataku (Ch. Shangling Chouzhou, 1065–1123 CE) said, "When somebody becomes conscious of mind, there isn't an inch of soil on Earth." When we become conscious of mind, heaven falls down and the Earth is torn apart. In other words, when we become conscious of mind the Earth grows three inches thicker.

Master Isan Reiyu (Ch. Guishan Lingyou, 780–841 CE) said, "Fine pure and bright mind is mountains, rivers and the Earth, sun, moon and the stars." This means when we're moving forward, not enough and when we're drawing backward, too much.

Mind as mountains, rivers, and the Earth is nothing but mountains, rivers, and the Earth. There are no additional waves or surf, no wind or smoke. Mind as the sun, moon, and stars is nothing but sun, moon, and stars. There is no additional fog or mist.

Mind as living and dying, coming and going is nothing but living and dying, coming and going. There's no additional delusion or realization. Mind as fences, tiles, walls, and pebbles is just fences, tiles, walls, and pebbles. There's no additional mud or water.

"Mind here and now is Buddha" is untainted mind here and now as Buddha. If we don't establish the will, undergo training, realize the truth, and experience nirvana, then the state is not "mind here and now is Buddha."

But if we establish the will and do even a molecule of practice/experience, then "mind here and now is Buddha." If we establish the will and practice/experience for a single instant, or for zillions of years, or inside half a fist (which means concretely), then this is "mind here and now is Buddha."

Anybody who says this isn't so doesn't understand what mind here and now is Buddha means.

— Preached at Kannon-dori-kosho-horin-ji Temple
near Kyoto on May 25, 1239

Obviously Dōgen really wants to pound in this idea that Buddhism is not the belief in an eternal, unchanging soul that transmigrates from body to body. I've already talked some about Dōgen's views on reincarnation, and here you get another taste of just how adamant he was about denying this belief, at least in the sense that it was commonly understood in his time and continues to be understood in ours.

The fact that this was so important to him tells me that he probably had a lot of folks come to him asking about this stuff, just the way Buddhist teachers often do today. It must have been annoying.

Dōgen's big question when he was a young monk was this: If Buddhism teaches that we're all perfect just as we are — and it does teach that — then why do we have to undergo training? A whole lot of *Shōbōgenzō* is Dōgen's attempt to answer that question.

When I say it's his attempt to answer that question, I don't mean that he was searching for an answer. He already understood deep in his bones why this was so. But he found it very difficult to articulate it so that folks would understand. The answer to the question comes in actually doing meditation practice. It's not an intellectual matter.

I once asked Nishijima Roshi why Dōgen spent so much time trying to explain this stuff, and why Nishijima also did so, and why he was encouraging me to do it too. He said, "People like to have explanations."

That's true. We don't just like to have explanations; we seem to need them. In the novel *Cat's Cradle*, Kurt Vonnegut has his character Bokonon, the founder of a religion based on lies that are actually true, compose the following poem:

> Tiger got to hunt, bird got to fly;
> Man got to sit and wonder "why, why, why."
> Tiger got to sleep, bird got to land;
> Man got to tell himself he understand.

I read that book a long time before I met Nishijima or read Dōgen, so I understood what Nishijima meant when he said we like explanations. We just need to feel we know, or we can't rest. And yet much of life is unknowable and will remain so. Lots of religions try to deal with this by inventing explanations and myths.

But myths only work if you don't try to turn them into factual explanations. If you try to turn your myths into literal, inerrant truths — if, for example, you start insisting that Noah really did build an ark or that the Earth was created in six days a few thousand years ago, it just becomes a big, huge mess.

The solution Buddhism offers is what the Korean Buddhist master

Seung Sahn called "Don't know mind." You know that you don't know. So at least you still feel like you know something, even if it's just the fact that you don't know.

The other point Dōgen makes in this piece is that if we say — as many Buddhist masters do — that the whole world is just mind, it doesn't mean the same thing as saying consciousness is the ultimate reality. It also doesn't mean that the physical world is either nonexistent or, at the very least, unimportant. The physical world as mind is still the physical world. It's real, even though our understanding of it is so messed up that we can call that understanding delusional.

Dōgen's Buddhism is not an idealistic or spiritual philosophy that denies the physical world. Nor is it a materialistic philosophy that considers the physical world the only reality. It says that neither of these positions is the right one. Reality, according to Dōgen, is neither matter nor spirit but something that transcends those categories. Saying that it is mind alone just reminds us that what we conceive of as mind is an intimate aspect of all things, even inanimate objects, and that we are so deeply connected with everything around us that we can say there is really no separation at all.

11. BANNED IN JAPAN: THE TWISTED HISTORY OF *SHŌBŌGENZŌ*

IT WOULD BE a massive understatement to say that *Shōbōgenzō* was not a bestseller when it was first written. In fact, hardly anyone in those days read it. The book was virtually lost for centuries and was even banned by the Japanese government at one point. It wasn't until the twentieth century that *Shōbōgenzō* really began to be regarded as the philosophical classic it's considered today. That's a full eight hundred years after it was written, folks! In my book *Sit Down and Shut Up* I also mentioned this and said that it was as if my book had to wait until the year 2807 to reach an audience.

I still think this is an interesting point. Just think about the differences between our era and Dōgen's. In the *Shōbōgenzō* chapter "The Dignified Behavior of Acting Buddha" ("Gyobutsu Iigi"), Dōgen compares the Buddha's practice to an iron rail thousands of miles long. When I first read that I envisioned a train track. But then I remembered that Dōgen lived hundreds of years before railways were invented. Who knows where he came up with that image! I don't really believe the guy was psychic, but that line makes me wonder sometimes. I hate to sound too much like Erich von Däniken here, but Dōgen also wrote lines that seem to indicate he understood that the Earth rotated and that landmasses could move, long before either of these ideas were widely accepted. My teacher believed he was able to intuit these things. I'm not so certain, but I think it's possible.

Let's talk about what *Shōbōgenzō* is and what it was. The current English- and Japanese-language editions of *Shōbōgenzō* are usually multivolume sets. My teacher's version is in four volumes, while Kaz Tanahashi's edition is in either two doorstop-size hardbacks or one Greater New York telephone directory–size paperback. But Dōgen originally wrote his stuff on papyrus scrolls, which were then hand copied by his students.

As I mentioned on page 1, the common term for the sections that comprise *Shōbōgenzō* is *fascicles*. According to Barbara O'Brien at About .com, the word *fascicle* is "a term borrowed from horticulture. An example of a fascicle in the plant world would be a cluster of needles on a pine tree. In literature, a fascicle is a discrete section of a book that could be pulled out and published separately." Professor William Bodiford likes to call the sections of *Shōbōgenzō* "books." But I prefer to talk like a normal human and just call them "chapters."

We know that Dōgen intended *Shōbōgenzō* to be a single massive literary work because while he was alive he compiled certain of his scrolls into different configurations, which he called *Shōbōgenzō*. His chief disciple, Ejo, said that before Dōgen became ill with the sickness that would kill him at age fifty-three, he had been working on creating a definitive hundred-chapter version of *Shōbōgenzō*. In the end he completed only ninety-five or ninety-six chapters, depending on if you count one of the pieces he split into two sections as a single chapter or as two.

During the Middle Ages a buttload of variant *Shōbōgenzō*s existed in Soto temples throughout Japan. Some had seventy-eight chapters, some had eighty-four, some had ninety. There was also a sixty-chapter edition and a twelve-chapter edition and one that had twenty-eight chapters. It's all very confusing. If you're really interested in getting all the details, check out a book called *Dōgen: Textual and Historical Studies*, edited by Steven Heine. The first chapter, "Textual Genealogies of

Dōgen" by William Bodiford, lays it all out in about as much detail as anyone could stand. Most of what I'm going to tell you in this chapter comes from what Bodiford wrote.

In the 1700s the Japanese government looked to the West and noticed that every Western religion was based on a book. So they decreed that all Japanese religions had to have some kind of book as their basis too. By then an organization called Soto-shu existed. This was a loose affiliation of temples whose practice was based on the style of Zen that Dōgen brought back from China and whose priests and abbots could trace their lineage back to Dōgen and his students.

Naturally, the Soto-shu chose *Shōbōgenzō* as their book. But there was a lot of dispute about how it should be interpreted. The Soto-shu responded by asking the government to ban the printing of the book so that only they could tell people what was written inside. The government agreed to this request, and for more than a hundred years nobody could even find a copy of Dōgen's masterwork unless they worked for Soto-shu.

Japan closed itself off from contact with the outside world from 1633 until 1853, when the American commodore William Perry arrived in Yokohama Harbor with three black ships and forced Japan to open up to international trade. This set off what is known as the Meiji Restoration, in which the Meiji emperor came back into power and Japan embarked on a period of rapid modernization.

You can watch *The Last Samurai* with Tom Cruise if you want to know more about the Meiji Restoration. But for the purposes of this book, what's significant is that, as part of their effort to remake their image as a country on a par with the West, the Japanese started looking for thinkers in their own history who could prove to the West that Japan was as smart as Europe and America. This led to the rediscovery of Dōgen's writing and the promotion of *Shōbōgenzō* and his other works as world-class examples of philosophy.

In the 1920s a Japanese philosopher named Tetsuro Watsuji published a book called *Shamon Dōgen* (*The Monk Dōgen*) that helped create a huge wave of popular interest in Dōgen in Japan. After this, Dōgen's writings, including *Shōbōgenzō*, began to be reprinted as different scholars searched among the variant texts stored away in rural Soto temples for the most accurate versions of each chapter and vied with each other to produce the most definitive and complete edition.

These days the ninety-five-chapter edition, originally complied by Hangyo Kozen between 1688 and 1703, is generally considered the most comprehensive edition. It was the first one to be printed on woodblocks in 1815. This is the edition that Gudo Nishijima used as the basis for his complete English translation, which I have used as the main basis for this book. Originally this version excluded certain chapters that were considered secret by the Soto-shu, including the chapter about Buddhist robes, which appears later in this book. In 1906 they put the secret chapters back in and reprinted it. Several other versions have come out since then, each with its own advantages and disadvantages to Dōgen scholars.

In the 1960s Shunryu Suzuki, a Soto-shu monk, was sent to San Francisco to preside over a Zen temple there that served the Japanese immigrant population of that city. But pretty soon Suzuki's morning meditation services began to be attended by a number of non-Japanese who were interested in learning about Zen meditation after reading about it in books by D. T. Suzuki and seeing references to Zen in the works of Beat poets such as Jack Kerouac and Allen Ginsberg.

D. T. Suzuki was of the Rinzai Zen lineage and didn't care very much for Dōgen, whose philosophy he considered to be a form of negativism and whose meditation practices he thought of as promoting mental stasis. Shunryu Suzuki, on the other hand, was a Soto monk schooled in the works of Dōgen. He often cited Dōgen in his lectures, some of which were compiled into *Zen Mind, Beginner's Mind* in 1971. Unlike *Shōbōgenzō*, *Zen Mind, Beginner's Mind* was a huge seller right from the start and remains in print today. That book was many Westerners' first encounter with Dōgen — me among them.

One of the people who deeply influenced Suzuki's love of Dōgen was a guy named Kodo Sawaki. Often called "Homeless Kodo," Sawaki was a Zen monk who maintained no temple of his own (until very late in life, anyway), but instead traveled around Japan, leading meditation sessions and lecturing about Dōgen. Sawaki was also a huge influence on my teacher Gudo Nishijima, who attended many of Sawaki's lectures and meditation sessions.

These days, as I've already mentioned, there are dozens of books about Dōgen in English, with more being published regularly, as well as several English translations of *Shōbōgenzō*. The TV series *Lost*, in which many of the characters were named after famous philosophers and religious thinkers, even had a character named Dōgen. To me his appearance — at least in name — as a major character in an American network TV show is definite proof that after eight hundred years Dōgen has been rescued from obscurity and now maintains his rightful place as one of the world's greatest philosophical thinkers.

Too bad the ending of *Lost* sucked so hard.

12. ZEN AND THE ART OF WIPING YOUR BUTT
Senjo
Washing

MAN, I ALWAYS dreaded when Nishijima Roshi would start reading this one during his Saturday-afternoon lectures on *Shōbōgenzō*. As I said before, every Saturday he would go through the whole thing, from start to finish, without skipping any chapters, including the weird ones, like this one. I don't know how many times I got to hear him lecturing on Dōgen's method of cleaning your butthole. But I am sure I did not want to hear it even once.

Yes, folks. Dōgen wrote a chapter of *Shōbōgenzō* all about how to keep your bum hygienic. Okay. There's more to it than that. But a significant segment of this chapter involves extremely detailed butt-cleaning instructions.

As I said when we looked at the chapter on temple rules, these kinds of writings by Dōgen give us an insight into how his is a philosophy of action. It's not just about what you think. It's about what you do, how you embody the attitude of Buddhism in your day-to-day activities. And that means all of them!

These butt-cleansing instructions were originally intended to be taken quite literally by Dōgen's monks. Don't worry, though. I don't know of any temple here or in Japan where the monks follow these rules to the letter anymore. However, they do suggest that bodily cleanliness was and still is extremely important to Buddhist practice.

Also, keep in mind that, as I pointed out before, Dōgen's monks were mostly young guys who'd been brought up in the boondocks of preindustrial Japan, back when it was largely regarded as a nation full of uneducated yokels. It was more crucial to teach those guys about personal hygiene than it is when dealing with the kinds of people one meets at Zen centers these days. Well, mostly, anyway. I've encountered some pretty stinky people in Zen places.

You'll see that Dōgen wrote this for his male students, but the instructions for women would be only slightly different. Let's take a look at what Dōgen has to say about butt washing.

The Buddhist patriarchs guarded and maintained the practice/experience called "not being stinky."

Master Daikan Eno (no relation to Brian) asked Master Nangaku Ejo, (Daikan Eno's successor), "Do you rely on practice and experience?"

Ejo said, "It's not that there's no practice and experience, but the state can never be stinky."

Eno said, "This unstinky state is what the Buddhas guard and desire. You're like this. I'm like this. All the masters of India were unstinky too."

The Sutra of Three Thousand Dignified Forms for Monks says, "Purifying the body means keeping your nails trimmed and washing your wiener and butthole."

There are dharma practices for cleaning the body and dharma practices for cleaning the mind. Not only do we clean the body and mind, we clean up around trees used for meditating under, even though they're outside and therefore can't really be considered dirty. This is a difficult point to understand but we do it anyhow.

In the Garland Sutra it says, "When we need to pee or poop, we should pray that all beings get rid of impurity and get free of greed, anger, and delusion. When we get to the toilet we should pray that all beings progress to the supreme state of the truth."

Water isn't originally pure or impure, and neither is the body. All dharmas are also like this. Water isn't sentient or insentient, and neither is the body. All dharmas are like this too. That's what Buddha said.

It's not that you clean the body by washing. Rather, we maintain the Buddha-dharma through the activity called washing.

At the moment we dignify body and mind through training, the eternal practice is totally realized and accomplished. That's how we manifest the original state.

We should cut our nails, all ten of them, both right and left hand, and trim them so they're shorter than a grain of wheat. These days in China lots of so-called Buddhist masters have long nails. Like four-inch nails! I've seen it! Others grow their hair long like a bunch of dirty hippies. They're not real monks. They're just posers.

My late master said, "Those who don't shave their heads aren't secular people or monks. They're just a bunch of dirty hippies! Since when did any real Buddhist patriarch not shave his head?" When he said this, lots of people who hadn't shaved their heads in years went and shaved them. My master was always going on about this kind of stuff. I think he was totally right.

Remember the famous story in which a passerby was so moved by the dignified way Buddha's disciple Shariputra took a poop that he decided to become a monk himself? When monks practice outdoors they don't have toilets. They clean themselves up with two rows of seven balls of clay.

First you take off your robes and fold them up. Then you find some soil — not the black stuff, but yellowish soil. Roll up the soil into balls, each about the size of a big soybean. Then arrange these into two rows of seven balls each and put them on a stone or someplace like that. Then get a rock you can use to rub your hands off with afterward.

After pooping some people use a stick or paper to clean off with. Then you go to the water to finish up, carrying three of those clay balls I told you to make. Take each ball in your hand and mix in a little water so that you get a kind of thin mud. Wash your wiener first, then use one ball like before to wash your butthole. Then use one of the clay balls to wash off the hand you used to wash your naughty bits with.

Ever since monks started living together they have built toilets.

Sometimes these are called the "east office" or the "brook house" or the "washhouse."

When you go to the toilet, take the "long cloth," which is a cloth around three meters (nine feet) long that is used as a towel, and a sash to hold up the sleeves of a monk's robe. Fold the towel in two and hang it over your left elbow. Then when you get to the toilet hang the towel over the clothes pole. If you're wearing your *o-kesa* or *rakusu* (Buddhist outer robes: the *o-kesa* looks like a big sash, while the *rakusu* is a hanging thing that looks sort of like a bib), hang those alongside the towel. And don't just toss them over the pole, either. Hang them nicely. You can put marks on sheets of paper next to the poles so you don't confuse your robe with someone else's.

When other monks come to the toilet, bow to them. You don't have to turn to them and make a formal bow, just fold your hands and kinda nod to acknowledge them. In case one of your hands is dirty do a one-handed bow.

The "Guidelines for Zen Monasteries" says, "When you have to go to the toilet, go early. Don't hold your pee so that you're in a big rush."

Before entering the toilet fill a bucket with water. Having entered the toilet, close the door with your left hand. Pour some of the water from the bucket into the toilet bowl, and then put the bucket in its place. Facing the toilet, snap your fingers three times. While you snap with your right hand, make a fist with your left hand and hold it against your hip.*

Pull up your undergarments, turn around so you're facing the door, squat down, and do your business. Don't miss and get stuff all over the toilet or outside of it. Keep quiet. Don't sing songs or chat with other people in the washroom. Don't write on the walls or make marks on the floor with a stick.**

Now use the shit-stick to wipe off any stuff that remains. You can use paper, but you shouldn't use old paper or paper with stuff written

---

* I did that just now to see what he meant. It makes you look like you're an arrogant hotel manager impatiently signaling for a bellhop.

** Just the fact that Dōgen had to specifically say this tells us a lot about the kinds of monks he had.

on it. Shit-sticks are a couple of inches long, and some are lacquered. There is a rack for clean sticks, and a box for dirty ones.

Holding the bucket with your right hand, dip your left hand into the water, scoop some up, and rinse your wiener three times, and then rinse your butthole. Don't tip the bucket or splash water anywhere. Wipe yourself dry, and make sure you dry off your bits too.

Put your clothes back on and wash your hands. Use ashes to clean the impure hand.

The Garland Sutra says, "When we wash our hands we should pray that all beings will get excellent hands with which to receive the dharma."

Don't do any of this noisily or hastily because actions like these purify the Buddha's Lands and adorn the Buddha's kingdom. You can apply fragrant wood to cover any unpleasant smells.

Privately consider that we don't try to explain the Buddha's dharma while on the toilet.

Cold water is used for cleaning the toilet because it's said that hot water gives rise to intestinal diseases, but you can use warm water to wash your hands. If the inside of the toilet is dirty, close the door and hang up the sign that says "dirty." If a bucket gets dropped in the toilet hang up the sign that says "fallen bucket." Don't go in a toilet that has one of these signs on it. If you're in the toilet and you hear someone outside snapping their fingers, leave and let them clean up the toilet.

Without washing, we shouldn't sit on the meditation platforms or receive people's prostrations. The Sutra of Three Thousand Dignified Forms says, "If we fail to wash the butthole or wiener we must not sit on the monk's pure sitting cloth. Even if we do, there is no happiness or virtue in it."

Thus, in the place of the truth where we pursue the truth we make cleanliness a priority. It's not our own intentional effort. It's a natural expression of dignified behavior. It's the ordinary behavior of Buddhas and the everyday life of the patriarchs.

Dumb people don't think that Buddhas have dignified behavior while on the toilet. We should remember that all the Buddhas have toilets.

Part 14 of the Precepts in Ten Parts says, "Rahula, Buddha's son, spent the night in the Buddha's toilet. When the Buddha woke up he patted Rahula on the head and composed a poem.

> You never lost your wealth
> You were never queasily poor
> You'll find the truth with stealth
> Problems you'll easily endure

There are toilet buildings in the places of pursuing Buddha's truth. The dignified behavior in the toilet is washing. We're lucky to have received it. Furthermore, the Buddha preached to Rahula in the toilet. The toilet was one of the assembly paces of the Buddhas.

Part 34 of the Mahasamgika Precepts says, "The toilet shouldn't be built in the east or north. It should be built in the south or west. The same applies to the urinal."

We should follow this rule of favorable directions. That's how they did things in the monasteries of ancient India during the Buddha's life-time. We should follow their example if we hope to practice like they did. The realization of the Buddha's body and mind in this very moment is like this.

— Preached at Kannon-dori-kosho-horin-ji Temple
near Kyoto on October 23, 1239

There you have it. Cut your nails, shave your head, and keep your naughty bits clean. Straight from the pen of Eihei Dōgen!

Dōgen quotes the Sutra of Three Thousand Dignified Forms for Monks several times in this piece. One of these I have paraphrased as, "Purifying the body means keeping your nails trimmed and washing your wiener and butthole." The word in the sutra that I've paraphrased as "wiener and butthole" is 大小便 (*daishoben*), which literally means "poop and pee." Most translators say "urine" and "feces." But the word is very colloquial and sounds more like poop and pee. The Nishijima/ Cross version has him saying "washing the anus and urethra," while Tanahashi has him saying "wash away excrement and urine." I figured you guys could handle what it actually says.

Dōgen quotes something from the Garland Sutra that I've para-phrased as, "When we flush, we should pray that living beings have patient endurance and become free from defilements." Of course, it doesn't really say "flush" here, but "wash away impurity with water," which in our modern idiom is to flush. Also what I've paraphrased as "get to the toilet" would be literally translated as "arrive at the water." Same difference.

After the stuff about all those clay balls, in their version Nishi-jima and Cross add the footnote, "It is not clear what was done with the remaining eleven balls of soil." This has been a mystery to Dōgen scholars for the past eight hundred years!

Even though it was excruciating to be read this passage aloud sev-eral times during my study with Nishijima Roshi, I learned a lot from it. I never attempted to do that whole thing about snapping your fingers and rolling up clay balls and all that. But it did give me the sense that Dōgen's Buddhist practice extended into all areas of life.

I think that's a great lesson. Because a lot of our philosophical stances these days are kind of half-assed. We're very bold in our proc-lamations of our own moral rectitude, but then we neglect to even keep our own toilets clean. You see a lot of that kind of thing. I used to see it all the time in my punk-rock days. Those guys were super-concerned with having the right political and philosophical views. But they never seemed to be able to keep their showers free from mold or their toilets free from horrible stains.

But what I think Dōgen is saying here is that if you want to be truly moral, truly ethical, you have to take things all the way. You even have to take a poop in an ethical manner.

Nothing in life was trivial for Dōgen. It was all important.

The men's room at Tokei-in Temple, where I attended many retreats with Nishijima Roshi, was a pretty normal men's room. I never heard anyone there snapping fingers. But there were poles inside that I assume were for hanging one's robes. Above the doorway was a small statue of an angry Buddhist deity called Ususama Myo. This character was derived from the more ancient Hindu god Agni, the god of fire. He is said to use his fire to burn away impurities. It was a pretty scary-looking little statue!

I always tried to observe some semblance of Dōgen's toilet rules while in that temple toilet, at least in general attitude if not in specific action. I usually ended up getting toilet-cleaner duty on those retreats. I tried my best to keep the place clean. But the temple was also a tourist attraction and the toilets were a little like the public facilities at a campsite. No matter how much you cleaned them they still had a pee smell that seemed to have seeped into the porcelain itself.

When we lived in Tokyo, my then-wife, Yuka, had a Xerox of Dōgen's toilet chapter tacked up inside our toilet room. I'd say "bathroom," but in Japanese houses the bathtub or shower is almost always in a different room from the toilet. Putting them in the same room is considered really gross, and I still think of it that way. It was a funny gesture to tack that up in there. But it always made me aware that I had a duty to maintain my principles even in such a private space and even when nobody was looking. To me, that is the great lesson of this chapter.

So don't worry about rolling up clay balls or figuring out what to do with the eleven you'd have left over if you followed Dōgen's instructions. But it can be a great benefit to try to keep your behavior properly dignified, no matter what you're doing, even if it's taking a dump!

13. THREE ENCOUNTERS WITH DŌGEN

THESE DAYS WE tend to put far more faith in concrete recordings, whether written or electronically preserved in audio and video, than we do in what someone remembers somebody having told them. The early Buddhists saw it differently. They thought the oral tradition was more likely to preserve the true essence and intention of what their master had said than if his exact words had been preserved on paper. Perhaps they believed that real people could translate the true meaning they'd received directly better than marks on paper could hope to convey. If you ask me, they were absolutely right.

I just watched the movie *The Treasure of the Sierra Madre*, starring Humphrey Bogart. That's the movie in which a Mexican bandito played by Alfonso Bedoya says, "Badges? We don't need no steeenkeen badges!" Only he never really says that. He actually says, "Badges? We ain't got no badges. We don't need no badges. I don't have to show you any stinkin' badges!" The oral tradition of movie lovers and popular culture changed the line. But although the words got a bit mangled, the essential meaning of the line remains the same.

The first real person I ever heard talk about Dōgen was Tim McCarthy. Tim was the teacher of a class I took at Kent State University sometime in the early 1980s with the very straightforward title of

Zen Buddhism. The class was part of something KSU called the Experimental College. This was a catchall term for a number of oddball not-for-credit courses the university offered.

The semester before I took the Zen Buddhism course, I took another Experimental College course called Introduction to Parapsychology. This course was all about the stuff the *X-Files* would base most of its episodes on a few years later, like out-of-body experiences, telepathy, telekinesis, and the rest. My favorite session was the one in which the instructor brought in a young woman who could supposedly channel the disembodied spirits of the dead.

Tim's class, like all the Experimental College classes, was a night course and an elective. Being a not-for-credit class, it doesn't even show up on my college transcripts, although it was the most important course I took in my entire university career and eventually formed the foundation for the way I earn my living. It says a lot about the blinkered conservative mentality of the folks who ran KSU in those days that a course about Zen Buddhism was deemed too freaky to get college credit for and was accorded the same level of respect as a course in which you got to see somebody channel the spirit of a dead motorcyclist.

Tim was an ordained monk in the Soto Zen tradition, of which Dōgen is often cited as being the founder, although he only claimed to have brought back to Japan a tradition that already existed in China. But Tim was also an academic with a master's degree in religious studies. So he structured the class not as a sectarian advertisement for the brand of Zen he'd been ordained in but as a serious scholarly overview of the history and practice of all forms of Zen. Though he talked in class about Dōgen's writings, this was not the point of the course. It was only later, when I continued hanging out with Tim and meditating with the tiny little group he put together, that I really started hearing about Dōgen.

Tim had absorbed most of what he knew about Dōgen through his teacher Kobun Chino Otogawa Roshi. Thus Tim's wasn't so much an academic study of Dōgen's writings as an experiential study of how Dōgen's philosophy was put into action by his teacher.

I didn't read Dōgen then, but I read *Zen Mind, Beginner's Mind* by Shunryu Suzuki, which I've mentioned a bunch of times now. Tim had assigned this book as part of the course. He said the chapters were short so you could read them on the toilet, which I sometimes did. But I also carried that book in my backpack and read it over and over between classes and on bus rides.

The book was created from transcripts of talks Suzuki gave. The editors did not correct the mistakes Suzuki made when he quoted Dōgen. Given the times, it's doubtful they even realized there were mistakes. Such mistakes, if one can even call them that, are part of what happens in an orally transmitted tradition like Zen Buddhism. Buddhism was a strictly oral tradition for some two hundred years before anyone attempted to preserve Gautama Buddha's words in writing. What we call mistakes today were simply part of the tradition. Teachers quoted the ancient founders of their tradition based on what they'd heard from their teachers, not from books.

Tim's way of teaching me about Dōgen was like Suzuki's. Sometimes he'd quote Dōgen's writings from memory, usually making more mistakes than Suzuki did in his book. But more often he just behaved in ways that were deeply informed by Dōgen's outlook, as he'd received it from Kobun, who in turn had received it from his teacher, and so on down the line for around eight hundred years.

But here's the weird thing. In his writings, Dōgen often comes across as one of the strictest, most rigid, even rule-bound Zen monks one would ever want to meet — or to avoid, if you feel the way I do about strict, rigid, rule-bound religious types. He spends a huge amount of time in his writings enumerating the most finicky minutia of Zen temple rules and etiquette. As we have seen, he even has a chapter in *Shōbōgenzō* dedicated to the proper way for monks to take a poop.

Yet Tim was nothing like that. He was very much a free spirit and tremendously antiauthoritarian. A friend of his who became his student said that, as a teacher, Tim so rejected the authority usually expected of teachers, especially religious ones, that it was hard to think of him as a teacher at all. This is the impression I got too. It seemed more like we were pals who meditated together rather than that I was his student. I still don't know whether calling myself Tim's student is really the proper way to characterize my relationship to him.

The next person I heard about Dōgen from was Gudo Nishijima Roshi. I met Nishijima about a year after I arrived in Japan, which would make it around ten years after I first encountered Tim and began a daily zazen practice. I guess it would've been 1994. I had spent my first year in Japan working as an English teacher for a high school in Toyama Prefecture on the remote western side of the country. Toyama was just north of Fukui Prefecture, which was formerly called Echizen and was the prefecture in which Dōgen established his temple Eihei-ji in 1244 CE.

I visited Eihei-ji once with this strange guy I'd met at a bar. Once a week this bar had a thing where they invited some of the English teachers who lived in town to hang out and speak English with locals, in exchange for free drinks. This guy and I spoke about Dōgen, and he invited me to come with him on a trip to see Eihei-ji. It was an uneventful visit, during which I mostly learned that Eihei-ji was a big tourist trap. I didn't do any meditating there, and in fact I don't recall even seeing any monks hanging around the place. Maybe they were hiding in the back.

At the time I met him, about a year after my Eihie-ji visit, Nishijima Roshi was working with Mike Cross on their complete English translation of *Shōbōgenzō*. As I've mentioned, every Saturday Nishijima met with a little group at a room in Tokyo University's Young Buddhist's Association, where we would do zazen for half an hour, followed by an hour-long discussion about Dōgen. Nishijima would read from his translation in progress and then invite participants to ask questions. These sessions were useful for him in refining the text. The first volume was already out when I started going to Nishijima's lectures.

The next three volumes came out during the ten years I attended those weekly meetings.

It was during my study with Nishijima that I decided it was high time I actually started reading Dōgen for myself. I saw how hard Nishijima was working on producing those translations, and I figured the least I could do was to read them. So I did. I was working for a film and television production company (founded by the man who invented Godzilla), and I had an hour-long commute each day to and from work. So I decided to spend those two hours reading *Shōbōgenzō* on the Odakyu train line between Nakano, where I lived, and Setagaya, where the company offices were.

At first I could barely understand what I was reading. Even so, I knew it was vitally important stuff. I had seen how it had influenced Tim and Suzuki and Kobun and now Nishijima. Living in Japan, I knew that Dōgen was significant, a cultural treasure. So I buckled down and read the damned thing, even when it made close to no sense at all. When I finally finished it I went back to the beginning and read it again. Then I went all the way through it for a third time, this time starting with the last chapter and making my way back to the first. At that point it started making some kind of sense to me.

Nishijima shaved his head and often wore the black robes of a Zen monk, neither of which Tim did. But he didn't live in a monastery and was largely ignorant of most of the ceremonial aspects of temple practice. He was married and lived in a house on the outskirts of Tokyo with his wife. He worked as a financial adviser for a soap and cosmetics company. He often advised his students *not* to become temple-living monks.

Nishijima ordained me as a monk. In fact, I took roughly the same ordination ceremony three times. Once it was called *jukai* and was what most people would consider a layperson's ceremony of accepting the Buddhist precepts. The second time was my wedding. Soto-style weddings are basically a dual *jukai* ceremony with a ring exchange at the end. The couple vows that, as married people, they will uphold the Buddhist moral regulations. The third time was called *shukke tokudo*, which means "home-leaving ordination." But I never actually left home. I continued to live in an ordinary house in Tokyo. Nishijima encouraged this, saying that he thought it would be a mistake to become a full-time monastery-bound monk.

Nishijima Roshi first started studying Dōgen when he was a teenager. He was a pretty good track runner in those days and said that he found an amazing sense of quiet stillness when engaged in particularly long runs. He looked into meditation as a way to find that same stillness when not running. As I said, he first encountered Dōgen's work at a used bookstore and was amazed that he could not understand this book written in his own language. That got him curious to learn more.

Nishijima was very different from Tim. As I said, Nishijima actually dressed like a monk. He was old and Japanese, much more typical of what one would expect of a Zen monk. Yet he was a unique individual, just as Tim was. While he was always open and friendly, he could also be extremely opinionated. He had tremendous confidence in himself and in his interpretation of Dōgen. To him, Buddhism was not a spiritual practice or a religion. It was simply a practical approach to real life that neither denied the spiritual side of things nor held that spirituality was better or nobler than the material side of life.

Whereas I actually lived with Tim for a couple of years, I never moved into the Buddhist center Nishijima established in the Tokyo suburb of Chiba. I spent a lot of time there, but I had my own place in the city. I got to know Nishijima mainly as my teacher rather than as a friend. Tim is only ten years older than I am and we're both from Ohio, while Nishijima was many decades older than me, and Japanese. Our points of contact were fewer. Yet over the years I did develop a strange friendship with the old man.

The third person through whom I encountered Dōgen was Kazuaki Tanahashi. I first met Kaz, as his friends call him, in person much later in my career as a Zen person. It was around 2008 when I was on a tour of Germany following the publication of the German edition of my book *Hardcore Zen*. My friend Regina Obendorfer, with whom Kaz was staying in Frankfurt at the time, invited me to come over and hang out with him. But I'd already met Kaz in writing many years before that. Until Nishijima's final volumes of *Shōbōgenzō* came out, Kaz's translations were the only places I could find certain of Dōgen's writing in English. So I had read a lot of Kaz's work already.

Kaz began translating Dōgen in the sixties after encountering Shunryu Suzuki in San Francisco, where both of them lived at the time. Kaz was deeply impressed with Suzuki and wanted to help him out any way he could. Suzuki suggested he translate Dōgen into English so that his students in San Francisco could read some of his works. Eventually Kaz published a volume called *Moon in a Dewdrop*, which contained a sampling of Dōgen's most important writings, some of which had not yet been published by Nishijima.

I'm not sure what I expected when I met Kaz. But I'm sure it wasn't the long-haired, wispy-bearded, almost-hippie-looking guy I encountered at Regina's house. Kaz is also a master calligrapher and painter, as well as a peace activist. He travels the world talking about peace, and finances his travels by selling some of the most innovative and interesting calligraphy I've ever seen. Instead of painting Chinese characters with black ink like most calligraphers, he does his in vibrant psychedelic colors. I became as big a fan of his calligraphy work as I am of his Dōgen translations.

None of these three men looks or acts very much like I would have imagined a person deeply involved in the study of Dōgen to look or act. Yet Dōgen had affected them all so profoundly that it wouldn't be wrong to say that their entire lives were shaped by the things Dōgen wrote.

A lot of people who study Dōgen worry about one specific and very glaring contradiction in his writings — which are often characterized by contradictions. In his earlier writings Dōgen is adamant that Zen practice and realization is available to anyone, regardless of whether they are monastics or laypeople, male or female, old or young, clever or stupid. He was extremely progressive in his attitude toward women, which in Japan is woefully behind the egalitarian ideals of the West, even today. Yet in his later writings Dōgen seems to have changed his mind and started to believe that only temple-bound monks — male and female, so at least he didn't change his mind about that part — could possibly attain the Buddhist truth.

Unlike the monks at Eihei-ji, who follow Dōgen's written rules to the letter even today (except for the stuff about balls of clay), Tim, Gudo, and Kaz regularly disregarded those rules and lived their lives pretty much like normal contemporary people. Were they just picking and choosing the parts of Dōgen's writings they liked, while ignoring the parts that didn't suit them? Somehow that didn't seem to be the case. They were all very disciplined in their own respects, even when that discipline sometimes manifested itself in ways that were not so obvious.

And I had my own doubts about the necessity of temple life. For example, if Dōgen really was as relevant to ordinary people living today as my teachers said he was, what good was that fact if the realization he wrote about was available only to culty-looking weirdos ensconced in remote temples following rules laid down eight hundred years ago? Was Dōgen right about some things and wrong about others?

That's one way of looking at Dōgen's writings. But then there's the fact that Dōgen reworked some of his classically egalitarian pieces like "Genjo Koan" right up till his final years. Even as he was writing other sermons that seemed to contradict its message that anyone could attain the highest truth. Even when he was simultaneously writing that realization was for temple-bound monks alone. Why?

The solution Nishijima proposed was that Dōgen was above all a practical person. He was trying to run a temple in the cold, remote mountains of rural Japan with a bunch of young monks who were probably pretty frustrated by the conditions there. He wrote many of his sermons to encourage them. And he was *always* contradictory, not just in his views about the cloistered life versus life as a layperson. He knew that often two contradictory statements can both be true, even if they can't be reconciled. We'll talk about that a lot more as we go along.

I still see Tim McCarthy pretty regularly. We often exchange emails or chat on Facebook. I'm not as close as that with Kaz, but then again I never was. Nishijima Roshi passed away in January 2014 at the age of ninety-four. I didn't hear much from him for the last two or three years of his life. He'd fallen ill and decided to move in with his daughter, who never really interacted with his Zen students that much to begin with. In some ways he had neglected her and her mother in favor of us, so I could understand her feelings. I just sadly accepted the situation. He continues to be a huge influence on my life. So do Tim and Kaz, whether or not I see them in person. And so does Dōgen, whom none of us has ever met.

14. WAS DŌGEN THE FIRST BUDDHIST FEMINIST?

Raihai Tokuzui

Prostrating to That Which Has Attained the Marrow

YOU CAN'T REALLY call Dōgen a feminist in the strictest sense because no equivalent to the word or even the concept of "feminism" existed in Dōgen's time. The word *feminism* derives from a term first used in France in the nineteenth century (*féminisme*) and didn't come into general usage in English until the 1960s. It's a bit like the way you can't really define certain ancient Greeks as homosexuals even though they had sex exclusively with others of their gender because there was no concept of homosexuality as a social identifier in those days.

Yet in this essay, written in 1240, Dōgen takes a very strong stand against the common idea held by many Buddhists of his time that women were somehow lesser spiritual beings than men. It's clear that Dōgen himself held a number of female practitioners and teachers in high regard.

This is extremely significant. The Buddhist tradition as a whole has a weirdly mixed track record when it comes to its female practitioners. On the one hand, it was the first of the great Indian religious traditions to admit women. I need to qualify that statement by saying that some archaeologists believe that there was a prehistoric matriarchal religion in India long before Buddhism. But since we know almost nothing about this religion except for the fact that its followers liked to carve feminine deities out of stone, I feel there's no choice but to leave it out of the current discussion.

According to tradition, the Buddha first established a male-only monastic order. When certain women who had listened to his teachings, including the wife he left behind when he decided to pursue the truth and the woman who raised him after his mother died, asked to join the group he refused. At this point his chief attendant, a guy named Ananda, asked the Buddha if women were any less intelligent than men. The Buddha said no, they were just as intelligent. Then Ananda asked if women were any less capable than men of realizing the truth. The Buddha again said no, women were just as capable as men of realizing the truth. "Then why can't they join our order?" Ananda asked. At this point the Buddha gave in and said that women could join.

However, the Buddha is supposed to have said that allowing women to join the order would cause the order to decline and finally disappear entirely in five hundred years. The mixed male-female order would not last as long, he said, as the all-boys club he had first established. We know now that this was not true, but we're not really sure the Buddha even said it.

In her book *Women of the Way*, Sallie Tisdale goes into great detail on the subject of women's historical involvement in Buddhist practice. Her research into the subject has led her to question the historical veracity of this traditional account. It may be that this story was a later invention or a mythologized summation of a few hundred years of the experiences of various people within the Buddhist lineages. Maybe she's right. Most of these ancient stories are fairly dubious as historical accounts.

Whatever the case, there is also a very strong misogynist undercurrent in a lot of Buddhist literature that seems to be totally at odds with the story that the Buddha himself did not regard women as inferior creatures. Tisdale quotes a sutra that says, "The dead snake and the dog are detestable but women are even more detestable than they are." Another Chinese Buddhist saying she discovered says, "If there were no women, every man would be a bodhisattva" and one more says, "The best thing about Buddhist heaven is that there are no women." So I guess Buddhist heaven is like the He-Man Woman Hater's Club from the old *Little Rascals* comedies. At any rate, it doesn't sound like much of a heaven to me.

Women were seen as obstructions to men's study and practice of the Buddhist way. One very early piece of Buddhist literature that Tisdale cites, the Anguttara Nikaya, says, "I see no other single form so enticing, so desirable, so intoxicating, so binding, so distracting, such a hindrance to winning the unsurpassed peace from effort...as a woman's form."

These are just a few examples of the attitudes Dōgen is responding to in this essay. There are a whole lot more where these came from. Dōgen is going against a very, very strong tide of tradition here. In that sense I think it's perfectly fair to retroactively call him a feminist. We have to remember that Dōgen lived a very long time ago in a world radically different from ours. So we need to cut him a little bit of slack when his attitudes are not quite in line with those of current feminism. Still, there's nothing in this particular essay or in any of the records of Dōgen's life and work that make him sound like anything less than a true feminist, in the contemporary sense of the word.

To be fair about some of the antifemale rhetoric that occurs in Buddhism, I don't think most of it was initially intended as a put-down of women. By that I mean that the writers probably weren't trying to send a message to women saying, "Hey, gals! You're terrible." Rather, they were heterosexual men trying hard to cope with celibacy and trying to help other hetero men do so by saying, "Hey, guys! The celibacy thing is tough, but if you think of women this way maybe you'll be able to deal with it better."

It's a lousy strategy, if you ask me. Obviously it had the unfortunate consequence of making celibate male monks think of women as almost demonic creatures and led to some of the discriminatory practices Dōgen denounces in this essay. It encouraged such frankly idiotic supposedly "Buddhist" customs as monks not being allowed to even so much as shake a woman's hand. This foolishness is still practiced today even by Western converts to certain traditions. Personally, I have no respect at all for that kind of nonsense, no matter how ancient or traditional it is. By the way, I do not particularly care if you're offended by my attitude. I find this repugnant misogynistic practice far more offensive than you could possibly find my attitude toward it.

I am amazed every time I read this part of *Shōbōgenzō* that a man of Dōgen's era was brave enough to say some of the things he says here. It makes me very happy to be part of his lineage. Let's take a look at what he actually said, and we'll discuss it some more afterward.

The most difficult thing about practicing zazen is finding a good teacher. A good teacher, whether male or female, needs to be a strong person.* The person should be someone who has that unspeakable "it" quality.**

They're† not a person of the past and present but they might have the naturally mystical spirit of a wild fox. This is the face of someone who has totally gotten wise to what Buddha was all about.

---

* The word I'm translating as "strong person" here is 大丈夫 (*daijobu*). In modern Japanese this word just means "all right." But it's actually a Confucian term meaning literally a "stout fellow." Thus Dōgen has to make a point of saying "whether male or female" here.

** That's almost literally what Dōgen says here. He says 恁麼人 (*inmonin*). The first two characters are a Chinese word meaning "it" or "what" and are used by Dōgen to indicate something that can't be named. The third character just means "person."

† In Japanese the subject of a sentence can be omitted if it is understood. Dōgen doesn't say "he" or "she" in this section. He just leaves the subject unstated. Clearly he means a person of either gender since he already said a good teacher is "beyond appearances of male or female" (男女等の相にあらず *Danjo-nado no sōni arazu*, which I paraphrased just now as "whether male or female"). I'm saying "they" here rather than "he or she" or "s/he" because it's just easier and reads more naturally. I know this usage is not necessarily grammatically sound.

They may be a guide or benefactor. They are never unclear about cause and effect. They may be you, me, him, or her.

Once we meet a good teacher we should throw away everything else and just get on with it. We should train with all our heart/mind, and train when we have no heart/mind, or train even when we have half a heart/mind. We should learn about walking on tiptoes as the Buddha did and about putting out a fire on our heads.*

When we do this demons can never mess with us. The person who cut off his own arm for his teacher — as Taiso Eka was said to have done for his teacher Bodhidharma — is none other than you! The master who drops off body and mind is you yourself!

You get the truth by sincerity and trust. This is not something that comes from the outside but is also not a direction that emerges from within. You leave the workaday world and make your home in the truth.

If you regard yourself as more important than the dharma, you'll never get the dharma. So don't take yourself too seriously. Those who regard the dharma as truly more important than themselves have the right humble attitude.

Just rely on whatever has the truth, whether it's a lamppost or a stop sign or a Buddha, whether it's a stray dog, a demon or a god, or a man or a woman.** It is common to be born with a body and mind. But to meet the dharma is really rare.

Shakyamuni Buddha said, "When you meet teachers who expound the supreme state of enlightenment, don't worry about their race or caste. Don't get hung up on their looks, and don't judge their conduct. Because you receive their wisdom, feed them thousands of pounds of gold every day, give them flowers, bow to them, and never get ticked off at them. Ever since I got enlightened, that's what I've been doing, and look at me! I'm Buddha!"

---

* This is a reference to the idea that Buddhist training is as urgent as putting out a fire on your head.

** Yes, Dōgen equates women with stray dogs and demons here, but note that he also equates men with stray dogs and demons!

So look to trees and stones to be your teachers,* even fields and villages might preach to you, as it says in the Lotus Sutra. Question lampposts and investigate fences and walls.

There's a story about the Indra, the most powerful of the Hindu gods, asking a wild dog to be his master, and Indra was regarded as a great bodhisattva. So the status of a teacher clearly doesn't matter.

Even so, dumbheads who don't listen to the Buddha-dharma think, "I'm a senior monk, I can't learn from a junior monk!" or "I'm an ordained master, I can't bow to somebody who's not a master!" and other such dopey things. Dunces like these are totally hopeless.

Master Joshu Jushin (Ch. Zhaozhou Congshen, 778–897 CE) said, "I shall question anyone who is superior to me, even a seven-year-old kid. I shall teach anyone whose understanding is inferior to mine, even a hundred-year-old codger."

When a female monk who has attained the truth becomes the master of a temple, male and female monks alike will join her order and bow to her, asking about the dharma. It's like a thirsty person finding a soda machine.

Master Rinzai Gigen (Ch. Linji Yixuan, d. 866 CE, the nominal founder of the Rinzai sect of Zen) grabbed Master Kankei Shikan (Ch. Guanxi Zhixian, d. 895 CE) when Shikan came to visit him. Shikan said, "I get it." Rinzai let go and said he would let Shikan hang out for a while. From that point on Shikan was Rinzai's disciple.

Shikan left Rinzai and visited the female master Matsuzan Ryonen (Ch. Moshan Liaoran, dates unknown, c. 800s CE). She asked him where he had come from. Shikan said, "From the front door!"

Matsuzan said, "How come you're naked, then?" This was her way of saying it was better to just be polite than to try to give a goofy "Zen" answer. Shikan was speechless and just bowed to her.

---

* This refers to an ancient Buddhist story in which a demon tells a child-bodhisattva the first two lines of a poem, and then tells the child he's too hungry to tell him the last two lines. The child offers his own body as food for the demon in exchange for the last two lines. As he's dying, the child writes these lines on nearby trees and stones in his own blood. The poem goes: "All actions are inconsistent / arising and passing is concretely existent / After arising and passing cease / This is quiet, this is peace." It's an okay poem but not worth getting eaten by a demon for, if you ask me.

Shikan asked Matsuzan later, "What is Matsuzan?"

Matsuzan, whose name, like those of many Buddhist masters, was also the name of the mountain where she lived, said, "Matsuzan never shows her peak!"

Shikan said, "No. I meant who is the person who lives in the mountain?"

Matsuzan said, "It's beyond male or female."

Shikan said, "So why don't you change?"

Matsuzan said, "I'm not the ghost of a wild fox. Why change?" The ghost of a wild fox means someone who is deceptive.

Shikan didn't know what to say to that, either, so he just bowed.

Eventually Shikan became a vegetable gardener at Matsuzan's temple and stayed there for three years. When Shikan became a master he told his monks, "I got half a dipper at Papa Rinzai's place and half a dipper at Mama Matsuzan's place. Now I've drunk a whole dipper full and am completely satisfied!"

Shikan's respect for Matsuzan is a good example to us all.

The nun Myoshin (Ch. Miaoxin, dates unknown, c. 800s CE) was the disciple of Kyozan Ejaku (Ch. Yangshan Huiji, 807–883 CE). When the chief of the temple's business affairs office retired, Kyozan asked his assembly who they thought was most qualified. Everyone agreed that even though Myoshin was a woman she had the balls to do the job.[*]

One day Myoshin was listening to seventeen visiting monks having a really dumb argument about an old Buddhist story concerning a flag waving in the wind. In the story, two monks were watching a flag flapping in the wind and arguing over whether it was the flag moving or the wind moving. Their master heard this and told them it wasn't the flag or the wind, it was their minds moving. When Myoshin heard the seventeen monks arguing about this she said, "Jeez-o-Pete! How many sandals have they worn out in vain visiting temples if that's the best they can do?"

They overheard her, but they didn't resent her criticism. Instead

---

[*] They said she was 大丈夫 — *daijobu* — which you'll recall means "big, stout fellow." In other words, they said that even though she was a woman she had the balls for the job.

they asked what she thought of the story they were discussing. "C'mere!" she said. While they were walking toward her she said, "This is not the wind moving. It's not a flag moving. It's not the mind moving." The seventeen monks were impressed, so they bowed and became her students.

This is the authentic Buddhist way. Even if a monk is senior, if he doesn't understand the dharma, what good is he? A leader needs clear eyes. But how many of them are just like a bunch of village idiots? Some of these dopes refuse to be taught by female teachers who are clearly their superiors. What a bunch of dim-witted weenies!

Over in China, if a female monk becomes a master everybody respects her. The male monks listen to her. That's an established tradition. Any male monk, regardless of his attainment, will bow and listen to a female monk who understands the dharma.

Why should men be higher? Emptiness is emptiness. The elements are the elements. Men and women are both able to attain the highest truth. Everyone who attains the truth deserves to be revered. Don't worry about whether they're male or female.

In China there's a word that translates as "householder." It means a working person, as opposed to a monk. Some live in actual houses and some don't. But if a householder attains the truth, monks should bow down and ask for his or her teaching just as they would of an ordained master.

Even a girl of seven can be a guide to monks if she's got the truth. We should venerate such a person just as we'd venerate an ordained master. That's the time-honored tradition, and those who don't know it are pitiful. Since ancient times there have been female emperors both here in Japan and in China. We treat female emperors with as much respect as male emperors. So when a female monk becomes enlightened, we respect her just as we do a male monk. If we fail to venerate such a person it's like failing to venerate our own supreme state. Such dim bulbs insult the dharma.

If you just shave your head and look like a monk but don't know even this, you're not worthy of being called a monk. People here in Japan follow such lousy customs of denigrating female monks without even realizing what a bunch of doofuses they are.

These days really stupid people think of women only as the objects of sexual greed. Disciples of the Buddha must not be like this. If anything that someone could possibly lust over should be hated, then all men should be hated too.

As for stuff people get their pervy jollies from, any damn thing can be the object! A man can be the object, or a woman, or what is neither man nor woman, or dreams and fantasies. There have been impure acts done while looking at images in water or looking up at the sun. Should we discard every single thing that could possibly be the object of lust?

The old Buddhist precepts say, "The abuse of the male or female sex organs is an offense, and the offender must be expelled from the community." This being so, if we hated whatever might become the object of sexual greed, then all men and all women would hate each other.

There are non-Buddhists who become celibate but still have wrong views and wrong understanding. There are Buddhist laypeople who are married and have better understanding than those people.

Even in ancient China there was an asinine monk who said, "In every life, in every age, I shall never look at a woman." What kind of morality is that crap based on? Is that Buddhism? Why would you say all women are bad? Why would you say all men are good? There are bad men and good women. Before they cut through their delusions, both men and women are equally delusional.

If a man vows never to look at a woman, must he disregard women when it comes to his oath to save all beings? This vow is like something a wino might mumble on a three-day bender! Don't be like that guy.

Look. If we hate others for the mistakes they've committed in the past, we should hate all the Buddhas and bodhisattvas too. We'd have to hate everyone. Where's the compassion in that?

Here in Japan we have a particularly laughable institution called "Places of Seclusion" or "Mahayana Practice Places." Female monks and female laypeople are not allowed into these places. This wrong custom has been with us so long that people don't even know how ludicrous it is. You could split a gut laughing at how absurd this is.[*]

---

[*] Dōgen really does say "you could split a gut."

Who are the "men of authority" who made up this garbage? Are they some kind of saints?

Moreover, if something shouldn't be changed just because it's an ancient tradition, shouldn't we give up the whole Buddhist training thing just because the "ancient tradition" in our own country is just to bumble through life aimlessly?

Shakyamuni Buddha established our tradition, and he admitted both men and women into his order. So what kind of so-called Buddhist order has no women in it? There have been women who were as fully enlightened as anyone else, so what kind of place could exist that enlightened women should be banned from just because they're women?

Those who exclude women from places of practice are a bunch of idiots. Yet in such places as these, any man, even if he's a total douche bag, can just randomly show up and hang out. What sense is there in that?

Whatever comes into this great world sanctified by Buddha is completely covered with Buddha's virtue. They will get free of all their attachments. When one direction is sanctified, the whole universe is sanctified.

Those who establish and maintain male-only sanctuaries don't understand that the whole universe is sanctified. They think their little sanctuary is so special! Let's hope they get over their stupor soon so they don't violate the whole world.

Who could deny that the very act of bowing to that which has attained the truth is the truth itself?

— Written at Kannon-dori-kosho-horin-ji Temple
on the day of the summer equinox, 1240

What amazes me most about this piece is how thoroughly Dōgen rips into those who think men are superior to women. I had to skip over a lot of this chapter in order to cut it down to a manageable length for this book. Yet even with all the cutting, it still comes off like a rant of epic proportions. In the actual piece he goes on for three or four more pages of this kind of stuff, just coming up with new ways of saying that anyone who thinks men are superior to women is an asshole. If you want to read it all, check out one of the complete translations of *Shōbō-genzō* and get an earful of Dōgen laying it on the line to misogynists everywhere.

Dōgen didn't keep a diary, so we don't know the backstories of his *Shōbōgenzō* pieces except where he explicitly tells them to us. But most scholars assume that he was preaching about things that were going on in his community. So I think it's safe to suppose that some of his monks, or perhaps others in the Buddhist communities around him, must have expressed the kinds of attitudes he is railing against in this piece.

Dōgen had a number of female students. There was Shogan, a distant relative of his who donated land and money to help build Kosho-ji Monastery, where much of *Shōbōgenzō* was written and preached. Ryo-nen was an older woman who had been ordained elsewhere but became one of Dōgen's students and was praised by him in *Eihei Koroku*, a record of his talks at Eihei-ji Temple. Egi was a nun who spent twenty years with Dōgen and was with him during the illness he eventually died from. She helped Koun Ejo, the guy who compiled Dōgen's writings, deal with some of the politics surrounding the transitional period after Dōgen died. We'll never know for sure, but I think it's safe to assume that Dōgen wrote this essay and preached it in his temple in part because he felt some of his male monks weren't showing these women proper respect.

This essay is one of the parts of *Shōbōgenzō* that convinced me Dōgen was worth paying attention to. Just before I encountered Dōgen's philosophy I'd been circling around the Hare Krishna movement wondering if maybe I should join. They seemed to be pretty happy and devoted to good principles. Plus the food was terrific, and the artwork at their temples and in their books was really pretty.

My biggest problem with them, besides how rigidly literal they were with their interpretations of Hindu scriptures,* was how blatantly

---

* They're the Hindu version of the Christians who insist there really was a Noah's Ark and spend as much time denouncing evolution as any blowhard televangelist.

and unapologetically misogynistic they could be. They really did believe that women were inferior to men and showed no compunction in saying so outright. A woman I knew who was part of the punk scene in Akron that I was part of at the time stayed at one of their temples in West Virginia for a summer. She came back with all kinds of horror stories about how women were treated at that place. It made me sick.

All the religions I'd encountered up till then had similar attitudes toward women. So I was really relieved to know that Dōgen didn't think this way. But there are plenty of others within Buddhism who are not nearly as liberal. In the intro to this chapter I mentioned some of what went on in the past. Unfortunately, that sort of thing continues even today.

In 2009 there was a huge ruckus when the Australian branch of the Thai Forest Buddhist tradition ordained four women as monks. Their parent monastery back in Thailand expelled the Australian branch from the order. The Thai group's view was that even though Shakyamuni Buddha did establish an order of female monks, that specific order of female monks vanished a few hundred years ago and nobody but Shakyamuni Buddha himself had the right to reestablish it. This kind of thinking ignores the fact that there have been female Buddhist monks in many other branches of the tradition. Anyway, that's what they said. Forgive me for thinking the real reason was because they were just a bunch of sexist jerks. The idea that only Shakyamuni Buddha himself could establish a monastic order of Buddhists is too absurd to even consider.

Lots of people I met at the time who were part of the Thai Forest Buddhist tradition wrung their hands over what to do. They were already committed to the tradition, but how could they go on? I personally thought it was a no-brainer. If I found out that an order of Buddhists I belonged to did this, I'd drop 'em like a hot potato. But I can see the dilemma. They had a lot invested in their groups. I also see the logic of remaining in the order and fighting against this kind of idiocy.

The controversy over this incident mainly had to do with money and institutional power. The conservative sexists back in Thailand and elsewhere who had funded the Australian temples didn't want to support people who didn't follow their own ridiculous customs. But the Australians couldn't abide by customs that were so nonsensical. In the end Ajahn Brahm, the guy who did the ordinations, was expelled. But he carried on in spite of it.

Even in the Soto Zen tradition there's what Dōgen said and there's what people really do. For example, Eihei-ji, the temple that Dōgen established, is these days an all-boys club. There is no specific rule against women practicing at Eihei-ji. It's just understood that they don't. Sallie Tisdale writes of asking the monk who took her on a guided tour of Eihei-ji about this. He said that officially women could practice at Eihei-ji but, "We have no facilities [for them]."

This is a lame excuse, but it's kind of typical of the Japanese way of dealing with stuff. When it's uncomfortable to make an actual rule against doing something, they often just make it really, really hard to do that thing. Most training temples in Japan these days are single-gender. A few are mixed, but not many, and most of those are places where Westerners train.

This also goes for the subject of monks who marry. In the late nineteenth century, Japan eliminated the laws requiring monks to be celibate and to refrain from eating meat. It seems pretty odd to us in the West, but these monastic regulations had become matters of law. The reason is that Japan has long been a very socially stratified society, with something very similar to the caste system in India. One way to leave your specific caste was to declare that you'd become a monk, since monks were considered to be outside that system. As you might expect, many people declared themselves monks just to escape the caste system. So laws were put into place requiring monks to behave like monks. In the medieval period there were times when being caught eating meat or having sex, if you were a monk, was punishable by death.

Nowadays both male and female monastics and clergy members in Japan are free to marry, and to eat meat, for that matter. In actual practice most male Buddhist priests in Japan get married, but the female ones rarely do. Just as in the case of Eihei-ji's no-girls-allowed policy, there is no actual rule against female priests marrying. It's just not done.

Although the Buddha did allow women into his order, in his day women had to train separately, and this remained the case up until Buddhism came to the West. Zen Buddhism arrived in America at the height of the civil and women's rights movements of the sixties and seventies, and so coeducational Buddhist monasteries were established. They were the first co-ed Buddhist monasteries to exist anywhere. Furthermore, the San Francisco Zen Center added the names of prominent female teachers to the traditional chanting of the Buddhist lineage, which had included only male teachers up till then.

This shift has not occurred without difficulties. The integration of women into what, in Asia, had been male-only monastic spaces and the elimination of female-only monasteries in much of the West has been blamed for some of the sex scandals that have happened in Zen communities here. I hope that such scandals are just a phase that will gradually fade away as people get more used to the idea of gender-integrated practice spaces. This is not to say that human lust will ever go away, or that the tendency of men to abuse their power and of some women to be attracted to powerful men will vanish. But I think we'll find better ways to deal with these facts of life as we continue with this experiment.

In an interview by Hakima Abbas (appearing in the October 24, 2014, edition of the website *The Feminist Wire*), Nigerian-British feminist Amina Mama said, "Feminism is the theory, philosophy, politics and practices of the movement for women's liberation. It has numerous manifestations all over the world. It offers us tools and strategies for demystifying and working to change the myriad historical and material realities that oppress and exploit women." I think it is vital for followers of Dōgen's feminist outlook to continue what he started and work to change the way women have been oppressed and exploited in Buddhist institutions — including the institutions founded by Dōgen himself.

15. HEARING WEIRD STUFF LATE AT NIGHT
Keisei Sanshiki
River Voices and Mountain Forms

THIS IS ONE of the most mystical and poetic pieces in all of *Shōbōgenzō*. I've tried my best not to do a hatchet job on the poetry of it in my attempt to paraphrase it.

The basic idea here is one Dōgen revisits several times. He believed that nature could often explain the dharma to people better than people could explain it to each other through words. That may sound abstract, but it's really not that difficult to understand.

You could say that nature explains science to people. It explains science by demonstrating scientific principles. The principles of science exist before we put them into words or write them out as equations.

It's the same with the dharma. Reality exists as it is. The words we use to explain our understanding of it are always pale reflections of the truth we are attempting to convey and of our own understanding of that truth.

To me this attitude of insisting that nature can explain Buddhism better than words is part of the bravery of Buddhism. I was initially impressed by Buddhism because, unlike every other religion I'd encountered up till then, it was not afraid of science. For example, these days a lot of misguided people in my country try to deny the observable fossil record and insist that the words of their religious book are truer than what nature tells them.

But Buddhism isn't like that. The Dalai Lama famously said, "If science proves some belief of Buddhism wrong, then Buddhism will have to change." Dōgen is expressing something very similar here, along with a lot of other good ideas.

There are loads of examples of great practitioners of the past, and we should learn from their determined effort. Be like the ancients who pulverized their own bones in pursuit of the truth, or like Taiso Eka, who sliced off his own arm just for the dharma, or like Buddha in his former lifetime when he spread his dreadlocks over a mud puddle for his master to walk on.

When we shed our old skin we're no longer stuck in our outmoded beliefs. Suddenly stuff that's been all fuzzy and weird forever becomes plain as day. In the here and now of that moment the self doesn't know it, nobody else is aware of it, you don't anticipate it, and even the eyeballs of Buddha can't get a glimpse. How could human thought contain it?

In China there was a poet named So Toba (Ch. Su Dongpo, 1036–1101 CE). He was really a whiz with the rhymes and a student of both worldly and Buddhist teachings. On a trip to scenic Lushan province he heard the sound of a mountain stream. He composed a poem and gave it to Master Shokaku Joso (Ch. Donglin Changzong, 1025–1091 CE):

The voices of the valley are Buddha's tongue
Mountains are nothing but his Pure Body
Through the night a thousand verses are sung
What can I say about this that's not shoddy?

Master Joso said that So got it. The preaching of the Buddha never stops. What made So understand what the river was saying that night? We should be glad causes and conditions sometimes make things like this plain.

Should we learn that these voices of nature are close when they're apparent, or that they are close when hidden? In past seasons So didn't hear the mountains and waters, but that night he did, even if just barely.

One night, before all this happened, So visited Master Joso and asked about the teaching that says insentient nature preaches the dharma, and Joso explained it to him. So didn't quite get the idea just from hearing Joso's words. But then when he heard for himself nature preaching the dharma, it was like massive waves crashing high into the sky. Now that So has been surprised by the voices of nature, is it because of the voices themselves or because of Joso's teaching?

I suspect that Joso's words hadn't stopped echoing but were mixed into the sounds of the river valley. Is it So realizing the truth? Or is it the mountains and waters realizing the truth? Who, today, can hear this?

Here's another story. Zen Master Kyogen Chikan (Ch. Xiangyan Zhixian, d. 898 CE) was studying with Zen Master Isan Reiyu. One day Isan said, "You're a pretty sharp cookie. Without quoting from any text, tell me something about yourself before your parents were born."

Kyogen couldn't think of a reply. He was so mad at himself for this that he burned all the writings he'd collected for years and said, "A commercial for Twinkies can't cure hunger.* I'm not even gonna *try* to understand Buddhist philosophy in this lifetime. I'll just be a monk who serves the other monks breakfast and lunch."

After doing this for a while he said to Isan, "I'm kind of a dope. Maybe you can tell me something about all this Buddhism stuff."

Isan replied, "I could tell you all kinds of things. But if I did you'd bear a grudge against me later."

After a few years of this, Kyogen went up in the mountains and built himself a hut. He planted some bamboo to keep him company because nobody ever came to visit. One day he was just sweeping up around his place when a pebble flew up from his broom and hit the bamboo. Upon hearing this sound Kyogen was suddenly enlightened.

He bathed himself, did some prostrations, faced the mountain where his master lived, and said, "If you'd explained it to me before, there's no way I would've gotten it now. That was totally cool of you not to tell me." Then he wrote a verse that went something like this:

---

* Actually he said, "A painted rice cake can't cure hunger." But since the painting he probably had in his mind was the kind one would see at a shop that sold sweet rice cakes as snacks, I think my version is pretty close.

In one moment all trace of me is lost
No need to struggle or get crisscrossed
The ancient way makes me glad
And I'll never be sad
'Cuz I've mastered the truth like a boss!

When his master heard this he said, "This disciple is complete."

And here's another story. Zen Master Reiun Shigon (Ch. Lingyun Zhiqin, dates unknown, successor of Isan Reiyu) had been a practitioner for thirty years. One day he was out walking and saw some peach blossoms in bloom. At that moment he got it. So he wrote a poem and gave it to Master Isan. It went a little like this:

For thirty years I looked for a sword
Blossoms opened and fell but I just ignored
Seeing them once
I said, "What a dunce!"
Doubts vanished and my heart, how it soared!

A sword is a symbol of intellectual understanding because it cuts through things, dividing them like the intellect divides things. Isan affirmed Shigon's understanding. "Somebody who has entered by relying on conditions," he said, "will never lose their way."

A monk asked Master Chosa Keishin (Ch. Changsha Jingcen, dates unknown), "How do we make mountains, rivers, and the Earth into ourselves?"

Chosa replied, "How do we make ourselves into mountains, rivers, and the Earth?"

Master Roya Ekaku (Ch. Longye Huiejiao, 1071–1128 CE) was asked by the philosopher Shisen (Ch. Zhixuan, 984–1038 CE), "How does that which is originally unconditioned give rise to mountains, rivers, and the Earth?"

Master Ekaku answered, "How does that which is originally unconditioned give rise to mountains, rivers, and the Earth?" By repeating Shisen's question Ekaku means that we shouldn't confuse mountains, rivers, and the Earth, which are purely unconditioned, with our abstract *idea* of mountains, rivers, and the Earth. The philosopher had never heard such a thing, so he didn't get it.

Remember, if it wasn't for the voices of the mountains and rivers, Buddha could never have become enlightened and his teaching could never have been transmitted. People of the past were like this. Those of us in the present should learn from them.

It's rare to encounter someone who is serious about this pursuit these days in this dinky little country. They're around, but it's hard to meet them. There are lots of jerks who become monks only for personal gain. What a waste! Even if they meet a real master they don't see the truth.

People make a vow and say, "I pray to hear the true dharma in this life and every life to come. If I'm able to hear it, I'll never doubt it. I will throw away the secular world and retain the dharma so that the Earth and sentient beings can practice together." This vow will naturally become the causes and conditions for authentic understanding.

When a person tells others about the truth, but those people have no will to attain it, their good advice just seems annoying. As a rule we don't talk to worldly people about this stuff. We don't even tell them we're Zen practitioners. We just stay unknown.

People today rarely seek what is real. They just want to be praised for their meager understanding, even though there is no practice in their body and no realization in their mind. That's what I meant in "Genjo Koan" about adding delusion to delusion.

It's all about attitude. What Buddha transmitted to us is really just that, an attitude.

You find a whole range of different types of people in temples. Some folks have it in their nature to learn the truth, while others are just hopeless. They figure they'll gain some kind of fame or profit from their practice. I don't know why people aren't more concerned about this. Maybe it's because they don't recognize greed, anger, and delusion as the poisons they are.

Dimwits, even if they have the will to the truth, forget about it as soon as people start praising them for their practice. That's one of the hazards that hinders the truth. Don't forget to be nice to people who praise you, but don't rejoice in their praise, either. Remember that igno-ramuses don't recognize sages, and weasels bite great saints.

Back in India the ancient ancestors were sometimes overpowered by kings, or non-Buddhists. It wasn't as if the ancestors lacked under-standing or that those guys were so brilliant, either.

For example, none of the Chinese rulers recognized Bodhidharma when he came to China. At the time there were a couple of jerk-wads known as Sanzo (Ch. Sung-shan) and Kozu (Ch. Guangting) who wor-ried that their empty fame might be thwarted by a true person. It's said they tried to poison Bodhidharma. But dogs bark at good people, and we bear them no grudge. Vow, instead, to lead them to the truth. On the other hand, sometimes even demons take refuge in the dharma.

In the Lotus Sutra an ancient Buddha said, "You shouldn't get close to royalty or secular people." Don't forget that advice.

There are stories of the god Indra testing a practitioner's resolve or the demon Papiyas hindering someone's meditation. This stuff hap-pens only to people who still crave fame and gain. It doesn't happen to folks with great compassion whose vow to save others is strong.

Because of the merit of practice you may be given a whole nation as a gift. But don't see that as a great achievement. Pay close attention when things like that happen. Wise people reject such gifts the way secular people would reject the gift of a bag of poop.

In general, beginners can't imagine the Buddha's truth. But the fact that you can't imagine it doesn't mean you lack understanding. You just can't recognize its deepest aspects.

Just make efforts to follow the truth, realizing there are mountains to climb and oceans to cross. A good teacher makes both sentient and nonsentient beings speak the truth.

Listening with the ears is normal. But listening with the eyes is the undefined intuitive state itself. Don't be scared of large Buddhas or put off by small ones. Recognize them as mountain forms and river sounds.

A student of Confucius said of him, "When I look at him he keeps getting higher and higher; when I bore into him, he gets harder and harder." The same is true of the dharma. A Buddha of the past said, "It covers heaven and encompasses Earth."

When you get to this place, you become a teacher of humans and heavenly beings. But if you teach others before you've arrived you'll just be a nuisance. If you don't even know pine trees and flowers, how can you cut through the roots of confusion?

If the mind and body get lazy, sincerely repent before the Buddha. When we do this we become pure. Once pure belief reveals itself, we and the external world are moved into action.

Here's what you can say:

"Although my accumulated bad actions hinder me, may the Buddhas of the past have compassion and get rid of my obstacles to learning the truth."

Before awakening, the Buddhas and ancestors were just like you. Upon awakening you will become Buddha ancestors. When you look at the Buddha ancestors, you are the Buddha ancestors. When you look at their will to the truth, you have their will to the truth. Working with compassion, you achieve skill and let skill drop away.

In the words of Master Ryuge Koton (Ch. Longya Judun, 835–923 CE), "If you didn't achieve perfection in past lives, do so now. With this life we deliver the body that is the accumulation of many lives. Before their enlightenment the ancient masters were like us. After enlightenment we'll be like the ancient masters."

Quietly reflect on this direct understanding of a great teacher. If you repent with your whole body and mind, you'll receive immeasurable help from the Buddhas. The power of repentance dissolves wrongdoing.

At the time of true practice, the mountains and rivers don't hold back their eighty-four thousand verses. Throughout the night they both do and do not actualize the eighty-four thousand verses. But if you haven't understood it through your effort, who can see you as the voice of the river and the form of the mountains?

— Preached at Kannon-dori-hosho-horin-ji Temple
on the fifth day of the ninety-day retreat of 1240

The night before I was ordained I stayed over at Tokei-in Temple in Shizuoka, Japan, where the ordination was to take place, alongside five other people who were going to be ordained early the next morning. That night we were put in a different, slightly fancier room from the one we usually stayed in for retreats. Although it was a better room than usual, the five of us ordainees still had to sleep on thin futons on the floor of that one big room.

This room happened to be right next to the creek that ran by the temple. Sometime during the night it got very, very quiet and the only sound I heard was the babbling of the water. All at once I remembered this chapter of *Shōbōgenzō*, and I understood what it meant. The stream really was chanting sutras all night.

This wasn't metaphorical, or just a pretty image. It wasn't like I heard the sound and thought, "It's almost like the stream is chanting sutras." No. The stream actually was chanting sutras. Like, actual sutras. Like, for real.

I wasn't hallucinating. It wasn't as if I heard human voices in the sound of the stream. It still sounded like a stream. And yet the sounds the stream was making had a depth of meaning that surpassed anything any sutra chanted by mere human voices could have equaled.

In this piece Dōgen says, "I suspect that Joso's words hadn't stopped echoing but were mixed into the sounds of the river valley." This just means that So Toba might not have noticed that the stream was chanting sutras if his teacher had not previously told him about how nature preaches the dharma. Yet just because he'd heard the principle before doesn't mean that So didn't authentically hear it for himself.

This is one of the values of a teacher. One of the most important ideas in all of Buddhism is the idea of "original enlightenment." We are all intrinsically enlightened, whether or not we are aware of it. What is often called "kensho" or "satori" or an "enlightenment experience" is not the introduction of a novel event into our otherwise mundane lives. Rather, it is the momentary recognition of our actual state from "before our parents were born," to paraphrase Isan's question to Kyogen from the story Dōgen tells in this chapter.

The phrase "before our parents were born" sounds pretty weird. I remember seeing some kind of a Christian book for kids when I was a child. It had a drawing of angels waiting to be born to human parents.

I later learned that a lot of Christians hotly dispute this idea, saying the soul is formed at conception. But in any case, the first time I heard that phrase my mind flashed back to that image. In many Buddhist societies there's a belief in reincarnation or of an endless cycle of births and deaths. So they too have an idea of an existence before our parents were born.

But that's not what this phrase is pointing to. Rather, it's referring to our most genuine, original nature, completely unadorned and indefinable. It's so ancient and basic that it is you before you were even you. That probably sounds pretty bizarre. But just keep it in your back pocket for the time being.

We all have this original nature. We *are* this original nature. But we might miss it if someone didn't point it out to us. It's ironic that this should be so. You'd think that if it was something that had been there all along you wouldn't need anyone to help you discover it. But in actual practice that's not the case.

In fact, within the Zen tradition there is a strong belief that no one ever gets this without some help, not even Buddha himself. The lineage of ancestors we chant in Zen temples includes six names that come before that of Shakyamuni Buddha to emphasize the belief that even the founder of our tradition had a teacher and that his teacher also had a teacher, and so on. These names are, of course, drawn from mythology rather than history. But still, the point they're intended to emphasize is important. You need a teacher.

Our friend Mr. So had to hear his teacher's words before he could experience the sound of the river chanting sutras for himself, and so did I. So will you.

Just after this story we get another story that explains why Zen teachers are always so frustratingly vague. Isan says to his student Kyogen, "I could tell you all kinds of things. But if I did you'd bear a grudge against me later." When Kyogen hears the pebble hitting the bamboo and suddenly gets it, he thanks his teacher for not answering his questions about original enlightenment. If his teacher Isan had filled Kyogen with too many stories of his own experiences, Kyogen would not have been able to truly experience his unique understanding because he'd have been too busy looking for his teacher's truth.

Dōgen then kind of shifts gears and moves into a discussion about people who get into Buddhist practice just to become famous. This seems to be a perennial problem with anything religious or spiritual. There's always a certain amount of fame to be attained by playing the role of the "enlightened master." In America and Europe we see all kinds of spiritual celebrities selling themselves to the masses as their saviors. This sort of thing is nothing new. It was going on in Dōgen's day too and for thousands of years before his time.

Dōgen spends a lot more time on this than I have indicated in my paraphrasing of this chapter. My guess is that in Japan during Dōgen's time there must have been a lot of guys setting themselves up as Buddhist masters in order to get close to the seat of political power. Dōgen must have thought there was a danger of some of his students going down this dark road.

He therefore suggests making vows that we will not get caught up in such things. Although Zen Buddhism is widely regarded as the kind of philosophy in which you'd never find anyone praying, these vows sound a lot like prayers. Dōgen advises us to ask for assistance from the Buddhist ancestors, from people who have been dead a very long time.

But this doesn't mean we are praying to the spirits of these dead guys to reach down from heaven and help us. Rather, we make a vow to learn from their examples and follow in their footsteps. Whether or not they are hanging out in the Buddha World listening to us invoking their names is irrelevant. We can still learn from them just by knowing what they did in the past.

Finally, Dōgen reminds us of the words of Master Ryuge Koton, who said, "Before their enlightenment the ancient masters were like us. After enlightenment we'll be like the ancient masters."

This line is part of what is known as "Eihei Dōgen's Great Vow"

(*Eihei Koso Hotsuganmon*). This particular part of this chapter of *Shōbō-genzō* is now used as part of the morning chanting liturgy in many Zen temples. They take the parts from what I've paraphrased as, "Although my accumulated bad actions hinder me" through the paragraph that in my version begins, "Quietly reflect on this direct understanding" and chant them during certain services as a way of renewing their own vows and taking encouragement from Dōgen's words.

These days whenever I read these lines I can't help but think of cold, early mornings inside the zendo at Tassajara with incense in the air and big bells ringing, and me chanting these words along with all the other poor souls who woke up way too early in the morning to attend service. As cynical as I am about things that other people gush about as being "moving," it is sort of...y'know...moving.

It's yet another reminder that the people who founded the Buddhist way of life were never to be regarded as anything beyond us. They weren't superhuman saviors or sacred prophets. Nothing they attained is unavailable to anyone else who seriously wants to pursue it.

Finally, I paraphrased one line of this piece as, "It's all about attitude. What Buddha transmitted to us is really just that, an attitude." This is a very crucial point. The word I'm paraphrasing as "attitude" is 正法の心術 (*shōbō no shinjutsu*). The first word, *shōbō*, is the first two characters in the word *Shōbōgenzō*. It means something like "correct dharma." The word *shinjutsu* means "heart surgery" in modern Japanese, but in Chinese and ancient Japanese it's usually translated as "intention." I prefer "attitude." The Japanese word *no* just means "of," so the whole thing means "attitude of correct dharma."

What Dōgen is trying to convey to us across the span of eight hundred years is not facts or information. He's trying to pass along an attitude. That's why he says again and again that it doesn't matter how smart or dumb a person is. It doesn't matter how many facts you've got in your head or how many sutras you can quote. Dōgen could quote all kinds of texts. But he still praises teachers who were illiterate and completely unschooled because they had the proper attitude.

This is why it's very good to have an in-person teacher. Without a teacher you can still absorb all kinds of facts and learn to regurgitate quotations on command. But you might never cop the proper attitude unless you see it in action in the form of an actual human being who lives it.

16. DON'T BE A JERK
Shoaku Makusa
Not Doing Wrong

THIS IS ONE of my all-time favorite parts of *Shōbōgenzō*. It's about how the Buddhist precepts have one very simple message. Don't be a jerk. That's pretty much all there is to it.

You officially become a Buddhist by making a vow to uphold ten precepts, which are, once again: Don't kill, don't steal, don't have excessive wants, don't lie, don't get high, don't criticize others, don't praise yourself and berate others, don't be stingy, don't give in to anger, and don't abuse the Three Treasures, which are Buddha, dharma, and sangha. In some sects the last five are different, but the first five are common to every form of Buddhism.

That's the set of vows you take nowadays. In the early days of the Buddhist order, there were no specific rules of conduct for monks. Whenever a dispute came up, someone would ask the Buddha his opinion. His answers were memorized by his followers and formed the first rules for the monks. By the end of his life there were hundreds of these rules, ranging from practical advice on maintaining good relations to weird stuff like whether or not it was a breach of decorum for a monk to run up a tree when being chased by an elephant (the Buddha said that it was okay).

At the end of his life, the Buddha told his fans and followers that it was important to keep the major rules but that the minor ones could be set aside. Unfortunately for the more pedantic and rule-bound of his followers, he never got around to explaining which rules were the important ones. This was left to future generations, which is how the precepts were winnowed down to just ten.

I could write a book just on the precepts. In fact, I have written a whole book just about the third precept. It's called *Sex, Sin, and Zen*. But you don't really need a lot of words explaining each precept if you get the basic idea behind all of them — don't be a jerk.

The title of this chapter is in four Chinese characters that break down as follows 諸 (*sho*), meaning "various," 悪 (*aku*), meaning "bad" or "wrong" or "evil," 莫 (*maku*), meaning "don't," and 作 (*sa*), meaning "do." So the phrase I'm translating in this chapter as "don't be a jerk" would probably be translated by a more philosophical type as "do not enact evil" or more generally as "don't do wrong things." Because Japanese doesn't have true plurals, Dōgen has to add a character meaning "various" to the word "wrong" in order to make clear that he is talking about individual wrong actions rather than the more generalized concept of evil. We'll talk about that later.

Within the text Dōgen takes this title phrase and sometimes uses it as a noun. I've tried to preserve that sense by hyphenating the phrase when it's used that way (being-a-jerk) or adding -*ness* to the end (being-a-jerk-ness), along with a few other variations on the same idea. I hope that's not too confusing. Take heart, though. It's way more confusing in Japanese! Dōgen often disrespects the grammatical rules of his own language. But it does help make the point he is trying to get across here.

Ethics and morality are practical matters. People get wrapped up in the words used to describe ethical action. But being ethical is just doing what's right and not doing what's not right. Simple as that. Of course, sometimes it's hard to know what's right. That's when we rely on the precepts.

In this chapter, Dōgen tries to indicate the basis of all ethical action. And it turns out it's as simple as just not being a jerk.

The phrase "be a jerk" has some unfortunate connotations due to the peculiarities of the English language. I'd like to address those by indulging in a bit of Dōgen-ism before we begin. *Ahem.*

A jerk is not something you *are*. Being-a-jerk is something you *do*. There is no jerk outside of you *being a jerk*. When you cease to be a jerk, the jerk that you were when you were being a jerk vanishes instantly. I'll let Dōgen take over from here.

The Buddha said:

> Don't be a jerk
> Do the right thing
> Then the mind is not irked
> And the enlightened ones sing

We should consider this ancient teaching in practice. This is the real message that has been transmitted through the ages to this concrete time and place. It's what the ten thousand Buddhas have been practicing all along.

Among rightness, wrongness, and it-doesn't-matter-ness, there is wrongness. Wrongness is what happens at the very moment you do something wrong. It's not an abstraction that sits around waiting to be done. It's the same with rightness and it-doesn't-matter-ness.

There are similarities between real wrong actions, no matter where or when they occur. And there is a big difference between right, wrong, and it-doesn't-matter-type actions. Right and wrong are time, but time is neither right nor wrong. Right and wrong are the dharma, but the dharma is neither right nor wrong.

When you yourself are in balance, you know right from wrong absolutely. The state of enlightenment is immense and includes everything.

We hear of this supreme state from our teachers and from what we read. Right from the start it sounds like "don't be a jerk." If it doesn't sound like "don't be a jerk" it's not Buddhist teaching.

"Don't be a jerk" wasn't a teaching someone intentionally invented. It existed before anyone put it into words. When we hear it, we hope that we can learn to do the right thing and not be a jerk. This is a pretty big deal. It's on the scale of the whole of time and the entire universe. The scale of not being a jerk is in the "not being" part. Just don't do jerklike things.

When jerk-type actions are not done by someone, jerk-type actions do not exist. Even if you live in a place where you could act like a jerk, even if you face circumstances in which you could be a jerk, even if you hang out with nothing but a bunch of jerks, the power of not doing jerk-type things conquers all.

Jerk-type action has no fixed form. It has no existence until some-one does it. If we don't act like jerks, jerk-type acts cannot exist.

You can do jerk-type things, or you can avoid doing jerk-type things. The moment you know that jerk-type action does not exist out-side your own conduct, that is realization of the truth.

This is not a once-and-for-all realization. It appears dynamically, moment after moment. When enlightened people understand that not being a jerk requires not doing jerk-type things, they behave like decent people at each moment in the past, present, and future.

At every moment, no matter what we're doing, we need to under-stand that not being a jerk is how someone becomes enlightened. This state has always belonged to us. Cause and effect makes us act. By not being a jerk now, you create the cause of not being a jerk in the future. Our action is not predestined, nor does it spontaneously occur.

By not being a jerk at this very moment, you enact non-jerk-ness and make it appear in the world. It's not that you, as a regular person, are destroyed by doing the right thing, and yet you, as a regular per-son, have dropped away and what remains is an enlightened being.

When you look at it this way, you realize that being-a-jerk is refrained from. Aided by this understanding we can penetrate "not-being-a-jerk" and realize it decisively through Zen practice.

There is no being-a-jerk apart from what you actually do. Being-a-jerk doesn't vanish as if it were a thing in and of itself. You just stop doing jerk-type things.

Some people think that being-a-jerk arises out of past causes and conditions but don't see how they themselves *are* those causes and conditions. Those guys are pretty sad cases. The seeds of Buddhahood also come from causes and conditions. Jerk-type actions neither exist nor don't exist. Evil doesn't exist or not exist. It is either done or not done.

Learning this in practice is the great universal realization. You can look at it subjectively or objectively.

When you finally grasp this point, even the thought, "Oh, hell, I was a jerk back then" is just energy arising from your desire not to be a jerk again. However, to say that this realization is some kind of weird rationale for being a jerk is totally stupid.

The relationship between being-a-jerk and the *not* of not-being-a-jerk isn't one of a donkey looking at a well. It's like a well looking at a donkey, a well looking at a well, a donkey looking at a donkey, a person looking at a person, and a mountain looking at a mountain. In other words, it's the mutual relationship of all things involved.

It is said, "The Buddha's true body is like space; it manifests its form according to circumstances like the moon's reflection in a pond." That means there's no division between subject and object. You can never doubt such instances of non-jerk-ness.

As for doing the right thing, there are all sorts of right things that can be done. But there has never been any kind of right thing that just sits around waiting for someone to do it.

The right thing never fails to appear once someone actually does it. The many kinds of right things converge like iron to a magnet, upon the place where *doing them* happens. Nothing can hinder them, not even all the bad things you've ever done in your whole life.

Different people in different places may have different ideas about what is the right thing to do. It's the same deal with what constitutes being a jerk.

What we can recognize as right, we call right. It's like how Buddhas preach the appropriate thing according to who they're preaching to and according to the era in which they appear. Nevertheless, underneath it all the dharma they preach is always fundamentally the same.

It's kind of like devotional practice and meditation practice. Though they're different, they're still the same thing.

Doing the right thing doesn't arise from causes and conditions, nor does it cease due to causes and conditions. Many kinds of right action are all phenomena, even though all phenomena are not examples of right action. What is truly right is right at the beginning, right in the middle, and right in the end.

Doing the right thing is not the self, nor is it known by the self. Nor is it someone else or known by someone else. In the act of knowing, there is self and other. In the act of seeing, there is self and other. But doing the right thing is beyond such distinctions. It is just the right thing doing itself.

Doing the right thing isn't something you can understand intellectually. It's beyond that. Doing the right thing is beyond existence and nonexistence, beyond form and emptiness. It's nothing other than *doing-the-right-thing* being done.

Wherever and whenever doing the right thing happens, it is, without exception, doing the right thing. The actual doing of the right thing is the universe itself. It doesn't arise or cease. All individual examples of doing the right thing are like this.

When we are actually doing the right thing, the entire universe is involved in doing the right thing. The cause and effect of this right thing is the universe as the realization of doing the right thing.

It's not that causes come first and effects come after. Rather, both cause and effect perfectly satisfy themselves. When causes and effects are in balance, the whole universe is in balance. Waiting for causes, effects are felt. But it's not a matter of before and after. The truth is present in each moment as it is.

The meaning of the old Buddhist phrase "purify your mind naturally" is this: It's natural not to be a jerk, and not-being-a-jerk purifies the mind. You yourself are the one who concretely doesn't do jerk-type things. What is referred to as "mind" is doing-the-right-thing-ness. What purifies it is doing-the-right-thing-ness. The concrete state is doing-the-right-thing-ness.

Those we call Buddhas are sometimes like Shiva, the Hindu god of destruction and regeneration. But some Shivas are different from other Shivas. Other Buddhas are like the legendary wheel-rolling kings, but not all wheel-rolling kings are Buddhas.

Basically, Buddhas are all different, so you should know that enlightened people may not look or act quite the way you think they will.

If you don't investigate what Buddhas really are, you're just wasting your time looking for them.

Not-being-a-jerk means this and that are done, and now you gotta do the other thing. It's an ongoing process.

Haku Kyo-i (Ch. Bai Zhuji, 770–846 CE) was a student of Zen master Choka Dorin (Ch. Niaowo Daolin, 740–824 CE). Kyo-i asked Dorin, "What's the meaning of Buddhism?"

Dorin said, "Don't be a jerk. Do the right thing."

Kyo-i said, "Jeez! Even a three-year-old could say *that!*"

Dorin said, "Sure, a three-year-old could say it. But even an eighty-year-old has trouble doing it!"

Kyo-i bowed in thanks and left.

Kyo-i was a super-respected poet. People thought he was one of the greatest who ever lived. But as far as Zen was concerned he was a rank amateur. It seems like he never even dreamed the phrase "don't be a jerk."

Kyo-i thought Dorin was just making an intellectual statement. He didn't know that "don't be a jerk" is the time-honored eternal Buddhist truth. As brilliant as he was in the world of literature, he was kind of a dummy when it came to Buddhism.

Even if you tell people not to intentionally be a jerk or encourage them to do the right thing, what really matters is the actual reality of not being a jerk in the here and now. This teaching is the same whether you hear it from a good teacher or whether it's being experienced as the ultimate state of realization.

Actual cause and effect is not concerned with whether we characterize it as being about some kind of divine principle or whether we think it's a natural process. This being so, we can't experience good effects without enacting good causes. Dorin expressed this, so his can be called real Buddhist teaching.

Even if the whole universe is nothing but a bunch of jerks doing all kinds of jerk-type things, there is still liberation in simply not being a jerk.

Kyo-i doesn't get this at all, so he says, "Jeez! Even a three-year-old could say *that!*" He says this because he is unable to express the truth.

What a dingbat you are, Kyo-i! What are you trying to say, anyway?

You've never understood the customs of Buddhists, so you don't even know the customs of three-year-olds! How could someone who has not understood the Buddhas understand small children? Someone who knows a three-year-old child also knows the Buddhas.

Don't think that just meeting face-to-face is the same as actually knowing someone. And don't think that not meeting someone face-to-face means you must not know them.

Someone who has come to really know a single speck of dust knows the whole universe. Someone who has penetrated one teaching has understood them all. Those who don't understand all teachings don't even understand one of them. When you study a speck of dust thoroughly and completely, you study the entire universe.

It's really stupid to think that a three-year-old can't express the essential teaching of Buddhism, or to think that whatever a three-year-old says must be easy.

The real point of all this is to thoroughly clarify life and death. It is the great matter of cause and effect. Master Nagarjuna said, "When you were born you could roar like a lion!" To roar like a lion means to understand the great Buddhist truth.

Zen master Engo Kokugon (Ch. Yuanwu Keqin, 1063–1135 CE) said, "Coming-and-going, birth-and-death are the true human body." So clarifying the true human body and being able to roar like a lion are the real point of all this Buddhist stuff. That's why clarifying the real motives and actions of a three-year-old child are also the real point of all this Buddhist stuff.

Of course, there are differences between what three-year-olds do and what the Buddhas do. That's why that dumbhead Kyo-i wasn't able to hear a three-year-old speaking the truth. He said what he said because he couldn't even imagine it was possible for a three-year-old to say something profound.

He doesn't hear the thundering of Dorin's voice, and so he pooh-poohs what he says. But Dorin was so compassionate he said, "Sure, a three-year-old could say it. But even an eighty-year-old has trouble doing it!"

He was saying that three-year-olds sometimes have profound things to say and that you should listen to them. He's also saying that old men of eighty have trouble practicing not being a jerk and you should listen to them. It's up to you to decide if a child speaks the truth, but it's not up to the child. It's up to you to decide if an old man speaks the truth, but it's not up to the old man. That's your job.

To realize, express, and live your life like this is the whole point of all this Buddhist stuff.

— Preached at Kosho-horin-ji Temple
on the evening of the full moon in August 1240

My favorite line in this is, "Even if the whole universe is nothing but a bunch of jerks doing all kinds of jerk-type things, there is still liberation in simply not being a jerk." When I posted this online, some people asked me what Dōgen "really said."

Dōgen did not speak English. So asking what he "really said" is problematic. What he actually wrote was 諸悪たとひいくかさなりの尽界に弥輪し、いくかさなりの尽法を呑却せりとも、これ莫作の解脱なり (*shoaku tatohi ikukasa nari no sankai ni binishi, ikukasa nari no sanbō wo tenkyakuseri tomo, kore saisaku no gedatsu nari*). Here are three translations: "Even if wrong upon wrong pervade the whole Universe, and even if wrongs have swallowed the whole Dharma again and again, there is still salvation and liberation in not committing" (Nishijima/Cross). "Even if unwholesome action fills worlds upon worlds, and swallows up all things, *refrain from* is emancipation" (Kazuaki Tanahashi). "Even if evils completely filled however many worlds or completely swallowed however many dharmas, there is liberation in not doing" (Soto Zen Text Project). I think my version is pretty close.

The so-called problem of evil has been a long-standing difficulty for Christian philosophers as well as for others of similar religions. If you believe in a God who is all-powerful and all-good, how can there be evil? Why wouldn't God just eliminate evil if he can do anything and if he's a good guy?

Lots of different solutions have been proposed. For example, the Gnostic Christians invented a sort of sub-God who was almost as powerful as the real God but who was evil, and they imagined a struggle between the two. That idea was pretty goofy, so it never caught on. A less goofy idea that has been pretty popular is that God gave us free will as a way to test whether we were good enough to come and live with him after we died. This never made much sense to me because he could have just made us that good in the first place. Why play weird games? Are we just God's entertainment?

The underlying premise of all these ideas is that something called *evil* exists. We don't know what exactly evil is. It's often personified as Satan, an intelligent and powerful supernatural being who is purely evil and makes people do bad things, just as God is a supernatural being who is purely good and makes people do good things.

But even people who don't believe in Satan or God tend to believe in the existence of evil and good. Reading this chapter makes it apparent that Asian Buddhists who knew nothing of the Judeo-Christian God or Satan nevertheless had similar ideas about the existence of something called "evil" and something called "good."

Dōgen takes an entirely different approach. He says that there is no evil or good as absolutes or as personified supernatural beings. There is only action. Sometimes you do the right thing, and sometimes you act like a jerk.

This is a much more straightforward explanation. In terms of Occam's razor, the principle that the simplest explanation accounting for the facts must be the right one, Dōgen's position makes tons more sense than theories about supernatural entities or about a kind of evil and good that sort of sit around waiting for people to do them.

I think Dōgen tried to be as straightforward as he could when he wrote. But much of his writing is hard for us because it's so removed from the way we express things today. I've tried to rewrite this chapter in order to make it as direct as possible. For example, there's a line in the original that literally translates as something like "donkey business not having gone away and horse business coming in." Horse and donkey business is just an old Chinese expression meaning something like "this, that, and the other thing." So I changed it to "this and that are done, now you gotta do the other thing."

That was pretty easy. And I already told you about how I got the phrase "don't be a jerk" and what I did about the places where Dōgen uses the phrase like a noun. I hope that wasn't too difficult to follow.

But there are some other parts of this chapter that are a little mystical sounding. In several lines, Dōgen indicates a very different understanding of the nature of cause and effect from the usual one.

He says, "It's not that causes come first and effects come after. Rather, both cause and effect perfectly satisfy themselves. When causes and effects are in balance, the whole universe is in balance. Waiting for causes, effects are felt. But it's not a matter of before and after. The truth is present in each moment as it is." My paraphrase is based on Nishijima/Cross. But other translations are pretty much the same. Tanahashi, for example, has, "Although effect is experienced as induced by cause, one is not before and the other is not after." Shasta Abbey's translation is, "Although depending upon the cause we feel effects, it is not a matter of 'before and after,' because 'before' and 'after' are merely ways of speaking." Nishiyama/Stevens have, "Cause is usually thought of as preceding effect, but actually neither one comes before or after."

Normally we think that cause always precedes effect. In fact, that's pretty much how we define causes and effects. Causes are the things that happen first, and effects are what happen afterward because of those causes.

But there's an idea in Zen that cause and effect are simultaneous and that time is illusory. This is a tough one to wrap your head around. Modern physics seems to be grappling with something like this idea. Einstein criticized Niels Bohr's theories about quantum mechanics by saying they produced what he called "spooky action at a distance." That is, two particles appear to change states instantly in relation to each other, even when widely separated. But there should always be some time lag between cause and effect, and that time lag would be influenced by the distance between the cause and the thing that responds to it.

Personally, I don't understand physics because I'm terrible at math. So I'm reluctant to say that Einstein and Bohr were looking at precisely the same problem as Dōgen. But I do know that modern physics does allow for an effect to precede a cause. There is nothing in the math that says it can't.

Yet Dōgen's idea is more immediate and personal than that. The jerklike actions that we engage in have an instantaneous effect, both on us and on whomever or whatever we're being a jerk to. Sometimes we might even feel the effects of our jerk-type actions before we do them. It's weird, but it has happened to me, and I'll bet you a doughnut it's happened to you too. In that case, we just need to *not* do those actions. The path to liberation is just to stop being a jerk.

This is something you can see clearly if you just get quiet enough and learn to be honest with yourself. We imagine that we can act like jerks and get what we want, thereby becoming happier. We always tend to think we can become happier by getting what we want, even if that means we have to make someone else suffer. There are entire segments of society whose existence is based on this principle. I live in Los Angeles. I think a lot of those people are my neighbors.

But it doesn't work that way. When you're a jerk, you know it even if you deny that you know it. Because you know you were a jerk, anything you gain from being a jerk is tainted by that knowledge and can never be a genuine source of happiness. On the other hand, doing the right thing always makes you feel better, even if some kind of loss is involved.

You might ask how I can know that. There are people who insist that this type of thinking is an example of the fallacy they call the "just-world hypothesis." Certainly there are plenty of people out there who appear to be happy, even though they're big, fat jerks to everybody.

Yet I know it doesn't work that way because I've seen how it does work over and over and over again in my own life. My daily zazen practice has helped quiet things down in my head so that I no longer listen to the ways my mind can justify any jerklike thing I do. Those kinds of justifications are endless, and some of them even sound pretty convincing.

But when you step back and look at what's actually going on, apart from how thought tries to frame it, you can see that being a jerk is always harmful to you, no matter what supposed rewards it may bring. And you see clearly that the effects of jerklike actions are always instantaneous. In other words, "both cause and effect perfectly satisfy themselves."

At the end of the chapter Dōgen makes a big point about how dirt-simple this idea is. It's so simple even a three-year-old can understand it. But then he gives us the example of Kyo-i, who is a great intellectual. He is so smart that he starts to believe more in his own intellect than in the reality right before his eyes.

I'm sure Dōgen was teaching this lesson to himself as much as to anyone else. Dōgen was, like Kyo-i, a very well-read guy and a master poet whose works were praised by lots of people. In the story of Kyo-i and his teacher, Dōgen must certainly have seen how he himself had behaved when confronted with teachers whose earthy, in-your-face lessons must have been shocking to someone as learned as he was. It's a touching example of Dōgen teaching himself something and letting the rest of us listen in.

One of the pivotal moments in Dōgen's life came when he first arrived in China and saw an elderly monk at a nearby temple setting out mushrooms to dry in the sun. Dōgen asked him why such a senior monk would work so hard in the hot sun. Why didn't he just stay in the temple and study and have one of the younger monks do the job?

The old monk laughed and said, "I am not other people." He told Dōgen that he seemed like a pretty smart young fellow. "But," the old monk said, "if I don't work, if I do not have this experience here and now, I cannot understand. If a young monk helped me to do the work, if

I were to stand by and watch him, then I could not have the experience of drying these mushrooms."

This moment so startled Dōgen that he had a major epiphany right then and there and later wrote about it in a short book called *Instructions to the Cook*. Many regard this as one of his most profound pieces of writing, even though it's pretty much exactly what its title implies, instructions on how to be a cook at a Zen monastery. It was one of the best expressions of how Dōgen's philosophy was all about real action here and now rather than a lot of lofty words and pretty proverbs.

I think this is why Dōgen spends so much time tearing poor Kyo-i — who was long since dead and buried by the time he wrote it — a new bumhole. He's really trying to remind himself of what the most basic teaching of Buddhism is.

At the end of the piece Dōgen says, "To realize, express, and live your life like this is the whole point of all this Buddhist stuff." That's a very big statement. A lot of people imagine that the point of Buddhist practice is to become enlightened just like Buddha did, and to know the complete truth of the whole universe. Yet Dōgen says the point of Buddhism is just to learn not to be a jerk. Furthermore, he equates this simple thing that every three-year-old knows with the grand enlightenment of the Buddha. He says that not being a jerk and becoming one with the whole of creation are the very same thing.

This is something I think all of us could stand to sit and ponder for a while.

17. PSYCHEDELIC DŌGEN
Uji
Being-Time

THE WORD *uji* (有時) that Dōgen uses as the title for this piece normally means "sometimes." But, being the punster that he was, Dōgen seized on the fact that the two Chinese characters used to spell out the word mean "existence" and "time." He then uses this commonplace word as the basis for a pun-filled essay about how existence and time are one and the same.

Depending on the context, I've mainly paraphrased *uji* as "sometimes" or "existence-time." I've seen people translate it as "being time" and "for the time being" too. Some translators try to be consistent so that you get the idea that Dōgen is using the same word to mean different things, but that just gets confusing. You don't get the sense of the pun anyway, no matter how you translate it because there's no English word or phrase that has the same dual meaning.

This is one of my favorite pieces of Dōgen's writing because it's so psychedelic. I'm a big fan of trippy stuff. Despite the fact that my few attempts at actually tripping out on hallucinogenic drugs were pretty disastrous, I still love stuff that sounds like it was created while on heavy medication. In this piece we can feel the purple haze of Dōgen's mind-train whisk us off in a strawberry fire to the Zen love-in beyond the realm of the phosphene dream.

By the way, you don't actually need drugs to get psychedelic. In fact, you're more likely to get truly and deeply tripped out when you're straight as an arrow. With a regular meditation practice you can find a way into the same places drugs can take you, but you can get there without any of the confusing and distracting side effects those drugs always produce. Plus, you can be more relaxed about the whole thing because you know you can turn it off any time you want to. So you lose that horrible sense of careening off into no-man's-land without a seat belt. And yet if you actually want it to be that way, you can even have that as well.

In any case, even the trippiest pieces of writing Dōgen produced are direct and to the point once you know how to understand them. He is always talking about real human experience. So swallow your Technicolor sugar cubes now and let's flip out on some primo Dōgen-o-delica.

Master Yakusan Igen said,

> Sometimes on top of a peak
> Sometimes at the bottom of the sea
> Sometimes a three-headed freak
> Sometimes a tall chill golden body
> Sometimes a stick or a flyswatter
> Sometimes a pillar or post
> Sometimes Bill or his daughter
> Sometimes Earth and space, it's the most

Which basically just means that time is existence and existence is time.

When you're as chill as a sixteen-foot golden Buddha, that's time. Because it's time, it's bright like time. Study the twenty-four hours of today as time.

When you're as furious as a three-headed demon with eight fighting arms, that's time too. Because it's time, it's not separate from the twenty-four hours of today.

Some days go by too fast, and some days drag on forever, but we still say each is twenty-four hours long. Nobody doubts that time comes and goes, and everyone sees the traces of time's passing. But even though nobody doubts time, that doesn't mean they know it.

The doubts we all naturally have about things we don't understand are never consistent. The doubts you had yesterday aren't the same as those you have today. But even doubt is just time.

When we get our acts together, we see ourselves as the whole universe. Each individual or object in the universe can be appreciated as an individual moment of time. You can't have two things in the same place, and two moments can't occur at once. That's why some people's minds arise in this moment, and this moment of arising is what those minds are made of.

The self lays itself out to look at itself. That's how you should understand time.

This is why all the stuff in the whole world exists. This understanding is the first step in Zen practice. When we arrive at real understanding there is just one concrete thing here and now. It's beyond our comprehension and beyond the comprehension of anyone or anything else. It's even beyond nonunderstanding.

Because there is nothing but this moment, all moments of existence-time are the whole of existence-time, and everything that exists is made out of time. The whole of time exists at just this moment. Let's stop and think about whether there's any place to which time could have leaked away from this very moment.

Yet regular people think, "Sometimes I'm pissed off like a three-headed demon, but sometimes I get real chill like a sixteen-foot golden Buddha. It's sort of like crossing the street on the way to the convenience store to get some chips and brews. The street and the convenience store still exist, but now I'm kicking back in front of the TV with my bag of Doritos and a can of Arrogant Bastard Ale."

But it's not limited to just that. When you were crossing that street or walking into the store, that was time. Time wasn't separate from you. And you actually exist now. So time hasn't gone anywhere.

If time is just one single moment, then the time of crossing the street is right now. But if time is linear, then you have this present moment, which is just time itself. Doesn't the time of crossing the street swallow and puke up the time of kicking back in front of the TV?

You were pissed off yesterday and that was time as yesterday. You're chill today and that's time as today. Even so, the Buddhist principle is that yesterday and today are both contained in the moment when you go down the street and end up at the convenience store. It hasn't passed.

Getting all cranky or taking it easy might seem far away now. But both are the present moment. Street lamps are time and sidewalks are time.

Don't think that time just flies away. Flying away isn't the only thing time can do. If it just flew away, you might be separate from time. Those who don't get what time is all about don't get it because they only think of time as having passed. To cut right to the chase: all the things in the whole universe are linked up in a series, and yet they're also individual moments of your own real time and my own real time.

Because time flows through a series of moments, moments of the past aren't piled on top of each other or lined up in a row. For the same reason, Jason is time and Dave is time and Kim and Julie are also time. Because subject and object are time, practice and experience are moments of time. Doing the dishes and cleaning the cat box are also time.

Regular people experience their own causes and conditions, but what they experience isn't reality itself. It's just that reality itself has made regular people into its causes and conditions. Because you think that time and existence are something other than what you are, you think you can never be as chill and enlightened as a Buddha. But attempts to evade the real issue by thinking you can never be a Buddha are just flashes of existence-time by someone who doesn't yet realize it.

Time also causes the hours to follow each other like they do. Midnight is time and 4:00 AM is time. You are time and Buddha is time.

Time experiences the whole universe by using a guy who's really pissed off and by using a girl who's chill as a cucumber. To universally recognize the universe using the universe is called universal realization.

Enacting Buddha by means of Buddha is establishing the will to train, is training itself, is the state of enlightenment and is nirvana as existence and time itself. It's nothing but realization that all of existence is all of time. There is nothing left over.

Because something left over is just something left over, even a half-assed realization is perfect as a half-assed realization. When it seems like we're just groping in the dark, that's also existence-time. Even such moments have their place and their function.

Just stick with what's really happening. Don't mistakenly say that it's nonexistence or existence. Don't just see how relentlessly time passes, without seeing that it never arrives. Even though intellectual under-standing is also time, such understanding doesn't matter much to real time.

People see time as leaving and coming, but nobody ever sees how it stays in one place. If you don't get that, how are you gonna get any-thing? Out of all those who are conscious of time staying in one place, none of them can express the inexpressible. The fact that all things are existence-time doesn't change, no matter how you explain it.

Time and existence are entirely realized, even though you still feel like you're being held back. Visions of marching bands and Elvises in jumpsuits appearing to your right and left are the time in which you make effort. All of time and all of being, in darkness and in bright-ness, continue from moment to moment as the realization of your own effort. Without this effort nothing could continue from moment to moment.

Get this. Passage from one moment to the next is like wind and rain moving westward or eastward. The whole universe is change and movement. It is passage from one moment to another. Take spring, for example. There are lots of aspects to spring, and we call those "time's movement."

But you should watch and see how the flow of time continues with-out there ever being anything external to it. Spring passes through itself moment by moment. The truth of the here and now is realized as spring. It's not like there's something called spring and then nature goes and embodies it.

If we think that time passes by us while we somehow remain the same, that's not real learning.

Master Yakusan Igen, the guy who wrote the poem at the beginning of this essay, asked his teacher Kozei Daijaku (Ch. Jiangxi Daji, 704–788 CE), "I've pretty much figured out the basics of Buddhism. But why did Bodhidharma come to China?" (You'll recall that Bodhidharma was the Indian teacher who brought Zen to China.)

Daijaku said, "Sometimes I make him lift an eyebrow or wink. Sometimes I don't. Sometimes that's the right thing to do. But sometimes it isn't."

Yakusan understands and says, "Sheesh! When I was with my last teacher I was like a mosquito trying to bite the statue of a picnicker!"

What Daijaku says isn't like what other people say. He understood things that nobody else understood, and he was a really strict follower of the precepts. Also, not doing right — in other words "being a jerk" — isn't just a matter of inaction. Sometimes doing nothing is the right thing to do.

Mountains and oceans are time. Without time there'd be no mountains or oceans. Don't think that the real mountains and real oceans aren't time. If time were destroyed, mountains and oceans would be destroyed. All these situations are examples of being-time. Buddha himself got enlightened in accordance with existence-time.

Zen Master Shoken Kisho (Ch. Yexian Guisheng, dates unknown) said,

Sometimes I've got will but no words
Sometimes I've got words but no will
Sometimes I've got both in big herds
Sometimes I've got neither, I'm still

The will and the words are both existence-time. Having them or not is also being-time. The moment they're here hasn't finished, but the moment they're not here has come. The will has been made into this and that. Presence isn't about having come from somewhere else, and absence isn't about going somewhere else. Real will is as it is. This is time.

The will is time as the realized universe. Things are only exactly what they are, nothing more or less. Here's what I say:

Making yourself lift an eyebrow or wink is half existence-time
Making yourself lift an eyebrow or wink is mixed-up existence-time
Not making yourself lift an eyebrow or wink is half existence-time
Not making yourself lift an eyebrow or wink is mixed-up existence-
    time
When we experience it like this, that time is existence-time.
— Written at Kosho-horin-ji Temple on the first day of winter 1240

Pretty far-out, right? I could probably spend the rest of the book trying to explain this piece. In fact, I've heard that someone is coming out with a whole book just about this chapter of *Shōbōgenzō*. It'll probably be on sale at your local Book Barn by the time this book becomes available, so go check it out.

It's not all that hard. What Dōgen is really trying to say is that time and existence are inseparable. Heidegger said it too, in his book *Being and Time*. We tend to think that they're not the same thing, though. Because of this mistaken understanding we suffer over a lot of things that aren't really worth suffering over.

For example, you might be doing something that you don't like and thinking, "I could be somewhere else right now." It seems like a small matter. But some of us go through life absolutely hating everything we do and everywhere we go because we imagine it could be other than it is.

I used to do this a whole lot. I'd be at work at one of the series of thankless jobs I held throughout much of my life, seething with anger over how I could have been doing something better, more interesting, more suited to my talents or just less tedious and awful. This didn't stop once I got finished with my shift, either. A huge segment of my life was given over to just feeling a kind of intense resentment toward whatever situation I was in.

In some cases this kind of feeling can spur you on to improving a genuinely bad situation. But a little of that goes a long way. Most of us overdo it to such an extent that we feel horribly depressed and drained by our own relentless attacks on ourselves and our situation.

It took years of really boring meditation sessions for me to finally get past this. And even so, I still slide into it sometimes and need to be reminded that things really aren't that way. At every moment of every day, no matter how I feel about the situation, whether it's mind-blowingly thrilling or completely brain-numbing, I am the totality of the universe experiencing the fullness of itself. Even if I don't notice it.

We are not entities who experience time. We are time itself. All Dōgen is doing in this essay is trying to get us to notice that.

As Dustin Hoffman's character says in the movie *I Heart Huckabees*,

> Say this blanket represents all the matter and energy in the universe, okay? You, me, everything. Nothing has been left out, all right? ...Let's just say that this is me, all right? [pushes hand up under the blanket] And I'm, what, sixty-odd years old and I'm wearing a gray suit. Blah, blah, blah. And let's say over here, this is you [pokes other hand up under another side of the blanket]. And, you're, I don't know, you're twenty-one. You got dark hair, etc. And over here, this is Vivian, my wife and colleague. Then over here, this is the Eiffel Tower, right? It's Paris. And this is a war. And this is, uh, a museum. And this is a disease. And this is an orgasm. And this is a hamburger.

To which Jason Schwartzman's character says, "Everything is the same even if it's different." Dōgen might have written, "Everything is time."

Anyway, Dustin Hoffman replies, "Exactly. But our everyday mind forgets this. We think everything is separate. Limited. I'm over here. You're over there. Which is true. But it's not the whole truth because we're all connected. When you get the blanket thing you can relax because everything you could ever want or be you already have and are."

I think that's pretty close to what Dōgen is saying in this piece.

I'll go through some of the weirder lines of Dōgen's and tell you what I think they mean.

Dōgen says, "Some days go by too fast and some days drag on forever, but we still say each is twenty-four hours." Dōgen's view was that time was flexible. Even though our clocks measure each hour as being exactly the same length, in actual experience we know that's not true. Some hours are way longer than others!

In scientific terms we'd say this is a mistake. Even if your subjective experience of an hour spent in line at the DMV is different from your subjective experience of an hour spent rolling on the beach with the one you love, science would disagree. Dōgen's view takes the Middle Way. Yes, our measuring devices tell us every hour is the same. But our subjective sense of time is just as real. So they're the same, but they aren't. Just like what Dustin Hoffman says in the quotation above.

My paraphrase of Dōgen says, "The self lays itself out to look at itself. That's how you should understand time." The Nishijima/Cross translation has, "Putting the self in order we see what it is. The truth that self is Time is like this." Tanahashi's translation is, "The way the self arrays itself is the form of the entire world. See each thing in this entire world as a moment of time." Shasta Abbey's translation is, "We human beings are continually arranging the bits and pieces of what we experience in order to fashion 'a whole universe.'" In Japanese it's わ れ排列しおきて尽界とせり (*ware hairetsushi okite jinkai seri*). A lot shorter than it is in English!

This idea may seem odd since it's all about self, and one of the foundational teachings of Zen is that there is no self. But when we say there's no self, we only mean that there is no fixed and limited entity that remains unchanging while life and time go on around it. Yet what we mistakenly call "self" still exists. We just have completely wrong ideas about what it is and make huge mistakes by acting on those wrong ideas. So sometimes Dōgen just calls this unnameable something "self" or even calls it the "soul," another taboo word in Zen.

Dōgen's understanding of life is that the universe is a living thing. In the Western tradition sometimes we use the word *God* to express that same idea. In order to understand himself,* God arrays his own features before himself and experiences them as if they were other than him. Yet ultimately God remains indivisible. This is one way of looking at it.

Another of my favorite lines in this piece is the one I paraphrased as, "To universally recognize the universe using the universe is called universal realization." In Japanese it's それ尽界をもて尽界を尽界するを、究尽するとはいふなり (*Sore jinkai wo mote jinkai wo jinkai suru wo, kyūjin suru to ha ifu nari*). Nishijima/Cross translate this as, "To Universally realize the whole universe by using the whole universe is called 'to perfectly realize.'" Tanahashi's translation says, "To fully actualize the entire world with the entire world is called thorough practice." And Shasta Abbey's translation has, "To universally penetrate the whole universe by means of the whole universe is called 'complete realization.'"

This means pretty much the same thing as the other lines we just looked at. The universe and the self are one and the same. Time is another name for this thing. So is the "present moment." You are not a person living in a time and a place. You are the person *and* the time *and* the place all rolled into one. See? I told you this piece was trippy!

The line I've paraphrased as, "Visions of marching bands and Elvises in jumpsuits appearing to your right and left are the time in which you make effort" obviously didn't refer to marching bands and Elvises in the original. It said, "Celestial kings and celestial throngs appearing to the right and to the left." But I didn't see any good reason to leave it like that. I like visions of Elvises better.

It's impossible for me to say exactly what Dōgen had in mind when he wrote that. No commentator I've come across has even tried. But, having done a lot of zazen myself, my best guess is that he's talking

---

* God has no gender, but the English language demands one, so I'm using the male pronoun because that's the norm.

about some of the freakier things that go through a person's mind while sitting and staring at the wall for a long time.

A lot of schools of meditation value having strange visions or communicating with supposed spiritual entities. But Dōgen didn't regard such experiences very highly. In Soto-style Zen, when such things happen, you're generally told to disregard them and keep on sitting. Dōgen is pretty much saying the same thing here. No matter what you encounter in your meditation, that's just part of your effort, which is time itself.

I have Dōgen saying, "Doesn't the time of crossing the street swallow and puke up the time of kicking back in front of the TV?" This is another one of those juicy lines that most commentators don't attempt explaining. Even Nishijima, who provides a lot of explanatory notes for this chapter, just lets this one go.

The only changes I made to this part were substituting *puke* for *vomit* and changing the metaphor Dōgen uses of crossing a stream while walking up a mountain to one about crossing the street to get to a store and buy chips and beer. Dōgen was talking to monks who lived in the mountains and probably had to cross lots of streams. In fact, just after Dōgen died one of his successors raised a bunch of money to build a bridge over a stream near his temple because so many people got injured crossing it. Maybe that's what Dōgen had in mind. I figure that you, my readers, are likely to live in more urban settings.

I take this line to mean that even if we're sitting and watching TV with our Doritos and beer, the time that came before is still part of that moment. We have those chips and that beer because we made an effort in the past. So the past doesn't leak away. It exists right there with us in tangible form. In this example, that tangible form happens to be Doritos and beer.

A little later on Dōgen says, "People see time as leaving and coming but nobody ever sees how it stays in one place." This just refers again to the idea that all of time is present in just this moment. It stays in one place.

Dōgen quotes Daijaku as saying, "Sometimes I make him lift an eyebrow or wink. Sometimes I don't. Sometimes that's the right thing to do. But sometimes it isn't." It's pretty common for Zen teachers to refer to themselves in the third person like this, as if they themselves are an object that they use. They're expressing things from the point of view of that universal something that is the universe considered as a single entity — from the point of view of God, if you like. It sounds weird. But sometimes I try thinking about it this way in reference to myself. I get a different perspective on things, and it's pretty interesting.

Finally, I want to talk about this notion of "half existence-time" and "mixed-up existence-time" that Dōgen refers to at the end. All translations I've seen agree on the translation of "half existence-time." But "mixed-up existence-time" is a different matter.

Kaz Tanahashi's translation says "the time being missed" while the Shasta Abbey translation has "counterfeit 'just for the time being.'" They use "just for the time being" in quotes as the translation of the word *uji* ("sometimes" or "being-time" in my version) throughout.

In the original Japanese it says 錯有時. The last two characters, 有時, are *uji* ("sometimes" or "being-time"). The character 錯 by itself is pronounced *kosuri* and in modern Japanese means "rubbing," "scrubbing," or "scraping." But in compound words it takes on the meaning of "mistaken," "illusory," or "confused." In other compounds it can also mean "mixed," "complex," or "complicated."

As you can see, it's difficult to come up with a single English word to translate this character. All these translators are just doing their best to come up with one that's on target. For my money, Nishijima and Cross get it as close to right as can be done. Of course I'm biased. But I think if you look at the various connotations of the Japanese word that Dōgen used, "mixed up" hits as many of them as you can in English.

Nishijima Roshi says that when Dōgen calls something "half *whatever*," as he often does, the word *half* indicates something concrete or real. Other translators tend to agree. In his online essay "Commentary on Dōgen's Text: Uji" for the International Zen Therapy Institute,

David Brazier says, "Dōgen likes to use the term 'half' in order to indicate what it is like for actual human beings rather than idealized ones. We do not necessarily do the best possible job every time."

In his blog, Nishijima Roshi commented on Dōgen's poem at the end saying, "In real situations, it is not always all or nothing, or right or wrong, but in actual situations there are also cases of different degrees of right and wrong."

To me the poem at the end of the chapter just means that even in our confusion there is the total, actual truth of confusion. Realization isn't always the absence of confusion. Sometimes it's the total acceptance and embracing of confusion. If you can completely accept and be perfectly comfortable with the fact that you don't know anything, then you know everything.

Sure, that's far easier said than done. But as Dōgen stresses again and again, anything the so-called Great Masters have achieved, you and I can achieve as well. Maybe we ought to get started.

18. THE MYSTICAL POWER OF THE CLOTHES YOU WEAR

Den-E

Transmission of the Robe

THE NEXT TWO chapters in the complete ninety-five-chapter version of *Shōbōgenzō* are two versions of the same thing. They're both about how to wear Zen robes. It is thought that the shorter version is the draft of a talk Dōgen gave and that the longer one is a transcript of the actual talk. If you're a completist or a scholar you want to have both.

But this book isn't for completists and scholars. In fact, it isn't really even for people who wear Zen robes, at least not exclusively. Heck, I have three sets of the things in my closet and I wear them as little as possible. They're uncomfortable and hot, and they make me look like a weirdo unless I happen to be hanging out in a temple. Even then it feels awkward.

But Dōgen was a big fan of wearing robes. Here he gives his reasons for why he thinks the robe is so important.

Even so, with apologies to Dōgen, I've chosen to paraphrase only the shorter version of this piece, with a few bits from the long version added in here and there. I'm also skipping over more sections of these chapters than I've been doing with the others. This is because I assume that you, dear reader, probably aren't going to be wearing Buddhist robes yourself or that, if you do wear robes, you have probably already read these chapters in their original form. I'm sticking mainly to the philosophical aspects Dōgen puts in between his instructions for the wear and care of big, black robes. I'm more interested in why Dōgen thinks the robes are important than in specifics about how they should be worn.

To read both versions, you can find them in the Nishijima/Cross translation or the Shasta Abbey translation. Kaz Tanahashi's translation combines both chapters into one.

Before we begin, though, I want to tell you my understanding of the significance of the robes. When I lived in Japan I worked for a company called Tsuburaya Productions. They were one of the nation's leading producers of wholesome children's entertainment. Their corporate image was kind of like Disney's image in America. They made a TV show called *Ultraman*, which is Japan's equivalent of *Superman*.

Every time they started up a new TV show or movie, staff members and company employees like me would get jackets with a design related to the new show. These were produced in very limited numbers and available only to people connected with the show or the company. I really liked Tsuburaya Productions, so I often wore mine around town. It was a conversation starter since it was amazing to Japanese people that a foreigner actually had one of those jackets.

So one day I was wearing my jacket while browsing in a video store. I happened to be in the back room of the store, ahem, conducting cultural research into the sexual mores of the natives. All of a sudden I realized I was wearing my Tsuburaya Productions jacket. Embarrassed, I immediately made my way to the front of the store and looked for some Studio Ghibli cartoons to rent.

By wearing that jacket I was representing the company and the things it stood for. It didn't matter that I knew that one of our execs was having an affair with someone from the events division, or that the idea of our employees being any kind of moral role models was pretty dubious. The jacket represented more than that. It represented an ideal that meant a lot to people.

The power of Buddhist robes is something like that. There's no magic involved. There doesn't need to be. When you wear a Buddhist robe you feel like you're representing the Buddhist tradition to the world at large. And you're representing it to yourself too. You behave differently, depending on the clothing you wear. Dōgen talks of the robe's mystical powers, but whenever I read this chapter I flash back to that day in the video store, and it all makes perfect sense.

Also a little note: Throughout this text Dōgen uses the term *Buddhist robe* (*kashaya*) to mean three different things, without making any distinction between them. One is the actual garment worn by Shakyamuni Buddha when he was alive. This was supposedly passed on to each person in his line of successors until it ended up in some temple in China, where I'm sure it was a big tourist attraction. The ones we wear today are supposedly based on that original robe. The second meaning of the word *kashaya* in Dōgen's usage refers to the copies of that original robe that are still worn by Buddhist monks today. The third meaning is a more conceptual sort of robe. For example, he says that every Buddha who realized the truth was wearing the robe. This isn't literally true. But in terms of their spiritual development they can be said to have been "wearing the robe" conceptually.

By the way, one of Dōgen's robe-related pieces I'm working with here — "Den-e," the one I've based most of this chapter on — was actually forbidden by the Soto organization to be published until the twentieth century. Specific instructions on how to make and wear a Buddhist robe were considered trade secrets!

Only Bodhidharma, who founded the Shaolin Temple (that's right, the one from all the kung fu movies) authentically transmitted Buddha's robe to China. This robe was passed from twenty-eight generations of teachers in India and six generations of teachers in China. The robe is still enshrined in Horin Temple on Sokei-zan Mountain (Baolin Temple on Caoxi Mountain, in Chinese). The early Chinese emperors revered it as a sacred relic and treated it with the utmost respect.

Monks and laypeople who have paid respect to Buddha's robe are, without exception, great people who believed in the dharma he taught.

Even worldly philosophies say that you can tell a lot about a person by watching how they behave. Admiring and bowing to the Buddha's robe is just like admiring and bowing to the Buddha in person.

It's a darn shame that later rulers in China didn't know what an important relic they had in their country and failed to pay it the proper respect. They were deluded by Taoist teachings and even abolished Buddhism. Instead of wearing stylin' Buddhist robes they wore tacky Taoist caps.

In the old days in India, even laypeople often wore Buddhist robes. Nowadays there are Buddhist monks who don't wear them. This is a truly pathetic situation.

We can understand and appreciate the dharma when we hear even a short verse about it. But the Buddhist robe is a concrete expression of the dharma. It can be just as valuable in transmitting the teachings.

Since way back in the day the robe has been called the garment that wards off suffering from heat and the clothing of liberation. When Buddhas realize the truth they're always wearing the robe. We, who were unfortunate enough to have been born in a dinky little country nobody cares about, should jump for joy that we can retain the tradition of the robe. If we wear the robe for just a single instant, there is huge merit even in that.

Everybody knows the saying "a king doesn't wear something different from the previous kings or follow laws different from the previous kings." We should be like that too. If our clothes and customs are different from those of our Buddhist ancestors, how can we expect to reach their level of understanding?

People who think that the robe is just a piece of clothing, while not understanding that it is a physical manifestation of the dharma, are a bunch of dopes. The material, color, and measurements of Buddha's actual robe have been retained in the customs of the traditional lineage.

When Shakyamuni named Maha Kashyapa as his rightful successor, he gave him his robe. Thirty-three succeeding generations received this very robe. The tradition of how to make and wear the robe was also passed down.

There are basically three types of robes: five-panel, seven-panel, and nine-panel. You wear the five-panel robe for work or traveling. You wear the seven-panel robe for conducting services or other formal activities. When you preach before a group, or go into a town or a palace, you wear the fancier nine-panel robe. You can also layer them on top of each other. When the Buddha got really cold they say he wore all three robes at the same time.

The Buddha said, "Even if somebody has great sins and wrong views, if they honor the robe with a sincere mind even for an instant they will be able to become a Buddha in the future. The power of the robe can make people feel compassion for each other. Even those on battlefields can achieve salvation through the robe."

Moment by moment thoughts appear and then vanish. Moment by moment our bodies appear and then vanish. But the power of practice goes on forever. The robe is the ultimate realm of the Buddhas. Anyone who receives it feels its power.

The Buddha said, "Those who are about to fall into wrong views hate the robe." So if hateful thoughts arise when you see the robe, you should feel sorry that you're falling into wrong views.

The story goes that when Buddha left the palace into which he'd been born and went out to pursue the truth as a penniless wanderer, the tree gods held up a robe to him and said, "If you put this on it'll protect you from demons." And it worked! For twelve years he practiced without disturbance. Nice one, tree gods!

There's a proverb, "Hearing a thousand times isn't as good as seeing once, and seeing a thousand times isn't as good as experiencing once." We should remember that when we put on the robe and experience its power.

If we cover our body with the robe even once it will be like a good luck charm that protects us and ensures our eventual enlightenment. The robe isn't our possession, nor does it belong to anyone else. Even so, it's hanging in your closet and there's another one in mine, and anyone who wears it gets loads of merit points.

The great nun and teacher Utpalavarna said that in a past life she was a comedienne. One time she put on a Buddhist robe as a joke and because of that she was reborn as a nun in the time of Kashapa, the Buddha prior to Shakyamuni.

But then, she said, she got all full of herself and broke the precepts. So she was reborn in hell. In her next life she was reborn at the time of Shakyamuni and practiced with him. Then she got right with Buddha. So you should know that the power of the robe is such that it can even save you from being a total jerk.

Lots of people doubt the power of the robe. But even the gods come down from the heavens to receive instructions from Buddhist monks. Anyone who insults the dharma is gonna have a hard time of it. The Buddha said, "You can repent for killing your mom and dad, but you can't repent for insulting the dharma."

The Buddha made his own robe out of rags. Some people get all hung up on what sort of material is used to make a Buddhist robe, saying that silk robes are too fancy to be authentic. But we should use whatever material we have, even if it's silk.

Some people say it's no good to use silk because silk is produced by killing silkworms. But even cotton plants are the habitat for many living things. So there is no special merit in using cotton and refusing silk.

When collecting rags to make a robe, just use whatever works. Don't worry about what it's made of. Sometimes silk looks like cotton, and vice versa. It doesn't matter, anyway.

When the Buddha was alive the only ceremony he established for taking the precepts was saying, "Welcome, monk!" Then the monk received the robe. Nobody worried about what their robes were made of.

Here are the ten kinds of material that are best for making a Buddhist robe: rags chewed by oxen, rags gnawed by rats, rags scorched by fire, rags used as rags by women who were "on the rag," rags used to clean up after childbirth, rags offered at shrines, rags left in graveyards, rags offered in prayer, rags discarded by royal officers, and rags brought back from funerals.

These sorts of materials are esteemed as best. In normal society they just toss these out, but we Buddhists use them. When we want pure materials, we should look for these kinds of rags.

Only a dumbass would think we use these kinds of materials just to deliberately make ourselves look shabby. Rags have always been used in Buddhism for their splendor and beauty.

In Buddhism we regard materials like brocade, embroidered silk,

silk twill, or materials encrusted with gold or precious gems as being truly shabby. We Buddhists use pure and beautiful material like those ten pure kinds I just described above. Such pure rags are beyond being shabby and beyond being extravagant.

It's regrettable that here in Japan there are monks and nuns who don't wear their robes. Even laypeople can wear the five-, seven-, and nine-panel robe if they've received the precepts. How can monks and nuns go without them?

Before you put on your robe you should first take it out and, with the robe still folded up, put it on top of your head. Then you kneel, fold your hands in prayer, and say the following verse three times:

Magnificent robe of liberation
Merit field of no creation
Wearing the teachings Buddha gave
All beings, we shall save

Then you stand up and put it on while thinking of your teacher or visualizing a Buddhist stupa. You should also recite this verse after you wash your robe.

When I was in China practicing at a temple there, I noticed the monk next to me did this every morning just after the first period of zazen before the chanting of the morning service began.

It was so moving to see this it brought me to tears. I had read in ancient sutras lines about "humbly receiving the robe upon the head," but I never understood what it meant until I actually saw it being done. At that moment I vowed to teach others to do this when I got back to Japan.

When I was in China I encountered a couple of Korean monks who didn't wear robes, even though they were very well versed in Buddhist literature. In China they looked like a couple of hicks from the boonies. I don't want my Japanese monks to be thought of like that.

So please take my advice and be joyful to receive and wear your Buddhist robes.

— Written and preached on October 10, 1240,
at Kannon-dori-kosho-horin-ji Temple

As I said in the introduction to this text, my version of this chapter is just the edited highlights. The chapters themselves are very long and detailed. For example, just like in the chapter about using the toilet, Dōgen goes into meticulous detail about how to wash the robe and how to hang it up to dry. I figured that after all the potty stuff you'd probably had enough of that sort of thing.

For every example of how great the robe is that I've given you here, I swear Dōgen lists ten more. I've tried to pare them down to the most interesting and relevant ones.

The little put-down here of Taoism is interesting. I often hear people who have apparently taken an Introduction to World Religions course somewhere say that Zen is a combination of Buddhism and Taoism. Dōgen was always very clear that even though Chinese Buddhism often uses Taoist language — such as referring to the Buddhist Way in Chinese as the Tao — it was very different from Taoism.

Also in this text, Dōgen refers to the Buddhist view of time that he wrote about in "Being-Time" ("Uji") when he says, "Moment by moment thoughts appear and then vanish. Moment by moment our bodies appear and then vanish. But the power of practice goes on forever." In Buddhism there is an idea that the universe — including our bodies — appears and disappears at every moment. This is a difficult concept, which he takes up in more detail later on in *Shōbōgenzō*. I just thought I'd draw your attention to its brief mention here.

The thing about killing silkworms is also very instructive. A few years ago there was a TV commercial for some kind of germ-killing Kleenex-type tissues in which a Buddhist monk sneezes into one of these killer tissues and then feels guilty for it. Although Buddhists do avoid killing whenever possible, we try not to take things too far. This statement by Dōgen is a good example of the actual Buddhist view, as opposed to the views of actors playing Buddhists on TV commercials.

As Dōgen says, "even cotton plants are the habitat of many beings." Even being a vegetarian or a vegan involves some degree of killing. So we can't be too proud of ourselves for those kinds of things. Using discarded silk is akin to what the Buddha told his followers about eating meat. He said they could eat whatever was given to them, even if it was meat, as long as they knew the animal wasn't killed specifically for them.

I've always loved the part about what kinds of rags can be used to make a Buddhist robe. All kinds of gross stuff is considered "pure" when it comes to making an authentic Buddhist robe. I've met a lot of Buddhists who have sewn their own robes, and some who've even used discarded cloth. But I've never met anyone who actually went so far as to get rags that had been chewed on by oxen or had been used as, you know, "rags" in the slang sense. It's also notable that you were supposed to wash these rags thoroughly before you sewed them together. So at least there's that.

Be that as it may, the custom of putting the robe on top of your head and saying that chant three times is still preserved in most Zen temples. I've never been moved to tears by it like Dōgen says he was, but every morning when I sit in a temple where they do this, I always find it oddly touching. As with all the poems I've quoted, I decided to make it rhyme (you wouldn't believe how hard that is, by the way!). The standard English version of the verse chanted in most American Zen temples goes, "Great robe of liberation / Field far beyond form and emptiness / Wearing the Tathagatha's teachings / Saving all beings." Actually, as goofy as my rhyming version is, I think it's a bit closer in meaning to the original chant in Chinese. I doubt it'll be widely adopted, though.

In any case, this robe chant is the first vocal sound anyone is supposed to make in the morning at a Zen temple. At night, you're supposed to observe what they call the Great Silence and not speak at all after the bell that ends the chanting of the Three Refuges (I take refuge in Buddha, I take refuge in the dharma, I take refuge in the sangha) at the end of evening zazen.

The first round of zazen in the morning is supposed to occur within this Great Silence, and then the robe chant finally breaks it. There are a few bells, drums, and wooden clacker things that happen before then. But you're not supposed to use your voice until the robe chant begins. Something about that feels really special, though it's hard to put into words exactly why.

Whether or not you ever decide to put on Buddhist robes for yourself, I think there's something to be learned from what Dōgen says in this chapter. As I said earlier, the clothes you wear can affect how you behave and can sometimes even make you a whole different sort of person. That's the real mystical power of the robe.

19. THE BEER AND DORITOS SUTRA

Sansuigyo

The Sutra of Mountains and Waters

I'M JUST PULLING your leg with the title. I'm not really going to be translating "mountains and waters" as "beer and Doritos" throughout this chapter. But since I did that in the chapter about Dōgen's concept of being-time, I thought I'd reference it again in the title of this chapter. Is joke! I making the joke!

In his introduction to this chapter, Nishijima Roshi says, "Buddhism is basically a religion of belief in the Universe, and nature is the Universe showing its real form. So to look at nature is to look at the Buddhist truth itself."

The introduction to the Shasta Abbey translation of this piece points out that the words *mountains* and *waters* also have a metaphorical sense in Chinese Buddhism. A Zen teacher is often referred to by the name of the mountain on which he or she resides. Such teachers are often compared to mountains because they sit immobile for very long stretches of time. The word *mountain* can also indicate our material nature. The word *waters* often refers to the flowing, spiritual side of our nature, as opposed to the more mountainlike, static, material side.

Both these sets of meanings come into play in this essay. Let's take a look at it, shall we?

The mountains and waters you see right now are the real forms of every-thing the ancient Buddhas ever said. Because they are just as they are, they always measure up to their full potential. They live in the timeless state, and live in the here and now. They're the self before the begin-ning of time. They're the real form of true emancipation. We get moral integrity by depending on mountains and waters because their virtue is so great. Their freedom can even inspire us to take the air like the wind.

Master Fuyo Dokai (Ch. Furong Daokai, 1043-1118 CE) said, "The blue mountains walk all the time. The stone woman gives birth at night." Mountains lack nothing that they're supposed to have. For this reason, although they're always still, Fuyo says they walk all the time. We need to pay close attention to the virtue of this walking.

Walking mountains are just like walking people. Even though the way that mountains walk doesn't look like the way people walk, you can't doubt that they are walking. We should listen to this teaching because the constancy of mountains depends on their movement. Human beings can't sense how mountains move. But they're faster than the wind.

To be among the mountains is to be in the real world where flow-ers bloom and real stuff actually happens. People who don't know the mountains never sense this concrete fact.

If you doubt that mountains can walk, you're also doubtful about your own walking. If you don't know your own walking, you can't under-stand how mountains walk. Once you really understand your own walk-ing, then you can understand how mountains walk.

Mountains are beyond being sentient or insentient. You yourself are also beyond being sentient or insentient.

You might not know what terms of measurement to use when talking about the mountains walking, but you should check it out thoroughly as well as thoroughly checking out your own walking. You should also look into that whole thing of "taking the backward step" that I talked about in "Fukanzazengi," as well as the concrete activity of actually stepping backward.

Dig this. From the moment just before the universe came into being, and since before the time of the first Buddha, who appeared during the Age of Emptiness, walking in forward steps and in backward steps has never stopped for even a second. If walking stopped there would've been no Buddhist masters. If walking were to end, the dharma couldn't reach us today.

Forward walking doesn't oppose backward walking, and vice versa. Each and every action occurs in its own independent present moment. We call this motion the flowing of the mountains.

Mountains, without being anything other than mountains, travel around and learn in practice. Don't insult them by saying they can't walk or move on water. Only dimwits doubt that mountains can walk or go slackjawed when they hear about "flowing mountains." Those who don't get this idea drown in their paltry understanding. These kinds of people think they know all there is to know about mountains.

Even if you're able to fully comprehend the nature of grass, trees, soil, stones, and fences, that isn't all there is to realize. Even if you realize mountains are decked out with seven treasures, that's not the real refuge. Even if you have visions of mountains as the place where Buddhas practice the truth, don't get too impressed by those visions. Even if you can see mountains as the magnificent merit of all the Buddhas, the reality is way more than just that.

Such realizations are objects realized by you as the subject. That's not what we esteem as true understanding. It's just like looking through a pipe at one corner of the sky. Buddha himself criticized the idea of the separation of subject and object. The ancient masters don't affirm what people call "enlightenment experiences" (the words Dōgen uses here are kenshin 見心 "seeing [the] mind" and kensho 見性 "seeing [one's true] nature," which generally refer to so-called enlightenment experiences).

Enlightenment experiences are the animated activity of non-Buddhists. Getting stuck in words and phrases isn't liberation. But there is a state that's free from such things. We express it by saying, "The blue-green mountains are constantly walking" and "the East Mountain moves on water." Get busy working on that!

Master Fuyo also said, "The stone woman gives birth at night." Sometimes we romantically call stones and other things male or female. In concrete terms we know they're not actually male or female. There are heavenly stones in the sense that we imagine things about stones, and there are earthly stones in the sense that we know the physical characteristics of stones. The secular world has terms for this, but few people really understand it.

And what do you know about childbirth? How could you think that one becomes a parent only at the time of birth? In real childbirth you become a parent and become a child.*

Zen Master Unmon Kyoshin (Ch. Yunmen Kuangzhen, 864—949 CE) said, "The East Mountain travels on water." The point he's making is that all mountains are East Mountain and that they all travel on water. So Mount Sumeru at the center of the world and its eight surrounding mountains appear and do practice-realization. But was Master Unmon really able to fully understand the life and activity of East Mountain?

These days in China a bunch of unreliable people have formed such a huge crowd that nobody can ever convince them they're wrong.

---

* Dōgen actually says 児の親となるを、生児現成と参学するのみならちや、親の児となるときを、生児現成の修証なりと参学すべし、究徹すべし (*ji no oya to naru wo, sei-ji genjo to sangaku suru nomin narachi ya, oya no ji to naru toki wo sei-ji genjo no shushō nari to sangaku-su beshi, kyūtetsu-su beshi*). I would translate this as, "To completely learn in practice-realization that in the actuality of childbirth (one/you) become parent to a child is to fully penetrate and verify in practice-realization that in the actuality of childbirth (one/you) become child of a parent." Nishijima/Cross has, "We should learn in practice, and should penetrate to the end, that the time of [the child] becoming the child of the parent is the practice-and-experience of the reality of childbirth." Kaz Tanahashi and the folks at the San Francisco Zen Center translate this as, "Study not only that you become a mother when your child is born, but also that you become a child." I like the nice nonsexist phrasing of the Tanahashi version. Since the subject is unstated, as is often the case in Japanese, it could be taken as addressing a hypothetical female "you." It could also be argued that "mother" is an acceptable translation of the word 親 (*oya*), which is usually translated as "parent." Maybe that's what Dōgen had in mind. Who can say? However, it tends to give the contemporary reader the impression that Dōgen's gender-neutral phrase is more definitely feminine, and for that reason it's not really a good translation, even if it is a translation I happen to like. What I've translated as "the actuality of childbirth" uses the same 現成 (*genjo*, or actuality/actualized) to modify the word childbirth as "Genjo Koan" uses to modify *koan*. In Nishijima's blog commentary he said about this, "All things and phenomena are always in mutual relations with each other."

They say that stories like this, about mountains moving on water and suchlike, are beyond rational understanding. Their idea is that Buddhist masters use weird irrational stories to try to convey a mystical truth beyond mere logic.

These imbeciles talk like they've never heard the truth. Guys like this have been spouting such nonsense in China for two or three hundred years. Nobody should even listen to these weenies. They're ruining Buddhism!

They don't know that images and thoughts become words and phrases, and that words and phrases transcend images and thoughts. When I was in China I laughed my butt off at these dumb-bums, but they couldn't say a word in response.

Their negation of logic is just plain stupid. Where did they even get such an idea? With no decent teacher to point out the truth, they have fallen into the non-Buddhist idea of naturalism.

Remember that rivers, streams, mountains, and suchlike aren't just abstractions. You realize real water at the foot of real mountains where real water is. Water is crowned by mountains whose walking is always on water and is always real. Mountain toes walk over all sorts of water in all directions, making it dance.

Water is not strong or weak, wet or dry, moving or still, cold or warm, existent or nonexistent. It's not delusion and it's not realization. When it's solid, it's harder than a diamond. Nobody can break it. When it's melted, it's soft as milk. And still, nobody can break it.

So don't doubt the real virtues of water! Human beings and gods see water. Water sees water too. Water practices and experiences water, and we can investigate water speaking water language. We should make real the path where self realizes self. We should move forward and backward on the living path in which the outside world completely exhausts its own total realization of the outside world, and then we should leap beyond!

Different types of beings see water differently. Gods and goddesses hanging out up in the sky see it as a string of pearls. But that doesn't mean they see strings of pearls as water. Maybe they see their version of water as something we call by another name. We just see their strings of pearls as water. Demons see water as raging flames or

as totally gross stuff, like pus and blood. Dragons and fish see water as
a beautiful palace they can live in. Many other beings see water in many
other ways.

But dig this. Is it that there are different ways to see one object? Or
have we mistakenly assumed assorted images to be one object? Really,
really look into this. By the same token, there are thousands upon millions of different ways to do practice and realization.

Keep in mind that although we sometimes say that there are many
kinds of water, there isn't one true original water, nor are there many
kinds of water. At the same time, the various kinds of water — which
accord with whomever or whatever is perceiving water — don't depend
on matter, don't arise from cause and effect, don't rely on themselves,
and don't rely on others. The liberation of water depends only on water.

For this reason water is beyond all categories, sensations, or properties. But water is naturally present as the element called water. Don't
be like small-minded people. They think that everything in nature
belongs to some category. In reality, we human beings create those
categories.

In the Mahūratnakūṭa Sūtra (J. Daiho Shakkyo) the Buddha says, "All
things are free as the breeze, they have no fixed address."[*] Remember,
even though they're free as a breeze, each lives in its own place. Even
so, when humans look at water, they only see its continuous flowing.

There are all kinds of flowing, each of which is an example of how
humans see things. Water flows over the Earth, it flows through the sky,
it flows up, it flows down. It flows in a creek and flows into the ocean. It
rises up to form clouds and falls down as rain.

The Taoist text Bunshi (Ch. Wenzi, probably composed in the first
century BCE) said, "The way of water is to ascend into the sky to form
rain clouds and fall to the ground to form rivers." Even a secular person
gets that. It would be a shame if students of Buddhism were more ignorant than secular people. Water doesn't notice the ways of water. Nor
does it not notice them. Even so, it flows.

Saying that there are places where water can't reach is the teaching

---

[*]   The standard translation would be, "All dharmas are ultimately liberated; they
have no permanent abode."

of fools. Water is present in flames, it is present in the mind as images, and it reaches into the realization of Buddha-nature.

Water falls into rivers. And the life of a river can become sages. Dimwits assume water is only in rivers. Not so! Rivers and oceans are realized in water, just as entity and substance are one. Understand that Buddha-lands exist where water has formed oceans and rivers.

In every drop of water there are a bazillion Buddha-lands. But that doesn't mean there are watery Buddha-lands or Buddha-lands in water. The place where water exists is already beyond past, present, and future and beyond the world of dharma. Even so, it is the actuality in which water just is.

Buddhist teachers go wherever water goes, and vice versa. That's why they always treat water as their own body-mind and as their own thinking. They never deny that water rises.

Still, sometimes the sutras say stuff like "fire and wind rise upward while Earth and water settle downward." But upward and downward are just concepts, not actual places. It's not like the world of dharma is up in the sky and hell is down underneath us, or anything like that.

Hell can be the whole universe, and so can heaven.[*] It's like fish. If you told them their "palace" of water was flowing, they'd never believe you. So it is with us when we want to see things in a certain way. Just sit quietly and see things as they really are.

Lots of people think they know it all because they know a little about how things are for human beings. But only a dunderhead assumes that the way things are for them is the way things are for everything in the universe. We need to learn in practice that there may be lots of things forever beyond our human understanding, yet there is a state of universal truth that we can be a part of nonetheless.

Since the distant past, great saints have lived in mountains. We might imagine, then, that mountains must be kind of like whole cities chock-full of saints. But when we go into the mountains ourselves,

---

[*] 阿鼻も尽法界なり、無想も尽法界なり。(*Abi mo jin hokai nari, muso mo jin hokai nari*). "The lowest hell is the whole world of dharma, the thoughtless realm [Heaven] is the whole world of dharma."

nobody's there. There's just the lively activity of mountains. There's not even a trace of anybody having gone up there.

When we're in the regular world looking up at mountains they look pretty different from when we're actually up there. When you look at stuff one way it seems like mountains flow, but when you look at stuff another way it seems like they don't. Since things seem very different depending on people's different perspectives, we ought to rely on the ancient masters whose view was clearer than ours.

Yoka Gengaku (Ch. Yongjia Xuanjue, 665-713 CE) in his poem "The Song of Enlightenment" (J. Shodoka, 證道歌), said, "To avoid the karma that leads to hell / Don't insult Buddhist teachings, treat them well." Carve these words on your bones. They're really true.

They say mountains belong to a nation, but really mountains belong to people who love them. And mountains love those who live on them. When sages live on mountains those mountains belong to the sages, and all the birds and animals and trees and even the rocks are the better for it. That's because of the virtue of the sages. Remember that mountains love sages, and sages love mountains.

Emperors and kings climb mountains to visit saints and sages. When they do so, these royal people bow to the sages rather than conforming to what goes on in ordinary society. Regal authority means nothing to mountain sages. Obviously mountains are beyond the human realm.

The Taoist text Soji by Chang-tsu says that three thousand years ago the Yellow Emperor went into the mountains, crawling on his knees, to beg the sage Kosei (Ch. Guangcheng) for the secret of immortality. Shakyamuni Buddha left the palace of his father the king to go up in the mountains, but his dad didn't resent the mountains. Prince Siddhartha (the Buddha's birth name) became the King of the Mountains.

Remember, we can't even fathom the mountains with our puny human minds. So how can we doubt their flowing or nonflowing?

Since ancient times, sages and saints have lived near the water too. Some of them fish for fish, and some fish for people, while others fish for the eternal truth. Master Sensu Tokujo (Ch. Chuanzi Decheng, dates unknown, successor of Yakusan Igen) left Yakusan (Ch. Yao) mountain to go live by the river and caught himself a sage in the form of Master

Kasan Zen-e (Ch. Hua-shan, d. 850 CE). Isn't that like fishing fishes? Isn't it like fishing people? Wasn't he fishing water? Wasn't he fishing himself? Tokujo was the only one able to truly meet Tokujo. Tokujo's teaching of people is a human being truly meeting a human being.

It's not just that there's water in the world. There are whole worlds in water. And not only in water. There are worlds of sentient beings in the clouds, and in the wind, and in fire too. There are worlds of sentient beings in the dharma world. There are worlds of sentient beings in a stalk of grass or in a walking stick. Pay attention to this.

Water is the palace of real dragons. It's beyond flowing or falling. If we think of water only as flowing, that's an insult to water. The word *water* forces water to be something other than flowing itself.

Water is just what water is. It's beyond any word we can use to describe it. When we realize the flowing and nonflowing of just one body of water, we understand everything else all at once.

Same deal with mountains. There are treasures in the mountains, and there are mountains in treasures. There are mountains in marshes, and in space, and there are even mountains in mountains.

Master Unmon Bun-en (Ch. Yunju Daoying, c. 835–902 CE) said, "The sky is the sky. The Earth is the Earth. Mountains are mountains. Water is water. Monks are monks. Laypeople are laypeople." That doesn't mean the word *mountain* is a mountain. Real mountains are real mountains. We should work on this in our practice. Mountains and water naturally produce sages and saints.

— Preached at Kannon-dori-kosho-horin-ji Temple,
October 18, 1240

This chapter is a difficult one for me. First off, Dōgen talks a whole lot about mountains walking and stone women giving birth. It just sounds kind of crazy. But then it settles down and gets a little more sensible. I'll try to walk you through some of the more difficult parts.

About all the stuff in here about mountains walking, Nishijima Roshi said, "I have some personal supposition that at the time when Master Fuyo Dokai lived (1043–1118), some Buddhist Masters had noticed the rotation of the earth, not scientifically, but intuitively."

That sounds reasonable to me. They might also have had some vague idea of plate tectonics since they would have already known about earthquakes.

We don't need to see this idea of mountains walking as anything more mystical than the understanding we have today that mountains move, even though we see them as static. They move as the Earth rotates and they move as the plates of the Earth gradually slide against each other. They grow and shrink too, even though the time scale in which they do so is too slow for us to notice. I think the ancient Buddhist masters got this even though it was hard for them to express it in the language available to them.

On the other hand, the fact that the Earth is a dynamic, moving, evolving system implies something further that few of us these days seem to notice. We make a sharp distinction between things we think of as alive and the rest of the universe, which we imagine is not alive. But nobody has ever been able to come up with a convincing definition of life that absolutely includes all things we imagine are alive while excluding everything we think of as lifeless.

For example, crystals can replicate themselves and grow, but we don't normally think of them as alive. Viruses seem to exhibit properties we associate with life but also a lot of properties we associate with nonlife. We generally don't imagine amoebas are self-aware, yet we think they're alive. Even fire feeds, grows, and reproduces, yet we don't generally classify it as a life-form. The dividing line between life and nonlife is already blurry, and as more research gets done it just keeps getting blurrier.

So even though we make distinctions between living and nonliving things, we really don't know precisely what we mean. If the ability to move and change is how we define life, then maybe the Earth is alive. Perhaps, in ways we don't yet fully comprehend, the Earth is as much of a sentient being as we are.

Nishijima Roshi was fond of saying, "God is the universe. The universe is God." While I grew up thinking that people and dogs and iguanas and bugs were alive while most of the rest of the universe was nonliving, he saw the universe as a living thing. That idea has been present in Buddhism from the beginning. Life is a common element to everything in the universe. Complex systems like human beings experience life in a particular way. But to say that things that experience life in different ways from us are therefore nonliving may be a mistake.

Later on in this piece Dōgen references his own statement from "Fukanzazengi" about "taking the backward step." There's an interesting footnote about that idea of the "concrete activity of stepping backward" in the Nishijima/Cross translation. In this footnote they give a few examples of concrete backward steps, which include sitting zazen, lifting weights, doing prostrations, and having a bath. I suspect Mike Cross, being a pretty athletic guy, was the one who stuck lifting weights in there as an example.

They also give some examples of the kind of conceptual backward step Dōgen talks about in "Fukanzazengi" such as reading *Shōbōgenzō*, researching the function of the autonomic nervous system, and drawing inferences from trial and error in daily life. Nishijima very much believed that much of what Dōgen describes in *Shōbōgenzō* was, in contemporary medical language, referring to the working of the autonomic nervous system.

I've found that in my own writing and speaking career, it's highly problematic to mention the autonomic nervous system. When an elderly Japanese monk uses terms like that, he seems to be very forward thinking, and his lack of specific medical knowledge is easily forgiven. But when I say the very same things, it sometimes feels as if people are coming after me with knives. Some folks get extremely upset that a young (well, young compared to Nishijima, anyhow) Western person without a medical degree would use words like that.

I don't really understand this reaction. After all, we use scientific terms all the time. How many books have been written about the similarities between Buddhist theory and quantum mechanics by people who don't know diddly about physics? Maybe the guys who write those books get raked over the coals too. But anyway, in the interest of maintaining a peaceful life I've stopped saying much about the autonomic nervous system.

I still think it's an intriguing idea, though. So I'll give you the quick version. Save your knives for Nishijima. He made it up. Plus, your knives can't hurt him because he's dead. Anyhow, basically he said that when the two halves of the ANS, the parasympathetic and sympathetic nervous systems, are in balance, this is the state Dōgen refers to as "dropping off body and mind."

The parasympathetic nervous system is associated with what they call the "rest and digest" response. When it's functioning more strongly, we feel relaxed and calm. This, Nishijima associates with "body" in Dōgen's terminology. The sympathetic nervous system is associated with fight-or-flight responses. When it's stronger we feel more alert and energetic. This Nishijima associates with "mind" in Dōgen's terminology. Zazen is a state that is neither too relaxed nor too alert and promotes the balance of the ANS.

I think the reason this idea upsets certain people isn't really because of an assumed misunderstanding of the medical terms. What really upsets them is that it seems to reduce a lofty mystical idea to something base and physical. But Buddhism says that body and mind are one. So why shouldn't a lofty, spiritual state also have a bodily manifestation that can be explained in medical terms? It's not so scary if you think of it that way.

Moving right along, Mount Sumeru is mentioned in this piece. We now know that this is a mythical mountain created by the writers of Hindu religious epics. But Dōgen and his audience most likely would have assumed it was a real mountain in India. So he probably uses it as a concrete example of an actual mountain.

Nishijima Roshi has a short footnote after the section that I've paraphrased as, "In every drop of water there are a bazillion Buddha-lands. But that doesn't mean there's watery Buddha-lands or Buddha-lands in water. The place where water exists is already beyond past, present, and future and beyond the world of dharma. Even so, it is the actuality in which water just is." Nishijima says there, "Reality includes both matter, as in the form of real water, and meaning, as in the idea of Buddha-lands."

Nishijima has a similar footnote after the bit I paraphrased as, "There are treasures in the mountains and there are mountains in treasures. There are mountains in marshes, and in space, and there are even mountains in mountains." He says here that, "treasure (value), marshes (nature), space (the state of action) and mountains (reality) correspond to the four faces of reality outlined in Buddha's four noble truths." This refers to the four-phase interpretation of Dōgen's philosophy I talked about in the introduction to this book.

One important part of this essay is the one in which Dōgen expresses his idea of the nature of koans. Koans are often explained as illogical stories whose intention is to make us break out of the bonds of mere logic as in, for example, all that stuff about walking mountains and stone women giving birth.

In his book *Introduction to Zen Buddhism*, D. T. Suzuki, one of the most influential writers on Zen, says, "The achieving of enlightenment in Zen is not at all a rational or methodical process. It is completely non-rational, unexplainable, and intuitive. The Zen training in concentration, in the characteristic cross-legged position, and the Zen teaching of koans (non-logical riddles and stories) are designed to put the student in a state where he can abandon logic and make the leap upward into enlightenment." The parenthetical part is in the original; I didn't add it. D. T. Suzuki's ideas about this represent mainstream thinking in Rinzai-style Zen Buddhism.

This notion that koans are illogical is not a new idea. Dōgen was aware of it eight hundred years ago. I've paraphrased what he says about it as, "These days in China there are a bunch of unreliable people (who)...say that stories like this, about mountains moving on water and suchlike, are beyond rational understanding. Their idea is that Buddhist masters use weird irrational stories to try to convey a mystical truth beyond mere logic....Nobody should even listen to these weenies. They're ruining Buddhism!"

My version is based on the Nishijima/Cross translation and mashes together a couple of paragraphs into a few sentences. But there isn't a lot of discrepancy here with other translations. Tanahashi has, "They say, 'Ancient masters used expedient phrases, which are beyond understanding, to slash entangled vines.' Those who say this have never seen a true master and have no eye of understanding." The Nishiyama/Stevens translation says, "[The notion that such stories are incomprehensible] is not the teaching of a real master and not the eye of proper study." Later the Tanahashi translation says, "The great road of Buddha ancestors is crumbling" because of these people who he calls "more stupid than animals." In other words, these weenies are ruining Buddhism.

There is a general misunderstanding that Rinzai Zen uses koan stories and Soto Zen does not. In fact, Soto Zen uses koan stories all the time. Much of *Shōbōgenzō* is based on those stories.

However, Dōgen did not regard these stories as beyond logic or as "irrational." Rather, he believed they expressed an uncommon form of logic and rationality that could be comprehended by those who trained and practiced zazen. He spends a lot of time in his writings and talks explaining the rational, logical basis for these strange-seeming stories.

Sometimes Dōgen's explanation of the uncommon logic of koans gets so weird as to seem incomprehensible itself. It's almost as if he's trying to prove his opponent's point! But I think if you take chapters like this one slowly and work with them, the underlying logic and rationality appear. It can also help to have a teacher and to be doing your own zazen practice.

This is a long chapter, and in the original it's even longer. While I think that my paraphrase of this chapter gives you the general idea of what Dōgen is saying, I also think it would be useful to read a more complete, more standard version if you want to get the whole picture. As I've said too many times already, my earlier chapter about different editions of *Shōbōgenzō* will point you in the direction.

20. THE BUDDHIST HALL OF FAME

Busso

The Buddhist Patriarchs

In its original form, this chapter consists of a short introductory paragraph, followed by a list of names. You never see this chapter translated except in complete versions of *Shōbōgenzō* because why would anyone bother to translate a list of names? And yet this chapter does express something important about Dōgen's philosophy. Dōgen was very pragmatic. Let me tell you what that means to me.

Early on, when I first started getting interested in Zen, my first teacher, Tim McCarthy, mentioned that he liked the writings of Jiddu Krishnamurti. I was such a nerd that if Tim said he liked something, I had to go seek it out and read all I could. Luckily it was pretty easy to find Krishnamurti's books in used bookstores. So I read a bunch of them.

The short version of Krishnamurti's life story is that when he was a little kid some people from the Theosophist Society saw him on a beach and decided he was going to be their new messiah. They adopted him from his parents and took him off to be groomed for his role as the Great Teacher for the New Age.

After about two decades of indoctrination, they set up this huge rally in which Krishnamurti was supposed to go up in front of thousands of people and declare that he was the New Buddha/Christ/Savior/

Whatever. But Krishnamurti pulled a fast one on them. He went on stage and formally disbanded the whole organization saying, "Truth is a pathless land" and that he was a seeker just like everyone else.

He went on to work as a teacher for the next fifty years or so. He rejected all forms of ritual as mere conditioning and essentially void of anything useful. His ideas made sense and for many years, that's the view I held too.

Tim didn't do many Buddhist rituals. I'm not really sure why. I think Tim's teacher saw Tim's role as being a bit different from the usual Zen priest and trained him accordingly. My ordaining teacher, Gudo Nishijima, didn't do many of the ceremonies Zen priests in Japan usually do because he felt that too many Zen priests in Japan cared only about rituals and knew nothing about meditation. So it was easy to maintain this rather negative view of ritual Zen practice while I studied with those two.

But then I started going to the Tassajara Zen monastery in northern California during their summer guest season to volunteer as a dining room worker. When you're a volunteer worker at Tassajara, you have to participate in their big morning ritual of zazen, followed by a whole bunch of bowing and chanting. At first this really bugged me because my teachers never did this stuff and I was convinced it was useless and not worth my time. Still, I had signed up for everything and I did it anyway. To my great surprise, after doing it for a while I started to see that it made a real difference in my practice.

Maybe Krishnamurti would say that the rituals simply made me dull and that the joy I felt from them was just the pleasure of mindless conformity. But I don't think so. I certainly think it *can* be like that with rituals, especially religious ones. They can be used in all sorts of horrible ways to make people stupid and obedient.

But there's also something deep within us that craves these rituals. It could be the social nature of the human animal. We're not the type of creature that can survive on its own the way many other animals can.

We're almost like ants, which die when taken away from their colonies. If a tiger survives for a year alone in the woods, nobody thinks that's much of an accomplishment. If a human being does that, it makes headlines. I think rituals can satisfy a need we have to feel connected with our fellow humans.

There may also be another practical side effect. In a recent study led by Dr. Kathleen Vohs at the University of Minnesota, it was found that doing a ritual before eating, which is a standard practice at all Buddhist temples, makes the food taste better. The researchers believe this is because the anticipation of eating makes food seem tastier. Also, they say that rituals draw people into what they're doing and make them more focused on it. This is, of course, one of the key elements of Zen practice.

Most Zen temples have some set of rituals they engage in. Sometimes there are a whole lot of them. In spite of Dōgen's oft-quoted phrase about people chanting sutras being like frogs croaking together in a pond, he led ritual chanting at his own temples. This chapter is evidence of his commitment to certain aspects of ritual practice. The names he lists here are the ones his group chanted, probably every morning, in order to pay respect to the masters who paved the way of the practice that he taught.

Rather than just giving you a list of names, as Dōgen does, I'm going to tell you a bit about some of these teachers. None of that stuff is in the original — after the introduction it's just a straight-up list. I got most of my info about these guys from the footnotes in the Nishijima/Cross translation of *Shōbōgenzō*.

The realization of the Buddhist ancestors lies in how we pay homage to them. This isn't limited to Buddhas of the past, present, or future but goes beyond them. It is Buddhas going beyond themselves. We venerate those who have the real faces and eyes of Buddha and thereby meet them for ourselves. They have upheld the virtues of Buddhas. They are as follows.

Great Master Vipashan Buddha, who in Japan is called Bibashi Butsu or Kosetsu, meaning "Universal Preaching."*

Great Master Shikan Buddha, who in Japan is called Shiki Butsu or Ka, meaning "Fire."

Great Master Vishvabhu Buddha, who in Japan is called Bishafu Butsu or Issai-ji, meaning "All Benevolent."

Great Master Krakucchanda Buddha, who in Japan is called Kuruson Butsu or Kinsennin, meaning "Gold Wizard."

Great Master Kanakamuni Buddha, who in Japan is called Kunagon-muni Butsu or Konjikisen, which, confusingly, means "Golden Wizard," as opposed to just plain Gold Wizard.

Great Master Kashyapa Buddha, who in Japan is called Kasho Butsu or Onko, meaning "Drinking Brightness." The first six names on this list are of mythical figures. At Tassajara they refer to them in the monthly Full Moon Ceremony as the "Seven Buddhas before Buddha," even though there are only six of them. I guess seven sounds cooler than six. These are in the list to emphasize the idea that everyone must have a teacher, including Buddha himself and that Buddhism embodies an eternal truth that stretches beyond mere historical time.

Great Master Shakyamuni Buddha (c. 563 or 480–483 or 400 BCE), who in Japan is called Shakamuni Butsu or No-nin-jakumoku, which means "Benevolence and Serenity." This is the historical Buddha.

Great Teacher Mahakashyapa, who is called Makakasho in Japan. He succeeded Shakyamuni Buddha as the leader of the Buddhist order after Shakyamuni died. He also presided over the First Council, which was held in 483 BCE. It was during this meeting that the monks went over what they remembered of the Buddha's teachings and codified them for future recitation. The teachings would not be written down until around two centuries later; up till then they were memorized and chanted.

---

* In Dōgen's original, he gives only the Japanese version of each name. I'm giving the Indian or Chinese names first because that seems more suitable for a book. When you chant the names at Zen temples following the Japanese tradition, they are chanted with the Japanese pronunciations.

Great Master Ananda, whose name is the same in Japanese. Ananda was either the Buddha's cousin or his half brother, depending on which source you trust. He was also the Buddha's personal attendant. He is said to have memorized all the Buddha's teachings.

Great Master Shanavasin, who is called Shonawashu in Japanese.

Great Master Upagupta, who is called Ubakikuta in Japanese.

Great Master Dhitika, who is called Daitaka in Japanese.

Great Master Micchaka, who is called Mishaka in Japanese and came from Magadha, where Buddha attained enlightenment.

Great Master Vasamitra (c. first century BCE), who is called Vashumitsu in Japanese. He organized the fourth Great Council of Buddhist Monks, where the Buddha's words were first committed to writing.

Great Master Buddhanandhi, who is called Butsudanandai in Japanese, which is a real tongue twister. When they get to this name during the morning chanting services at Tassajara, everybody just mumbles it.

Great Master Baddhamitra, who is called Fudamita in Japanese.

Great Master Parsva, who is called Barishiba in Japanese. He presided over the fourth Great Council of Buddhist Monks. He's called the "side saint" because he vowed never to sleep on his side. Which is a funny thing to vow. But there ya go.

Great Master Punyayasas, who is called Funayasha in Japanese.

Great Master Asvaghosa, who is called Anabotei in Japanese. His name means "Horse Whinny," and he wrote a biography of Buddha in poetry. If he had been someone's aunt they could have called him "Aunt Whinny."

Great Master Kapimala, who is called Kabimara in Japanese. He is supposed to have popularized Buddhism in Western India.

Great Master Nagarjuna (c. 150–250 CE), who is called Nagyaharajuna in Japanese. He's one of the most famous of the early Indian Buddhist masters. He wrote extensively about the Middle Way and produced the highly regarded text *Mula Madhyamika Karika*, which is usually called "Fundamental Wisdom of the Middle Way" in English.

Great Master Kanadeva, who is called Kanadaiba in Japanese. His

Sanskrit name means "One Eye" because he was missing one eye. If he'd had a peg leg they would have called him "Peg Leg."*

Great Master Rahulabhadra, who is called Ragorata in Japanese.

Great Master Sanghanandi, who is called Sogyanandai in Japanese.

Great Master Geyasata, who is called Kayashata in Japanese.

Great Master Kumaralabdha, who is called Kumorata in Japanese, and thank God for that, because I'd never be able to pronounce his actual name!

Great Master Gayata, who is called Shayata in Japanese.

Great Master Vasubandhu (c. fourth century CE), who is called Bashubanzu in Japanese. He was one of the most prominent Buddhist philosophers of his time. His teachings formed the basis of the Yogacara school, which is commonly mislabeled as "radical Buddhist idealism" in the West because of its "mind only" philosophy. This philosophy doesn't say that all things are in the mind, as idealism has it. It says that we only know what we know through our minds and insists that the most valuable subject of study is the mind itself.

Great Master Manura, whose name is the same in Japanese.

Great Master Hakulenayasas, who is called Kakurokuna in Japanese.

Great Master Simhabikkshu, who is called Shishibodai in Japanese.

Great Master Vasasuta, who is called Bashashita in Japanese.

Great Master Panyamitra, who is called Funyomita in Japanese.

Great Master Prajnatara, who is called Hannyatara in Japanese.

Great Master Bodhidharma (470–532 CE), who is called Bodaidaruma in Japanese. He is said to have brought Zen Buddhism to China.

Great Master Dazu Huike (487–593 CE), who is called Taiso Eka in Japanese.

Great Master Jianzhi Sengcan (d. 606 CE), who is called Kanchi Sosan in Japanese. He wrote a famous poem called "Shin Jin Mei" (信心銘), or "Inscription on Believing Mind," which is often chanted in Zen temples today. The first line is, "The Great Way of the Buddhas is not difficult, just refrain from picking and choosing"; sometimes

---

* This is a reference to an old obscure joke that you're better off not knowing.

the last bit is translated as "just avoid love and hate" (至道無難唯嫌揀擇).

Great Master Dayi Daoxin (580–651 CE), who is called Dai-I Doshin in Japanese.

Great Master Hung Jen (601–674 CE), who is called Daiman Konin in Japanese.

Great Master Dajian Huineng (638–713 CE), who is called Daikan Eno in Japanese. Dōgen was a big fan of Huineng and mentions or quotes him often throughout *Shōbōgenzō*, sometimes calling him the "Founding Ancestor."

Great Master Quingyuan Xingsi (660–740 CE), who is called Seigen Gyoshi in Japanese.

Great Master Shitou Xiqian (700–790 CE), who is called Sekito Kisen in Japanese. He built a hut on top of a rock and thus received a name that means "On Top of a Rock." He wrote a poem called "Sandokai" (参同契), "The Harmony of Difference and Equality," which is often chanted at Zen temples. It starts off, "The mind of the great sage of India is intimately transmitted from East to West; while human faculties are sharp or dull, the Way has no northern or southern ancestors."

Great Master Yueshan Weiyan (745–828 CE), who is called Yakusan Igen in Japanese.

Great Master Yunyan Tansheng (780–841 CE), who is called Ungan Donjo in Japanese.

Great Master Dongshan Liangjie (807–869 CE), who is called Tozan Ryokai in Japanese.

Great Master Yunju Daoying (d. 909 CE), who is called Ungo Doyo in Japanese. They say he had fifteen hundred disciples!

Great Master Tongan Daopi (dates unknown), who is called Do-an Dohi in Japanese.

Great Master Tongan Guanzhi (dates unknown), who is called Do-an Kanshi in Japanese.

Great Master Liangshan Yuanguan (dates unknown), who is called Ryozan Enkan in Japanese.

Great Master Dayang Jingxuan (943–1027 CE), who is called Taiyo Kyogen in Japanese.

Great Master Touzi Yiqing (1032–1083 CE), who is called Tōsu Gisei in Japanese.

Great Master Furong Daokai (1043–1118 CE), who is called Fuyo Dokai in Japanese. The Chinese emperor tried to give him a regal purple robe but he refused, so the emperor banished him. The emperor later felt bad about that and pardoned him.

Great Master Dangxia Zichun (d. 1119 CE), who is called Tanka Shijun in Japanese.

Great Master Zhenxie Qingliao (dates unknown), who is called Choro Seiryo in Japanese.

Great Master Tiantong Zhongjue (dates unknown), who is called Tendo Sogaku in Japanese.

Great Master Xuedou Zhijian (1105–1192 CE), who is called Seccho Chikan in Japanese. He was the teacher of Dōgen's teacher.

Great Master Tiantong Rujing (1163–1228 CE), who is called Tendo Nyojo in Japanese. He was Dōgen's teacher, who gave him dharma transmission in China.

I, Dōgen, during the summer retreat of 1241 in China, met and served my late master, the eternal Buddha of Mt. Tendo. I prostrated to him (literally "received him upon my head") and realized the true meaning of the phrase "Buddhas alone together with Buddhas" (唯仏与仏 yui-butsu yō-butsu) from the Lotus Sutra.
— Written and preached at Kannon-dori-kosho-horin-ji Temple,
January 3, 1241

Lineage is a very important matter in all forms of Buddhism, and, in fact, in most Indian-derived religious and philosophical traditions. I first came across the idea of lineage when I was hovering around the Hare Krishna movement during my first year at Kent State University in Ohio. They used the term "disciplic succession." In their way of thinking, you had to receive your mantra from someone whose disciplic succession went all the way back to Krishna. One of their guys told me that anything other than that would be like receiving milk from the lips of a viper. It was a bizarre image that stuck with me for a very long time, mainly because it didn't really make any sense. How would you even do that? I thought about that a lot. I think about weird stuff too much.

In Zen, there's a tradition that your teacher's enlightenment was verified by someone whose enlightenment was verified by someone whose...and so on, all the way back to Buddha himself and beyond. This is what is known as "dharma transmission." If you believe in it, it means that your own teacher's enlightenment right now in twenty-first-century Poughkeepsie or Rotterdam or Nairobi or wherever is exactly the same as the Buddha's enlightenment in Magadha, India, five hundred years before Christ.

To prove this really happened, for centuries Zen Buddhists have been producing lineage charts to show the exact line of transmission they received. This idea seems to have emerged in China around the seventh or eighth century CE. At first only the Chinese ancestors were listed. Then it was decided that it sounded better if it went all the way back to India, and a tradition developed that Bodhidharma, who brought Zen Buddhism to China, was number 28 on the list.

The creation of a comprehensive list of the ancestors before Bodhidharma required a lot of research and a certain degree of creativity. Teachers who had produced a lot of writings, or a few very famous poems or other literary pieces, were well-known, and so naturally the folks who made these lists wanted to claim them as part of the lineage. Some of the earliest history of the order following Buddha's death was known, so those guys would obviously be included. But the rest of the names on the first part of the list Dōgen left us were probably mostly educated guesswork.

The historical accuracy of the Zen lineage has been severely questioned in recent times. Even the story of the very first dharma transmission from Buddha to Mahakashyapa is regarded these days with a great degree of doubt. The story goes that once, when he was supposed to give a lecture, the Buddha just went up on stage, held up a flower, and exchanged a knowing look with Mahakashyapa. This supposedly confirmed that Mahakashyapa was just as enlightened as Buddha himself.

Unfortunately for those who'd like to believe in a literal interpretation of Buddhist scriptures, this story did not emerge until hundreds of years after the event. And it first appeared in Chinese sources at a time when the Chinese were highly invested in creating complete lineage charts, going all the way back to India. The rest of the lists those guys made are equally questionable.

In Dōgen's day nobody really questioned the historical accuracy of the ancient lineage. Still, I tend to think someone as intelligent and well-read as Dōgen probably had doubts about it. Just look at the chart reproduced here. Note that Taiyo Kyogen died in 1027, but his successor Tōsu Gisei was born in 1032. Apparently a guy named Fuzan Hōon (Ch. Fushan Fuyuan, 991–1067 CE), who was a priest from a different lineage somehow posthumously delivered Taiyo Kyogen's transmission to Tōsu Gisei. Don't ask me how this was accomplished. It's just another one of those Zen mysteries, I suppose!*

I don't know if Dōgen knew this. My guess is he probably did. But even if he didn't know this particular point, he did openly express doubts about certain of the sutras, which shows that he was not one of those people who just bought into the literal truth of the dogma that was handed to him. In the *Shōbōgenzō* essay "Shizen-Biku" ("The Monk in the Fourth Stage of Meditation," contained in volume 4 of the Nishijima/Cross translation), he calls the highly regarded Platform Sutra a fake, based on its use of language that was uncharacteristic of the era in which it was supposedly written. If he was smart enough to use one of the key tools of the contemporary historical-critical method hundreds of years before the historical-critical method was invented, he was probably smart enough to wonder whether the lineage chart he received from his teacher was historically accurate.

---

* I got this info from the essay "Dharma Transmission" by William M. Bodiford in the book *Zen Ritual*, Oxford University Press, 2008.

My guess is he really didn't care. It's not absolutely necessary to believe in the literal accuracy of the lineage. That's a very modern idea. The idea of the importance of the literal historicity of ancient texts has been highly detrimental to current Christianity, with people trying to prove that Noah's Ark could really hold two Diplodocuses, and so on. It seems to me that if the lessons of the Bible are true, it doesn't matter who wrote them or when, or whether or not that person could walk on water and feed a multitude with two fishes.

For my part, I tend to believe that the lineage actually is accurate, even if some of the names are wrong. What I mean is that I do believe that the Buddha's original, fundamental enlightenment has managed to reach us in the present day through a line of teacher-apprentice relationships that stretches all the way back to the beginning.

I don't think this requires a belief in anything miraculous. I believe it because I have experienced something extraordinary when in the presence of my own teachers and in the presence of others who have also apprenticed with advanced teachers. I recognized this even before I had any clear idea what it was.

When I received dharma transmission from Gudo Nishijima I had to write out the entire lineage in black ink on a big piece of silk. The list I had to write was about twice as long as this one, by the way. After all, eight hundred years have passed since Dōgen's day. Then I had to use red ink to draw a line through all the names and connect them up to my own name at the very end. In the old days you didn't use red ink. You were supposed to poke your finger with a needle and use your own blood. That's probably how Dōgen did it. In the next chapter we'll hear all about that.

21. BUDDHIST PAPERWORK
Shisho
The Certificate of Succession

DŌGEN WAS WHAT is now called a "Zen master." The word usually translated as "Zen master" is 禅師 (*zenji*). And it does mean quite literally "Zen master." But in the tradition Dōgen established, nobody is called *zenji* unless they're dead. It would be weird in Japan to call a living person *zenji* to her or his face. In fact, it is such a high honorific that it could sound sarcastic and could more likely be taken as an insult than as a compliment. It could also sound as if you're saying the person's already dead.

Nonetheless, the English translation of this term has unfortunately been adopted by quite a few Western Zen teachers to describe themselves. Nobody should ever describe themselves as a "Zen master" unless they're making a joke — which I have done in my own previous books and elsewhere. It's a ridiculous term. As the late Kobun Chino Roshi — a Zen master if there ever was one — said, "Nobody masters Zen!"

And yet I see people all the time in America and Europe confidently announcing themselves as Zen master this or that without the slightest hint of irony. They apparently have no idea how goofy that sounds.

In any case, when someone calls her- or himself a "Zen master," what that normally means is that they have gone through a ceremony called 嗣法 (*shihō*), which means "dharma transmission." In this ceremony, your teacher confirms that you are authorized to teach Zen on your own, no longer as an apprentice but as a full-fledged teacher. These days some of the more institutionalized Zen institutions have added a few more steps to the process. Some now consider *shihō* to be just the first step. But in Dōgen's time, receiving dharma transmission was as far as you could go. It wasn't the entrenched hierarchical process it became later on.

As evidence of having gone through this ceremony, you're given a certificate called 嗣書 (*shisho*), or "transmission document." This is the tangible proof that you have received full permission to teach. In a way it's a lot like a diploma or other similar documents.

Nishijima Roshi's introduction to this chapter notes that "the certificate is only cloth and ink and so it cannot hold religious meaning or be revered as something with religious value. But Buddhism is a realistic religion, and Buddhists find religious value in many concrete traditions."

Dōgen very much revered these documents of transmission or succession. In this chapter he tells us about some that he saw as a student in China.

Every Buddha there ever was received the dharma from another Buddha, and every Buddhist ancestor there ever was received it from another Buddhist ancestor. Who but a Buddha or ancestor could certify another Buddha or ancestor?

When you get the certification of a Buddha you realize the state independently without a master and independently even of your self.* Even so, Buddhas and ancestors all experience the same state

---

* "Independently without a master" is 無師独悟 (*mushi dokugo*), which means, word for word, "no master independent realization." "Independently (even) of your self" is 無自独悟 (*muji dokugo*), which means, word for word, "no self independent realization."

of realization. Great bodhisattvas don't know it, and teachers of sutras don't know it. Even if you explained it to them, they still wouldn't get it. That's because it passes from Buddha to Buddha.

This state is outside of time. It's like pine trees succeeding each other as pine trees. The former pine is as real as the latter pine. They are both truly as they are. People who don't get this just don't get it even if they encounter somebody who does, and even when some of these people are supposedly "Zen masters."

Daikan Eno said, "From the Seven Buddhas till me there are forty Buddhas, and from me to the Seven Buddhas there are forty ancestors." He's right. Some of those Buddhas appeared in former eras, and some in our own era. The continuation of the face-to-face succession is the truth of the Buddhas.

Without experiencing the state of a Buddha or ancestor, we don't have the wisdom of a Buddha or ancestor. Without the wisdom of a Buddha or ancestor we don't believe in the state.

These forty Buddhas and ancestors are just the recent ones. It goes way, way back, much farther than that. Although Shakyamuni realized the truth before the Seven Buddhas, it still took him a long time to succeed Kashyapa Buddha, his teacher. Even though he got enlightened on December 8 of his thirtieth year, his realization is the truth before the Seven Buddhas and is shoulder-to-shoulder with all the Buddhas, and is a realization both before and after all the Buddhas.

Pay attention. Kashyapa Buddha, although he is Shakyamuni's predecessor, also succeeds the realization of Shakyamuni Buddha. If you don't get this, you don't get the truth. One time Shakyamuni Buddha's attendant, Ananda, asked him, "Whose disciples are the ancient Buddhas?" Shakyamuni said, "They're my disciples." That's the Buddhist doctrine.

Whenever a Buddha succeeds a Buddha there is a document of transmission. Without transmission we'd be a bunch of naturalists. Without transmission how would the Buddha's truth have reached us today?

Buddhas succeed each other in lots of different ways. Some receive a robe, some get a flyswatter. Sometimes the certificate is written in blood from a poked finger, and sometimes a teacher pokes their tongue and writes it in tongue blood! Whatever it's written with, it's still a transmission certificate. Sometimes the person who receives the transmission of the dharma doesn't expect it. But even if they didn't seek it out, they still succeed their teacher's dharma.

Ever since Bodhidharma came to China from India we've known about the tradition of succession. Before that nobody knew about it, not even in India. People who just study ancient literary works don't know it at all. It's a shame. They've been lucky enough to be born as human beings but they're clueless. We should instead study the state of Buddhas in detail.

When I was in China I got the chance to see and bow down before a few certificates of succession. One was owned by a master who'd retired from his own temple and lived in the west hall of the temple I was living in. He said to me, "Have you seen any old Buddhist calligraphy?" I said I'd seen a few pieces. He said, "I have a scroll in my room if you want to see it." I said I did, so he went and got it. It wasn't his own certificate but one from the lineage of Hogen Bun-eki. It said, "Mahakashyapa realized the dharma from Shakyamuni Buddha, and so forth." Upon seeing it I believed in the succession of the dharma. I had never felt so grateful.

The head monk at Mt. Tendo showed me a certificate of succession from the Unmon (Ch. Yunmen) lineage. It had the names of all the ancestors from India and China arranged in columns, under which was the name of the person who received the certificate. It was as if the names of the more than forty previous ancestors had converged on this one person's name.

I asked the head monk, "These days there are differences among the five sects of Zen (Rinzai, Igyo, Soto, Unmon, and Hogen) in the way they list the names of the ancestors. I mean, if the tradition came directly from India, shouldn't they all be the same? What's up with that?"

The head monk said, "Listen, kid, even if they were very different, just know that that's how it is in the Unmon lineage. How come Shakyamuni is revered? It's because he realized the truth. How come Master Unmon (Ch. Yunmen Wenyan, 862- or 864-949 CE) is revered? Same reason!" I think it got a little clearer for me when he said that.

In the Rinzai lineage there are some dingbats who hang out around the fringes of a teacher and then ask for a portrait or some calligraphy, which they then stash away. They collect a bunch of these things, and later on they bribe some government official to give them a temple. When they get one, they go to a famous teacher who hangs out with the local government big shots and get a half-assed dharma transmission from him. They don't give a rat's ass about the dharma. They're just in it for the money and prestige. It really sucks that things have gotten so bad these days.

These kinds of portraits and scrolls and things are often given to lecturers, or laymen and laywomen; even workers and servants get them. Sometimes some undeserving guy is in a big rush to get evidence of having succeeded the dharma and he'll go pester a teacher for a scroll. Teachers hate doing this, but occasionally they give in and write something. In such cases the certificate doesn't follow the regular form. It'll just be, like, a brief note saying, "This guy studied with me."

My teacher, Tendo Nyojo, told his students never to brag about having received the dharma. He himself never wore a fancy robe, although Master Dokai of Fuyo-zan Mountain (Ch. Furong Daokai, 1043–1118 CE) gave him one. Even so, everybody liked my teacher.

Once he said, "These days there are people who don't know much about anything, who put on robes, grow their hair long, and call themselves Zen masters. What a bunch of jackasses! It's a real shame how few people really go the full distance with this Zen stuff. Not even one in a thousand! That's how much Zen has declined!"

The Rinzai sect has a different way of writing their certificates. The most important thing in succeeding the dharma is the relationship between teacher and student. So they write out their certificates to reflect this. I saw a few of them in China too.

One time one of my brother monks showed me a transmission certificate. I first saw it on January 21, 1224. Around July of the previous year he told me about the certificate in secret. I happened to ask, "Who might have one?" He said the abbot had one and that if I asked nicely he might show it to me.

After that I really wanted to see it. So a while later I asked. It was written on a piece of white silk, and the cover was red brocade. The scroll was about nine inches wide and seven feet long. Not many people ever get to see them. The abbot said, "Now you've seen something very special." I was really happy.

Another time I was out visiting another temple. A teacher there said, "Have I ever shown you the transmission document I keep in my room?" I said no and asked if I could see it.

He said, "It's against the ancient custom to show it to anybody. But I had a dream the other night in which Zen Master Hojo of Daibai-zan Mountain (Ch. Damei Fachang, 752–839 CE) held up a branch of plum blossoms and said, 'If you meet a true person who has stepped off the side of a ship, show him these blossoms.' Then he gave me the blossoms. And what do you know? Here you are, someone who came to China on a ship. You must be the person Hojo told me about. If you want to get dharma transmission from me, just say the word, and I'll do it."

I didn't get his transmission, but I lit some incense and prostrated to him. I was thinking, "Why should some twerp like me, a kid from a backward island country, get so lucky as to see such a thing? And not only one of them, but several?"

The room was quiet and nobody else was around except for one attendant monk who said he'd never seen a certificate of succession before. The master brought out the certificate, and it was written on white silk with plum blossoms printed on the bottom of it. I was so happy I cried.

That night I stayed in another temple on my way back home and I had a dream. In it, the master who had founded that temple showed up and handed me a branch full of plum blossoms. The blossoms were more than a foot wide. Those plum blossoms must have been udumbra flowers, you know, those blossoms that are so rare that almost no one ever sees them. Maybe the state in a dream and the state in waking consciousness are equally real. I've never told anybody about any of this stuff since returning to Japan.

These days in our lineage the certificates are written in a different way from the Rinzai certificates. Seigen Gyoshi, one of the founders of our lineage, supposedly poked his finger to copy the lineage chart that Master Daikan Eno kept rolled up in his sleeve. Legend has it that it was written in a mixture of Seigen's blood and Daikan Eno's blood.

Supposedly Bodhidharma and his successor Taiso Eka did the same thing. We don't write "my disciple" or "studied with me" on ours. We just write the names of the ancestors. Know then that this certificate written in blood confirms that only Seigen was the true dharma successor of Daikan Eno.

Tendo Nyojo said, "Every master without exception received the dharma from a teacher. That means Shakyamuni Buddha got the dharma from Kashyapa Buddha, who got it from Kanakamuni Buddha, who got it from Krakuchanda Buddha, and so on."

I said, "Kashyapa Buddha had been dead a very long time before Shakyamuni was even born. How could he have received the dharma from Kashyapa?"

Tendo Nyojo said, "That's the way intellectual people see things. But our way isn't like that. We learn in practice that Kashyapa Buddha didn't die until after he had transmitted the dharma to Shakyamuni. If Shakyamuni didn't receive the dharma from Kashyapa, that would make him spontaneously enlightened, which is not the Buddhist way. If the dharma was something that was newly discovered by Shakyamuni, then it's only two thousand years old, which isn't very old. We learn that Shakyamuni was the successor of Kashyapa and that Kashyapa was the successor of Shakyamuni. When we learn it that way, it's the true meaning of succession."

When I heard it put this way, I accepted it and rid myself of my nagging doubts.

— Written at Kannon-dori-kosho-horin-ji Temple, March 7, 1241

When referring to the state of a teacher and disciple at the time dharma transmission takes place, I have Dōgen saying here, "This state is outside of time." This is my spin on what's actually written. I haven't done much of this in my paraphrasing. I've been trying to stick as closely as possible to the more standard translations.

Dōgen says 仏道はただ仏仏の究尽にして、仏仏にあらざる時節あらず (*Butsu-dō wa tada butsu-butsu no kyūjin ni shite, bustu-butsu ni araʐu jisetsu araʐu*). Nishijima/Cross translate this as, "The Buddha's state of truth is perfect realization only of buddhas, and without buddhas it has no time." Tanahashi's translation is, "There is no moment of the way without a Buddha and a buddha." Shasta Abbey's version is, "There has never been a time when there was not a succession of Buddha after Buddha."

I paraphrased it the way I did because it fits in well with the next part about pine trees succeeding pine trees. Dōgen also talks about jewels succeeding jewels, flowers succeeding flowers, and stones succeeding stones. These are not one-after-another successions. He's pointing to an idea in which our concept of linear time is irrelevant.

My first teacher told me that realization of the Buddhist truth takes place outside of time. I just remember thinking it was a weird thing to say. But I filed it away in my head. Later on it made perfect sense.

Normally we think that nothing can be outside of time. Everything that happens, we think, happens at some specific time. When people investigate a crime, for example, it's assumed that every event leading up to that crime, as well as the crime itself, could be pinpointed precisely in time if you had the necessary information. We tend to believe that any event can be pinpointed at a specific time.

But in Zen we have this weird idea that things can happen outside of time. In fact, we believe that everything happens outside of time. Time is just an abstraction we overlay on top of the event. The state of Buddhist realization is eternal. But it's not just eternal in the sense that it has existed forever and will never vanish. It's eternal in the way the present moment is eternal. It's always now, no matter what time it is. I once saw a cartoon of a Zen wristwatch on which there were no numbers. It just said "now, now, now, now," and so on.

Some things are more clearly outside of time than others, though. In the moment of realization you find yourself standing outside of time. It's a very peculiar thing, in retrospect. But when it's happening it feels absolutely natural. You suddenly understand very clearly that time is an abstraction. We *say* time is an abstraction a lot. But really feeling it deep in your bones is an entirely different matter.

A little after this we come to a section about how undeserving people sometimes pester a teacher for a certificate, and then get something hurriedly written, which they later claim is a transmission document. This is still very relevant today. In the past few years, I've known of at least two cases in which some Western person did exactly what Dōgen describes here. One guy I heard about got some fairly irrelevant piece of calligraphy from a Zen teacher in Japan, then went back to his own country and set himself up as a "Zen master." Of course, the folks there couldn't read the certificate and they wouldn't know what a real certificate looked like anyway. Up until recently this was a fairly safe con. The chances some old master back in Asia hearing about what guys like this were doing have been pretty slim.

These days, though, with even old Asian Zen masters knowing how to use the Internet, it's a bit harder to get away with this kind of swindle. The guy I was telling you about just now got busted after a few years when the Japanese master he'd claimed to have gotten transmission from heard what he was doing. In another case, I was asked to verify a certain person's so-called dharma transmission certificate. It was so obviously thrown together I wondered how anybody had ever fallen for it. It was just some random calligraphy that he'd apparently been passing off as an official certificate for quite a while.

Generally scamsters like that end up digging their own graves. They're often able to fool people for a time, but eventually things start getting weird. It's a good idea to ask about this kind of stuff. If someone says they're a successor of some master over in Asia, you can usually look that person up online and often even ask them directly if things seem iffy. Just keep your bullshit detector turned on.

You can be a very enlightened individual without having received any sort of official transmission from anyone. Jiddu Kirshnamurti, who I mentioned earlier, was a good example of that. But if you claim to be a "Zen master" you'd better have the paperwork to back that up because this sort of paperwork is an essential part of the Buddhist tradition. It's kinda like this: you can make a perfectly delicious burger without getting a McDonald's franchise. But if you're going to put a set of golden arches on top of your restaurant and thereby benefit from the advertising and reputation of the McDonald's brand, you need to have an official license from their corporate headquarters. It's not exactly the same, I know, but it's similar.

There's one line in this chapter that had me going for a long time. It says, "Maybe the state in a dream and the state in waking consciousness are equally real." Over the years I forgot where Dōgen said that. I looked it up in several places where I thought it might have been but I couldn't find it. I started thinking maybe the line was something I dreamed up myself! I only realized precisely where it was when I worked on this chapter for this book.

In Japanese it says 夢中と覚中と、おなじく真実なるべし (*Muchu to kakuchu to, onajiku jinjitsu naru beshi*). The Nishijima/Cross translation makes this a general statement about dreams and waking consciousness, as I have done here. However, the Tanahashi translation says, "This dream was as real as being awake," thereby making it refer specifically to Dōgen's particular dream about flowers.

In Japanese it's ambiguous, so both translations are technically correct. This phrase forms the ending of a sentence about how the plum blossoms were really the mythical udumbra flower — since udumbra trees have flowers that don't look like flowers, ancient people thought they didn't have flowers at all, so the udumbra flower was the symbol of something impossibly rare. Anyway, since it follows on from that phrase, I can see why Tanahashi chose to translate it as referring to the specific dream Dōgen is speaking about here. But since it would have been easy enough for Dōgen to make this phrase refer unambiguously to that specific dream and since he's been talking about dreams for a couple of paragraphs already, I believe it was intentionally ambiguous.

At the time I first read this I was a huge fan of science fiction writer Philip K. Dick. A lot of his books are about the relationship between dreams and waking life or between what happens in the mind and what happens in physical reality. The movie *Total Recall* was based on one of Dick's short stories. You'll recall that in that film Arnold

Schwarzenegger is implanted with memories of a vacation he took on Mars. The idea in the story is that in the future, people who can't afford real vacations will have the memories of vacations put into their heads so that they feel like they've actually gone someplace. But in a clever plot twist (spoiler alert!) it turns out that Arnold's supposedly fake memories of Mars are real memories of an actual trip to Mars. It's a very cool movie. (I haven't seen the remake.)

Obviously there is a difference between what goes on in a dream and what goes on when you're awake. Dōgen knew this. He often criticized people by saying they haven't even dreamed of whatever it is they're telling people they know. So dreams and waking reality aren't the same thing.

And yet Dōgen says here, "Maybe the state in a dream and the state in waking consciousness are equally real." He's not saying that they're the same, just that they may be equally real. This doesn't mean that if you dreamed you punched your sister she'll wake up with a bloody nose. But in some sense the dream state is another aspect of reality, rather than being, as we commonly think, totally unreal. It's not unreal. It's real, but very different.

People who do a lot of meditation often end up having lucid dreams — dreams in which they realize they're dreaming and can do cool stuff like flying through the air or whatever. At one point in my practice lucid dreaming went from being fun and fascinating to being a serious annoyance. I was having so many of the damned things it was making me a little loopy. I remember that I deliberately worked on stopping them. These days I don't get them very often.

Some people can get really seduced by various kinds of unusual states of consciousness, from those induced by drugs to those induced by dreaming or isolation tanks or any number of things. In Zen practice that's usually seen as a mistake.

We don't put any extra value on these kinds of surreal experiences or think of them as being somehow better than our usual state. Rather, we think that our usual state — because it's the one we experience more than any other — is the state we should pay the most attention to. For me, that attitude makes the most sense.

Yet we can learn from dreams. Dōgen paid attention to his dreams, as we can see in this chapter. He often writes about significant dreams and tries to understand their meaning. But he never does so at the expense of waking life. For him, even if dreams were another aspect of reality, waking life was far more relevant.

The other part of this chapter that interests me a lot is that bit of business at the end where Dōgen asks his teacher how Shakyamuni could have received the dharma from Kashyapa Buddha, who supposedly lived millions of years before him. Dōgen doesn't say it outright, but I think the subtext here is that Dōgen knows Kashyapa Buddha is a mythical figure. Nowadays we know that human beings hadn't even evolved at the time Kashyapa Buddha supposedly lived. And there are five other Buddhas before him!

Dōgen didn't know about human evolution, so it's possible he believed people could have been around that long. But I tend to doubt he regarded Kashyapa Buddha as an actual historical person. Anyhow, it doesn't matter because in either case there's still no way Kashyapa could ever have met Shakyamuni.

Dōgen says that Tendo Nyojo told him only intellectual people thought that way. What it actually says in the text is that this kind of thinking is that of "bodhisattvas of the ten sacred and three clever stages." Tendo Nyojo says that Buddhists think of things differently.

Here we're getting into an area that might be called "mystical." In Buddhism, just as in Catholicism, there's the idea that certain things are just mysteries. No one will ever really understand them. But in some way we can feel the truth of them even when they don't make a whole lot of sense intellectually.

As for me, I find that I do accept this myth even though I don't believe it in a literal sense. As I said earlier, I've always found people who try to do things like prove that Moses really parted the Red Sea or that Jesus actually turned water into wine kind of silly. These myths contain a kind of truth that goes beyond whether or not they are factual.

I feel it's the same way with the myth of Buddhist succession. It may not be factual, and yet at another level it's still true. It's metaphorical, but that doesn't mean it's untrue.

As far as we know, the standard Buddhist lineage charts used these days in most Zen places have been pretty much historically accurate for around the past thousand years or so, which is already no mean feat. They're probably not 100 percent factually accurate all the way back to the time of Buddha. However, my intuitive sense is there is good reason to believe that even if some of the names are incorrect, there really is an unbroken line of face-to-face transmission of the dharma all the way back to Buddha's time, and perhaps even beyond.

22. TWIRLY FLOWERS
TWIRL TWIRLY FLOWERS
Hokke Ten Hokke
The Flower of Dharma Turns the Flower of Dharma

I'VE ALREADY MENTIONED the legend that Shakyamuni Buddha transmitted the dharma to Maha Kashyapa by standing on the platform where he was supposed to deliver a sermon and just picking up a flower and twirling it. As I said, it's probably not literally true. In any case, the title of this piece refers to that story.

This is Dōgen's famous chapter on the Lotus Sutra. I remember once, after a lecture about this piece, someone asked Nishijima Roshi which translation of the Lotus Sutra was best. Nishijima said he thought all the available English translations were pretty good, and then he added, "Just read Dōgen's essay on the Lotus Sutra. That's enough." That being said, I happen to know he tended to favor the translation by Bunno Kato, published by Weatherhill/Kosei in 1975, but there are a number of other good translations too.

This piece was written by Dōgen for a guy named Etatsu on the occasion of his taking the precepts and becoming a Zen monk. We can surmise that Etatsu must have studied the Lotus Sutra and considered it really important. Nothing in the little sign-off at the end indicates that this chapter was ever preached aloud, like many of the *Shōbōgenzō* pieces were. So it really needs to be read. It's full of quotations, which would not have been apparent if you were just listening to it.

The Lotus Sutra might be the closest thing Zen Buddhism has to the Bible. By that I mean that it's a very old book, that all the various sects within what we now call "Zen Buddhism" esteem it (which doesn't mean all Buddhists esteem it, just that Zen Buddhists especially esteem it), that it's very long and difficult, and that even though lots of people quote bits of it, few of them have ever read it all the way through. It even has Buddha doing miracles like shooting laser beams out of his forehead, for gosh sakes!

It also has its own equivalent of the "begats" that hang people up when they read the Bible. You know, all that stuff about how Abraham begat Isaac, and Isaac begat Alouicious, and Alouicious begat Harvey, and on and on. The Lotus Sutra begins with the Buddha about to preach a sermon, but before he can talk the author name-checks every single person, deity, or garden gnome who was there — for about twenty pages. Maybe I'm exaggerating. But it's pretty tedious.

Also, like much of the Bible, the Lotus Sutra is what we would now call a work of fiction. Whereas many of the Buddhist sutras are probably reasonably historically accurate accounts of what the Buddha said and did, the Lotus Sutra, like the Heart Sutra, which we looked at earlier, is one of a group of sutras that appeared hundreds of years after Buddha's death. Nonetheless, the words the unknown authors put in Buddha's mouth are regarded by many as expressing Buddha's truth even if they know full well the historical Buddha didn't actually say them.

Some argue about whether the Lotus Sutra and others like it are truly "Buddhist" since Buddha was long dead when they were composed. But there is no evidence I'm aware of that Gautama Buddha intended his words to be the final revelation of the truth. During his lifetime he named a successor, and he granted a number of people permission to teach his way independently of him. Those aren't the actions of someone who believes his word alone should be taken as gospel.

Like many other Buddhists, I've never read the Lotus Sutra all the way through. I suppose that's blasphemous to admit, but it's true. It's just too dense. I'm a huge fan of Dōgen's work. But I have to say I'm not terribly interested in a lot of the rest of the Buddhist literature. Some of it is really lovely. But there's far too much of it for me ever to read it all, and things like the Lotus Sutra are a lot of hard work. One of these days I'll read it, though.

Luckily for me, the Nishijima/Cross translation of *Shōbōgenzō* cross-references all the quotations Dōgen uses in this chapter. It even includes an appendix with all the relevant Lotus Sutra quotations in full. I have made extensive use of that in putting together this chapter.

Taigen Dan Leighton, who I am certain *has* read the Lotus Sutra, wrote an entire book mainly about two chapters of the Lotus Sutra and Dōgen's views of them. It's called *Visions of Awakening Space and Time: Dōgen and the Lotus Sutra*. It's well worth reading if you want to get a better handle on what this chapter is all about.

According to Nishijima, the title 法華転法華 (*Hokke Ten Hokke*), which translates as "The Flower of Dharma Turns the Flower of Dharma," means "the wonderful Universe which is like flowers is moving the wonderful Universe which is like flowers itself." Buddhists don't believe in a God who stands outside the universe and makes it work. Instead, the universe itself is God. The universe has all the attributes we commonly ascribe to God. It's everything, and it's intelligent and all-powerful. But there is no subject-object relationship between God and the universe. They are fully unified.

In a sense this chapter is Dōgen doing for the Lotus Sutra what I'm attempting to do for Dōgen's writing with this book. He's trying to cut through the denseness of the Lotus Sutra and eliminate some of the parts that aren't really necessary to get to the heart of what the Lotus Sutra means for his students. Let's watch!

The whole universe in all directions is the Flower of Dharma.* All Buddhas everywhere and all enlightened beings twirl and are twirled by the Flower of Dharma. This is the Buddha's calm and clear state, which is difficult to enter.

As Manjushri, the bodhisattva of wisdom, it has the as-it-is-ness of "Buddhas alone together with Buddhas who can perfectly realize that all dharmas are real form."** The many stories written in the Lotus Sutra all point to the Buddha's truth, wisdom, and virtue. The method taught by the great master Daikan Eno, the customs of Master Seigen Gyoshi, and the philosophy of Master Nangaku Ejo are all the real Buddha's wisdom as contained in the Lotus Sutra.†

When Daikan Eno was at his temple in China, a monk named Hotatsu (Ch. Fada, dates unknown) showed up. He bragged, "Dude! I've recited the Lotus Sutra three thousand times!"

Daikan Eno said, "Feh! Even if you recited it ten thousand times it wouldn't matter, if you don't actually understand it."

Hotatsu said, "I'm just a dopey monk, man! How could someone like me ever understand what the Lotus Sutra means?"

Daikan Eno said, "Here. Recite the sutra, and I'll tell you what it means."

Hotatsu started reciting. He reached chapter 2, in which a father lures his three children out of a burning house by saying that there are three carts outside. When they run out through the gate he gives them one cart drawn by a white ox — which was considered more valuable than the three he offered combined. Daikan Eno said, "Hold up! The whole point of all the stories and stuff in the sutra is just that the wisdom of the Buddha is your own natural state right now!"

---

* Like many lines in this piece, this opening phrase is strung together from phrases found in the Lotus Sutra. I'm not going to note every place he does this. But I encourage you to seek out the Nishijima/Cross translation of *Shōbōgenzō* if you'd like to find them all.

** 唯仏与仏乃能究尽諸法実相 (*yui-butsu yō-butsu nani gujin shohō jisso*). This is a quotation from the Lotus Sutra.

† I've cut a massive section out of here in which Dōgen references a number of stories from the Lotus Sutra.

Then he recited a poem that went as follows:

When you're deluded, the Dharma Flower twirls you
When you're enlightened, you twirl the Flower, it's true
If you recite when you're unclear about who you are
You'll make an enemy of the sutra and never get far
Thought beyond thought is thought that is right
Thought within thought is thought that's just trite
When we transcend with and without
We ride the white ox cart everywhere all about

Hotatsu said, "Wait up! The sutra says that even if all the smartest people in the world tried to figure it out, nobody could grasp Buddha's wisdom. Unless we're geniuses like that, how could we help but doubt and deny it? Anyhow, in the sutra it talks about three carts. So what's the difference between them?"

Daikan Eno said, "It's perfectly obvious! You're just thinking too much! The three carts represent the Three Vehicles, which are forms of Buddhism: Hinayana, Mahayana, and Tantrayana. When people who follow those sects don't get the Buddha's wisdom, it's only because they're trying to understand it intellectually."

Daikan Eno went on, "The Buddha preached for regular people, not for enlightened people. Some of them didn't know that they were already sitting in the white ox cart, which represents a teaching beyond the Three Vehicles, so they walked out on him, just like the story in the Lotus Sutra says. Remember how a bunch of people walk out on him when he's talking and he says it's fine if they leave?"

Then Eno answered himself, "The sutra is clearly telling you there are no 'carts'! How come you don't get it? There's only one vehicle, one way to the truth. It exists in the here and now. Reality is not a concept. Reality is real! Everything you already have is a treasure, and it all belongs to you to do with as you please. From the beginningless past to the endless future and also right here and now you embody every truth of the sutra without ever having to read it."

Hotatsu jumped for joy as he heard this and then made up his own poem:

My three thousand recitations, like mere child's play
By one word from Eno were blasted away
Misunderstanding why Buddha appeared
How could we help but get really weird?
The sutra says that the carts number three
But start, middle, and finish are okay by me
'Cuz even if the house burns and folks they just ogle
Originally we each are the great dharma mogul!

Daikan Eno said, "From now on we'll call you Sutra Reading Monk!"

The point of this story is that you should always study Buddhism with an actual teacher. You can't learn it just by reading sutras. The present moment is the real form, the real nature, the real body, the real energy, the real causes and the real effects of the Flower of Dharma turning. Nobody ever heard it in China before Daikan Eno.

The deluded mind is just the Flower of Dharma twirling. So when we're in delusion, we're being twirled by the Flower of Dharma. Don't get excited about this fact of being twirled, and don't look forward to it. It isn't something that just happens and it isn't something you deliberately do. The twirling of the Flower of Dharma is the one vehicle. It doesn't matter if it's the twirler or the one being twirled.

We rely only on the sincere mind that manifests moment by moment. Don't worry about delusions. Your actions are the bodhisattva way of compassion. What you do at each moment is the Flower of Dharma twirling.

Getting back to the parable from the Lotus Sutra about the burning house, there is delusion inside the burning house, there is delusion at the gateway leading out of the house, and there is also delusion outside the gate. It is delusion that has created the gate and the burning house. Maybe the whole escape takes place on the white ox cart (of Buddhist practice).

Should we think of the open ground (of enlightenment) as the place to enter or the burning house (of delusion) as the place to leave? Is the gate between them just a place we pass through for a moment? Remember that in the white ox cart there is the twirling of the Flower of Dharma that makes us realize and enter the burning house, and on the open ground there is also the twirling of the Flower of Dharma that makes us enter the burning house. There are many, many ways in which the twirling of the Flower of Dharma unfolds the teaching inside the house, at the gate, and on open ground.

So the burning house is beyond understanding. The open ground is beyond understanding. Who is gonna make real circumstances into a vehicle for realization? When we seek to get to the white ox cart from the burning house it looks really far away! Should we come to the conclusion that Buddha's favorite hang-out spot exists in the peace and tranquility of the open ground? Or should we consider that the open ground is peace and tranquility in Buddha's favorite hang-out spot?

The Lotus Sutra talks about "wholeheartedly wanting to meet Buddha." Is this about you or about someone else? Pay close attention. There are times when realization occurs within the individual, and there are times when realization occurs throughout the entire universe.

Buddha was able to appear on Vulture Peak and preach the Lotus Sutra because of his past actions of never begrudging his body or even his life. He teaches by always abiding in the dharma and by using expedient means. Even when you're so close you can't see, how can you fail to wholeheartedly understand nonunderstanding?

When we look at the material world it doesn't mean we can't see the world of the dharma. When we experience the world of the dharma it doesn't mean we fail to experience the material world. When Buddhas experience the world of dharma, they don't exclude us from the experience. It's all good!

Because this is so, your present form as you are is the real state of experience. Alarm, doubt, and even fear are nothing but reality as it is. Within Buddha's wisdom, fear is only the difference between looking at stuff as if you're apart from it and really being right there with it. When we truly sit with what's real, it doesn't matter if it feels confining. You're thoroughly experiencing the blossoming of the Flower of Dharma.

Our profound, eternal state is the twirling of the Flower of Dharma. It's beyond alarm, doubt, and fear. When the Flower of Dharma twirls, we understand it as Buddha's wisdom on display. Know that in the state of delusion, the Flower of Dharma is still twirling away!

"The enlightened mind twirls the Flower of Dharma" describes the twirling of the Flower of Dharma. Which is to say, when you are fully twirled by the Flower of Dharma, you have the power to twirl the Flower of Dharma. Even though the twirling never ceases we naturally twirl it ourselves. It's just "this and that being done, now you gotta do the other thing." It is realized at every moment on Earth and throughout the universe.

·Don't fall for the way the world disbelieves this stuff and then be surprised. Even their disbelief is the twirling of the Flower of Dharma. At the time of the twirling of the Flower of Dharma, realization exists as the twirling of the Flower of Dharma, and the twirling of the Flower of Dharma exists as realization. This is the eternal life of the Buddha.

We shouldn't await some state of awareness. And we shouldn't assume our current state is without awareness. Every possible state *is* awareness. There's not even a gap big enough for a speck of dust.

The twirling of the Flower of Dharma is "form is emptiness." It "neither appears nor disappears." The twirling of the Flower of Dharma is "emptiness is form." It is "no birth, no death."*

In the Lotus Sutra there's a story about how a guy gets totally wasted and passes out. His friend, who is going away for a long time, sews a priceless jewel into the guy's clothes so that he'll have something to bargain with in case he gets in trouble later. A long time passes, and they run into each other again. The guy who'd gotten wasted is a mess. He's got nothing to his name except the clothes he had when they last met. His friend is like, "What are you, completely stupid? I gave you a priceless jewel! You could've lived comfortably for a long time with that!" The Sutra says that's how we are. We were given priceless wisdom, yet we wander around as if we know nothing at all.

Remember that when someone is a close friend to us, we're a close friend to that person too. We have to carefully examine moments of having been given a priceless jewel sewn into our clothes. These stories are metaphors for real life.

Don't just see this twirling of the Flower of Dharma as something the great saints did a real long time ago. The Buddha preaches the great vehicle today! When the Flower of Dharma is the Flower of Dharma, we

---

* The phrases in quotation marks are from the Heart Sutra.

don't sense it and we don't realize it. It's beyond knowing and understanding. A million, bazillion, quintillion years are just an instant of the Flower of Dharma twirling.

It's been hundreds of years since the Lotus Sutra was introduced to China and twirled like a Flower of Dharma. Lots of people both in Japan and China have written commentaries and interpretations. Some have even become enlightened by reading the sutra. But nobody ever really got it the way Daikan Eno did!

Now that we've been able to hear what he said about it, it's as if this very place is the eternal Land of the Buddhas. How cool is that?

Reality as it is is a treasure and an eternal seat of the truth, profound, great, and everlasting. Mind in delusion or mind in realization, the Flower of Dharma twirls the Flower of Dharma.

The Dharma Flower twirls while we're in delusion
We twirl the Dharma Flower when we're free of this confusion
When you perfectly realize this you can't be dour
'Cuz it's just Dharma Flower twirling Dharma Flower

— Written on a day during the summer retreat of 1241 and presented to Etatsu on the occasion of his becoming a monk. Good luck in your life as a monk, and never forget the Lotus Sutra

This was a bear of a chapter to summarize. I feel like I didn't really do it justice, but I hope I've given you just enough to get a taste of what's in the actual chapter. As I keep saying, there are plenty of standard translations, several of which you can access free of charge online. Check 'em out.

There are a couple of things you should know about the Lotus Sutra in general. The first is that it was the first sutra to introduce the idea of the Eternal Buddha. This doesn't mean that it was about how the Buddha lived forever and ever. Well, not exactly, anyway.

The idea is that Shakyamuni Buddha was the physical manifestation of something living and eternal that still remains with us today. In some sense it's like the Christian notion of the Holy Spirit. It's not necessarily that the Buddha is eternal in the temporal sense, although that's included too. It's more that the Buddha is a living and eternal principle.

Often Buddhist teachers and writers play fast and loose with the word *Buddha*. Sometimes it means the historical figure from India, and sometimes it means this eternal principle. Many Christian mystics used the word *Christ* in much the same way. Dōgen does this throughout this chapter.

Then there's the idea of *upaya*, or "expedient means," which also first appears in the Lotus Sutra. The story of the kids in the burning house is the classic example. In the story the father lies to his children about there being goodies outside in order to save them from dying in the house. The idea is that the children are too dumb to know what's actually going on, so their dad uses his wits to come up with the best idea he can for getting them to leave the house.

All the Buddhist teachings, then, are kinds of expedient means. We shouldn't take them too literally, or we miss the point. This also has some parallels in Christianity. If we take Jesus's parables or some of the Christian imagery and mythology too literally, we end up missing the point there too.

Let's look at the last four lines of Daikan Eno's poem:

Thought beyond thought is thought that is right
Thought within thought is thought that's just trite
When we transcend with and without
We ride the white ox cart everywhere all about

In the original Chinese this is 無念念即正、有念念成邪、有無俱不計、長御白牛車 (*Munen nen soku jo, Unen nen sei jaku, U mu ku fukei, Chogo haku-gyusha*). Nishijima/Cross has, "Without intention the mind is right / With intention the mind becomes wrong / When we transcend both with and without / We ride eternally on the white ox cart." Tanahashi has, "Thinking beyond thinking is right / Thinking about thinking is wrong / If thinking and beyond thinking do not divide the mind / You can steer the white ox cart endlessly." The Shasta Abbey translation says, "To read It without opinion's bonds is the proper way / But read It bound to fixed ideas, and It becomes error's way / When you cease to judge whether you are bound or not / You ride forever long within the cart by the White Ox drawn."

As you can see, this is a hard poem to translate! The character (*nen*) is usually translated as "thought," which is why Tanahashi translates it as "thinking." But this character has more a sense of deliberate thought or consideration than of the more passive kind of images and words that run through your mind seemingly at random. This is why Nishijima/Cross say "intention" and Shasta Abbey's translation has "opinion."

So what in holy heck is "thinking beyond thinking?" A lot of people, both here and in Asia, imagine that meditation means making your mind a complete blank. The great twentieth-century Zen teacher Kodo Sawaki used to say, "The only time your mind is a complete blank is when you're dead!"

When you do zazen, you're not trying to achieve a totally empty mind. That would be impossible. But you are trying to avoid the deliberate habitual manipulation of thoughts and images we usually engage in. To me, that's all this whole "thinking beyond thinking" stuff actually means. You point your brain toward something beyond thought, and hope for the best.

Later on we get a lot of stuff about the burning house, the gate, and the open ground. This business goes on for a whole lot longer in the original than what I used in this book. It consists mainly of a very complex set of rearrangements of strings of Chinese characters from the Lotus Sutra. I went over a few different translations as well as the original for quite a while trying to come up with an adequate way of summarizing it.

Basically, the point is that the burning house represents delusion, the gate represents the moment of transcending delusion — an "enlightenment experience" — and the open ground represents enlightenment. But Dōgen never explains Buddhist practice as a nice linear movement from delusion through an experience of realization and ending with a permanent state of enlightenment. Lots of people imagine Buddhist practice to be like that. I know I certainly did. But it's not that way at all.

The Nishijima/Cross translation offers a few explanations in the footnotes. He says that Dōgen here denies "the idealistic idea that delusion only exists in the burning house." So delusion can exist even in a supposedly "enlightened person." There is no permanent state of enlightenment, and there are no forever-enlightened beings. This is a really important point.

Lots of people claim to be enlightened beings, and some of them probably even believe they are. But to imagine yourself as fully awakened and as forever incapable of being deluded is the worst kind of delusion. Dōgen emphasizes this over and over in this chapter, and elsewhere. His language is highly metaphorical and depends on his audience knowing the Lotus Sutra thoroughly. As we have seen, this chapter of *Shōbōgenzō* was specifically written for a person who had studied the Lotus Sutra extensively. For those of us who don't know the Lotus Sutra well, or at all, it takes a bit of digging to get to the meaning.

In another footnote to this chapter Nishijima says, "Even people who are in the state of Buddhist wisdom can experience realization by recognizing their thoughts as thoughts." I feel like the single most important thing I ever learned from Buddhist practice is that my thoughts are just thoughts. That doesn't sound like much. Most of us believe we already understand this. I know I did.

But after many years of practice I became aware for the first time that my thoughts were far more dominant in my life than I'd ever imagined. My entire reality could be shifted by a change in thinking. It was scary to see. I'm talking here about massive shifts in perception, not just a matter of changing my mind about some idea. It was incredible how deep into my system certain thoughts had gone.

After working with this for a couple of years it started dawning on me that, as powerful as these deeply entrenched thoughts were, even those deeply entrenched thoughts were still only thoughts. Even the really, really important and vital-seeming ones were made of the same stuff as, say, a passing thought about a plate of shrimp or whatever. None of them mattered nearly as much as they seemed to. Most of them didn't matter at all.

The first moment of understanding that clearly was shocking. Although it had been building for years, it seemed to happen all at once. It felt like a huge shift in absolutely everything. Even the outside world seemed to change completely. I've lived with this state for a number of years now, so it's become my "new normal." It's much better than the previous state. But, as Dōgen keeps pointing out, it's not a permanently fixed condition. It's still quite possible to fall right back into the old patterns even while knowing full well that it's a mistake to do so.

Another of Nishijima's footnotes to the burning house story says that Dōgen denies the "idealistic interpretations of entering and leaving — reality is where we are already, and so there is no area to be entered and no area to be left." This is another crucial part of Dōgen's philosophy. Things can change, we can come to see reality more clearly, but we don't go anywhere. What we experience at every moment is beyond being categorized as delusion or enlightenment. Even our delusion takes place within, and is part of, enlightenment. That's why we don't direct our efforts at attaining enlightenment as a goal. Rather, we try to sit quietly within our delusion until we can see it clearly for what it is.

Another Nishijima footnote says, "Buddhist teaching always affirms the reality of the not-ideal situation, even for those who have real wisdom and are living in the peaceful state." So we enter the burning house even while remaining on the open ground. It's not an

either-or situation. Our lives continue, even when the balanced state is
established.

Nishijima also notes, "Buddhist wisdom can still be realized even
after the process is complete." It's not that enlightenment is a finishing
line, after which we're all done. Our training continues forever.

Nishijima says in yet another footnote, "We can sometimes realize the state in painful or emotional experiences." So, again, we're not
aiming at an idealized state of pure, blank tranquility. Even in our pain,
there is enlightenment.

The sentence I've summarized as, "Even when you're so close you
can't see, how can you fail to wholeheartedly understand nonunderstanding?" in the original Japanese this is 而不見の雖近なる、たれか
一心の会不会を信ぜざらん (shi fuken no suigon naru, tare ka isshin no
kai fukai wo shinzaran). Tanahashi translates this as, "Who has trust in
understanding and trust in beyond understanding when Buddha says,
'They do not see me, although I am close to them'"? Nishijima has,
"In the state of being so close yet failing to see, who could not believe
in understanding of non-understanding by wholeheartedness?" Shasta
Abbey's translation says, "It is our not seeing Buddha, though Such is
near; so who, pray, lacks the faith to wholeheartedly grasp That Which
Is Beyond Our Grasp?"

The key part for me is 会不会 (kai fukai), which is "understanding nonunderstanding" or "understanding beyond understanding" or
"grasp(ing) That Which Is Beyond Our Grasp" (the odd capitalization
is in Shasta Abbey's original). Dōgen asks us to wholeheartedly trust
this understanding of nonunderstanding.

This is what the Korean Zen teacher Seung Sahn calls "don't know
mind." It's difficult to fully trust in our nonknowing. To do so is to act
from intuition rather than concrete understanding. We're trained not
to do that. But Buddhist practice emphasizes this kind of nonunderstanding. Our knowledge is always incomplete, and our brains always
misinterpret so much, that the only thing we can truly trust is intuition.

The next chapter gets into this concept even more deeply. Let's
take a look!

23. STOP TRYING TO GRAB MY MIND!

Shin Fukatoku

The Mind Cannot Be Grasped

THIS IS ONE of my all-time favorite parts of *Shōbōgenzō*. Dōgen liked it too, apparently, because he wrote it twice. Complete editions of *Shōbōgenzō* include both versions. The first is a lot shorter, and some people think it might have been notes someone took during a lecture based on the second piece, which they say may have been Dōgen's draft of that lecture. We'll probably never know.

In any case, I have combined the two pieces into one and, as usual, left out a lot so as to get at what I feel are the most relevant points.

Nishijima Roshi's brief introduction to this chapter is almost as good as the chapter itself. He says that we tend to believe in the substantial existence of something called "mind." He cites the work of German idealists such as Kant, Fichte, von Schelling, and Hegel, who argued for the existence of mind.

Nishijima loved to read Western philosophy. He even studied German so he could read the German idealists in their own language. Me, I've never been that much of a fan of philosophy. I majored in it for a semester at Kent State. While it was fascinating, it also seemed kind of pointless. Plus, some of the philosophy profs I encountered at KSU seemed kind of nutty.

So I don't know about the German idealists, nor do I feel confident in commenting on their beliefs. But it doesn't really matter. Nishijima is right. Plenty of people do believe in something called "mind." You can see that all around you in just about every philosophy or religion you encounter.

As I write this book, Deepak Chopra, the holistic health doctor turned new age guru to the stars, is challenging skeptics to prove that the universe is not the product of what he calls Cosmic Consciousness. He believes that "mind" underlies and creates "matter," and he'll pay $1,000,000 to anyone who can prove otherwise. I wonder if that's an imaginary million in the "mind," or an actual million with which I could buy a bunch of bass guitars. If there is a difference...

Be that as it may, every philosophical or religious movement I've ever encountered other than Buddhism takes as its starting point the real existence of something called "mind" and something else called "matter." They accept the absolute separation of these two as a given. Religious types usually identify mind with spirit or soul or God, who is seen as the ultimate mind, a disembodied super-being made of pure consciousness.

Materialists, on the other hand, see mind as just a secondary manifestation of material processes. We only think that we think. Actually, thought is just an illusion caused by material energy bouncing around inside our skulls. When I hear this, I always wonder who is experiencing this illusion.

In Western philosophy this idea of the eternal separation of matter and mind is usually traced to Plato, who saw an absolute distinction between the two. His philosophy influenced the early Greek Christians, who made it a cornerstone of their philosophy as well. In India the idea of the absolute separation of spirit and matter was already well established by the time Buddha came along. Many believed that the immaterial atman (soul) resided in the material body and animated it, and was in turn connected or even identical to Brahman, a sort of super-atman — often referred to in English as the "super-soul" — that animated the otherwise dead material universe. Others in India rejected this idea completely and went the other direction, becoming some of the world's first true materialists, in the modern sense.

In any case, Buddhism does not accept this hard division between mind and matter. The Heart Sutra's famous line "form is no other than emptiness, emptiness no other than form" points to this notion. What we conceive of as matter and what we conceive of as spirit/mind are actually one and the same. Nishijima liked to emphasize this by translating that line as "matter is no other than the immaterial, the immaterial is no other than matter." But, as much as I loved the old man, I never really liked the clunkiness of his version.

This chapter (or these chapters, since there are two with the same title, but let's just call it one, okay?) is one of many in *Shōbōgenzō* dedicated to explaining this notion. In his introduction Nishijima says, "Buddhism says that all existence is the instantaneous contact between mind and the external world." Mind does not exist separate from matter, nor does matter exist separate from mind.

Before we begin, I should note that the word I've translated as "grab" throughout this piece is normally translated as "grasp." I mostly did this because it made for a funnier image. Grasp is probably the better choice. But enough of me. Let's see what Dōgen has to say about it, shall we?

In the Diamond Sutra, Shakyamuni Buddha says, "You can't grab the mind of the past, you can't grab the mind of the present, you can't grab the mind of the future."

Buddhist ancestors study this in practice. From the ungrabbable bottom they have scooped out the caves and cages of past, present, and future and brought them here. They have used these caves and cages of the ungrabbable mind itself to do this. The thinking you are doing right at this very moment is "mind cannot be grabbed." The whole body and all of concrete time is just "mind cannot be grabbed."

We understand "mind cannot be grabbed" from our teachers. Before we have a teacher we don't know "mind cannot be grabbed" well enough to even have questions about it. People who just study books haven't got a clue. Here's a story that illustrates my point.

Before he became a Zen master, Tokuzan Senkan (Ch. Denshan Xuanjian, 780–865 CE) was called the King of the Diamond Sutra. He edited twelve bundles of commentaries on it. One time he heard there was a teacher named Ryutan Soshin (Ch. Longtan Chongxin, dates unknown, c. ninth century CE) who was supposed to be the best. This really riled Tokuzan, so he crossed over mountains and rivers carrying all his commentaries with him to challenge the master.

On the way he stopped for a rest by the side of the road, and an old woman happened along. Tokuzan said, "What do you do for a living, lady?"

She said, "I sell rice cakes."

Tokuzan said, "Would you sell me some?"

The old lady said, "Why do you want them?"

Tokuzan, being Chinese, used a common Chinese phrase that translates as, "I want to refresh my mind."

The old lady said, "What's that huge bundle you're carrying?"

Tokuzan said, "Haven't you ever heard of me? I'm Tokuzan, King of the Diamond Sutra! There's not a single bit of it I don't understand! I've got all my commentaries on the sutra in this bundle."

The old lady said, "Can I ask you a question, then?"

Tokuzan said, "Ask away, lady!"

The old lady said, "I heard that the Diamond Sutra says, 'You can't grab the mind of the past, you can't grab the mind of the present, you can't grab the mind of the future.' So what mind do you intend to refresh with my rice cakes? If you can tell me, I'll sell some to you."

Tokuzan was dumbfounded. The old lady just walked away from him, swinging her sleeves, which was a sign of contempt in those days.

What a pity such a learned scholar was so defeated by an old lady that he couldn't even manage a polite reply! That's the difference between someone who has an authentic teacher and someone who doesn't. Tokuzan said to himself, "A picture of a rice cake doesn't cure hunger!"*

Listening to this story, we can almost hear Tokuzan's lack of clarity. Even after he met his teacher he was probably still scared of that little old lady. But I'm not so sure the old lady was all that brilliant herself. She seems to think "mind cannot be grabbed" just means there really is something called "mind" but that it can't be grabbed, or that mind doesn't exist at all. If Tokuzan had been gutsier he probably could have beaten her at her own game. From just this story we don't know what the deal was with her.

Over in China, monks hear this story and think Tokuzan was a dope while the old lady was pretty smart. But that's kind of stupid.

For instance, how come after Tokuzan couldn't reply, the old lady didn't say, "How about you ask me and I'll give you the right answer?" If she had, we might know whether she was any better than Tokuzan. Instead, she just asks questions but has no answers. People who never assert their own views can't be trusted.

Let me see if I can say something for Tokuzan. Maybe just as the old lady's about to question him, he could have said, "If you're gonna be like that, don't sell me any rice cakes!" If he'd done that he might have been an inspired practitioner.

Or Tokuzan could have asked the old lady, "You can't grab the mind of the past, you can't grab the mind of the present, you can't grab the mind of the future. So what mind do you intend to refresh with your rice cakes?"

Then the old lady could have said, "You only know that rice cakes can't refresh the mind. You don't know that mind refreshes rice cakes and mind refreshes mind!" If she'd said that, Tokuzan surely would have hesitated.

At that moment when he was hesitant the old lady should've taken three rice cakes and handed them over to Tokuzan. Just as he was

---

* Back in chapter 15, "Hearing Weird Stuff Late at Night," Kyogen Chikan is credited for coming up with that phrase. In my version I had him saying, "A commercial for Twinkies can't cure hunger."

about to grab them she could've said, "You can't grab the mind of the past! You can't grab the mind of the present! You can't grab the mind of the future!"

Or if Tokuzan would've not taken them she could've smacked him on the noggin with a rice cake and said, "You spiritless cadaver! Don't be so dumb!"

If she'd said this and Tokuzan had been able to reply, that would've been good. Instead she goes away, swinging her sleeves. It's not like she had a bee in there!*

Tokuzan doesn't say, "I have nothing to say. Why don't you speak for me, old lady?" So not only does he not say what he should've said, but he even fails to ask what he should've asked. The moral here is that you have to be diligent in your practice and not just take it easy.

Mind is never separate from past, present, and future. But as soon as we imagine it is, we get completely lost. We don't say that there is a mind but it just can't be grabbed. We only say, "Mind cannot be grabbed." We don't say it's possible or impossible to grab the mind. We just say, "Mind cannot be grabbed."

If someone asks about the state of the past, present, or future ungrabbable mind, we can say, "Living and dying are coming and going." Everything in the material world is the Buddha-mind itself. The state of "it cannot be grabbed" exists as mountains, rivers, and the Earth. "It cannot be grabbed" in the form of material objects is just mind. There are times when the phrase from the Diamond Sutra "even with no fixed address, the mind arises" is the state of "it cannot be grabbed." "It cannot be grabbed" preaches all the dharma throughout every age.

In conclusion, "mind cannot be grabbed" means you buy a painted rice cake and eat it up in one mouthful.

Here's another story. There was a guy who we call National Master Daisho (Ch. Nanyang Huizhong, 675–775 CE). A guy named Daini Sanzo (Ch. Daer, dates unknown), who was a master of ancient Buddhist literature, came to the capitol of China from India, claiming he had attained the power to know others' minds, which is supposed to

---

* That's really what it says. I didn't add this line.

be one of the effects of enlightenment, according to the ancient scriptures. The emperor told the National Master to go see what was up with the guy. When Sanzo met the National Master he prostrated himself.

The National Master said, "I hear you have the power to know others' minds. Is it true?"

Sanzo said, "I wouldn't be so bold as to say." Which, in those days, was a polite way of saying yes without seeming like a braggart.

The National Master said, "Okay. Tell me where I am right now."

Sanzo said, "You're the teacher of a whole county. Why are you at the West River watching a boat race?"

The National Master said, "All right. Where am I now?"

Sanzo said, "You're the teacher of a whole country. Why are you on a bridge watching somebody play with a monkey?"

The National Master said again, "Okay. Tell me where I'm at now."

Sanzo tried for a while, but he couldn't see anything. The National Master said, "You charlatan! Where is your power to know others' minds?"

Sanzo said no more.

Sanzo never saw the National Master even the first two times. He didn't know anything of the National Master's mind. The National Master asked him three times where he was, but Sanzo never paid any attention to the question. If he'd listened, maybe he could have answered. Although he was fortunate enough to meet a great master, he just passed up his big chance. How could a mere scholar ever hope to understand a true Buddhist master?

Lots of great Buddhists have discussed this conversation. Some of those discussions have survived, so let's look at them.

A monk asked Master Joshu Jushin how come Sanzo didn't see where the National Master was the third time. Joshu said, "Sanzo can't see him 'cuz he's up his nose!"

Another monk asked Master Gensa Shibi, "If the National Master is already up Sanzo's nose why doesn't Sanzo see him?"

Gensa said, "Because he's so very close!"

Master Kai-e Shutan (Ch. Haihui Shouduan, 1025–1072 CE) continued on from what Gensa said, saying, "If the National Master was right up Sanzo's nose why would it be difficult for Sanzo to see him? It's because the National Master is up in Sanzo's eyeballs!"

Gensa also criticized Sanzo by saying, "Did you even see the National Master the first two times?"

Master Seccho Juken (Ch. Xuedou Zhongxian, 980–1052 CE) said, "Defeated! Defeated!"

Then one time a monk asked Kyozan Ejaku how come Sanzo didn't know where the National Master was the third time. Kyozan said, "The first couple of times, the National Master's mind was wandering. Then he entered the self-using self-receiving *samadhi*, and Sanzo couldn't see him."

All these masters made good points, but they still didn't really get what the National Master was doing. They only talk about how Sanzo failed the third time. Yet they seem to think he got it right the first two.* That's their mistake, and students nowadays should learn it.

I have my doubts about these old masters. First off, they don't know why the National Master questioned Sanzo and second, they don't know the National Master's body/mind.

Here's why I say they don't know the National Master's purpose for questioning Sanzo. The National Master says, "Tell me where I am right now."** His intention is to see if Sanzo really understands the Buddha-dharma.

In Buddhist terms, what the National Master is asking is, "Am I here? Am I over there? Am I in the most awesome state of enlightenment? Am I in the state of super-intense wisdom? Am I floating in the air? Am I standing on the ground? Am I in a Pizza Hut somewhere?† Am I in a place where there's treasure?"

Sanzo didn't get this at all and just presented a lower-level answer. The National Master asked again, and again Sanzo missed his big chance. Then he asked again, and Sanzo couldn't answer, so the National Master told him to take a hike.

The old masters who think Sanzo got it right the first two times were wrong. The National Master never says Sanzo was right even once.

---

* Dōgen didn't forget Gensa mentioned that. He'll come back to it.

** Literally, "Tell me where this old monk is."

† Okay, he actually says "grass hut" not Pizza Hut.

The National Master wants to know if it's possible to call the Buddha-dharma "the power to know other's minds." If so, then we have to ask about the meaning of *others* and the meaning of *minds*, and finally what it means to "know" them. Even if Sanzo did say something the third time, if it was like the first two answers, it still would've been wrong. The National Master is asking three times if Sanzo really understands the Buddha-dharma.

Second, as I said, the old masters don't know the National Master's body/mind. The National Master's body/mind can't be known or grabbed by scholarly teachers. It's beyond even the most enlightened bodhisattvas. How could a guy like Sanzo know it? Nobody can know the body/mind of the National Master, even if they've read and recited every sutra there is to read and recite.

Furthermore, the body/mind of the National Master cannot be known by those who acquire mystical powers. That's because the National Master is beyond wanting to become a Buddha. Even the eye of a Buddha couldn't see the National Master's body/mind. His comings and goings have transcended any cage you could possibly put them in.

Joshu said the National Master was right up Sanzo's nose. That's what happens when you look at the details without understanding the foundation. How could that be? Sanzo has no nose! There's no way the National Master and Sanzo could even see each other.

Gensa says it's because the National Master was too close for Sanzo to see. I'll give that a pass. Just about. But what does he mean by "too close"? Gensa doesn't understand true closeness. He's the furthest of them all from really getting the story.

Kyozan says Sanzo can't answer the third time because the National Master had entered a state of *samadhi*. Even though lots of people revere Kyozan, he still bungled this one. If he's saying that Sanzo knew where the National Master was the first two times I'd say Kyozan doesn't know squat about the National Master.

Gensa asks if Sanzo has seen at all. But that's still not right because it suggests that Sanzo's seeing was like not seeing. But that's not it either.[*]

---

[*] See? He did remember what Gensa said! I'll discuss this comment below.

Seccho says, "Defeated! Defeated!" But you'd only say that if you thought Gensa had it right.

When Kai-e says it's because the National Master was in Sanzo's eyeballs, he's still only talking about the third time. How could he know the National Master was up Sanzo's nose or in his eyeballs?

All five are unclear about the National Master's virtue, and none of them has the power to get at the real Buddhist truth. The so-called power to know others' minds that people talk about should really be called the "power to know others' thoughts." The National Master criticizes Sanzo not because he got two out of three answers right but because he got them completely wrong. The five ancient masters who commented on the story completely miss the point. That's why I have to talk about "mind cannot be grabbed." Even old masters made mistake after mistake.

Once a monk asked the National Master, "What's the mind of eternal Buddhas?"

The National Master said, "Fences, walls, tiles, and pebbles." That is "mind can't be grabbed."

Another time a monk asked him, "What's the constant and everlasting mind of the Buddhas?"

He said, "Fortunately you've met the old monk who became the head of this temple." That's also the mastery of "mind can't be grabbed."

The god Indra once asked him how to be free of existence and change. The National Master said, "You get free by practicing the Way!" Indra asked him what the Way was. He said, "Mind in this moment is the Way!" Indra asked him what the mind of the moment was. He said, "This place is the base of wisdom. This place is like a net of pearls." Indra did prostrations.

People often like to discuss the body and the mind in terms of Buddhist truth. When we study them together in practice, that's the state beyond the intellectual understanding of the common or the sacred. Work on mastering "mind can't be grabbed."

— Written at Kannon-dori-kosho-horin-ji Temple
during the summer retreat of 1241

You're going to have to bear with me a little on this one. This particular chapter contains a number of important lines that have been translated very differently by different scholars. So I'm going to be throwing a lot more Japanese and Chinese at you here than I have been up until now. If you can't read that stuff, just skip past and read what it says in English.

The quotation that forms the basis for this essay, the one about the past, present, and future mind being ungrabbable, is 過去心不可得、現在心不可得、未来心不可得 (*kako-shin fukatoku, mirai-shin fukatoku, mirai-shin fukatoku*). It comes from the Diamond Sutra. A copy of this sutra, dated to 868 CE, is said by the British Library, which owns it, to be "the world's earliest complete survival of a dated printed book."

But as old as it may be, it is far from old enough to be a transcript of anything the historical Buddha actually said. In fact, it is one of the group of sutras we've been looking at that were composed centuries after Shakyamuni Buddha died. The particular subset the Diamond Sutra comes from is called the Prajña Paramita, or Perfection of Wisdom, sutras. Dōgen unapologetically attributes this quote to Shakyamuni, although he must surely have known that its historical accuracy was doubtful.

Anyhow, as I mentioned, most translators say "ungraspable" rather than "ungrabbable," although Shasta Abbey's version says "cannot be taken."

Just after this we come to a line that I have paraphrased as, "From the ungrabbable bottom they have scooped out the caves and cages of past, present, and future. In Japanese this is 不可得裏に過去、現在, 未来の窟籠を剜来せり (*fukatoku-ura ni kako, genzai, mirai no kurou wo wanraiseri*). Let's see what other folks have done with this phrase.

Nishijima/Cross have, "Inside *cannot-be-grasped* it has scooped out and brought here the caves of past, present and future." Tanahashi and his cotranslator have, "Buddha ancestors...have gouged out the caves and baskets (limited dualistic views) from what is ungraspable in the past, present and future." They added the explanation "limited dualistic views" as if it was there in the original, but it isn't. Nishiyama and Stevens go even further in reinterpreting the passage. They translate this line as, "The only way to understand past, present and future is by using your own 'ungraspable mind.'" Shasta Abbey has, "They have fashioned the niches and baskets of Their own past, present, and future. Even so, They have made use of the niches and baskets of others in Their tradition." I guess they figured the word *bottom* (裏 *ura*) means "others in Their tradition." They capitalize the words *they* and *their* to make *Shōbōgenzō* seem more biblical.

I think the Nishiyama/Stevens translation has the right idea, but they take such liberties with the text that it's not even as much of a straight translation as what I'm doing in this book. Tanahashi adds his own interpretation of caves and cages, which may be correct but belongs in a footnote. Nishijima/Cross actually added a footnote to the word they translate as "caves" by first noting that it actually means "cave-cages" and saying it "suggests the regulated and concrete conditions of a buddha's daily life." That's a very different interpretation from Tanahashi's! As for Shasta Abbey, well, I'm just confused by their version.

The upshot is that we're all just kind of guessing, at least about the caves and cages stuff. Yet I find that the variations of this chapter in English all say pretty much the same thing in the end, when you set the caves and cages bit aside. They say that these masters use the ungrabbable mind to look at the ungrabbable mind, and so can we.

Philosophers and others who study the mind often have trouble with this idea. We look at the mind with the mind itself, so we can never be completely objective. In Dōgen's style of Buddhism we just accept this as a given, acknowledge that we can't really grab (or grasp) the mind, and continue working on it anyway.

Moving right along, I remember an incident in which the phrase about the mind of the past, present, and future being ungrabbable popped into my own ungrabbable mind and I felt like I understood at least one aspect of it. I was at work at the sci-fi/superhero TV and film production company in Tokyo, where I was employed for most of the time I studied with Nishijima Roshi. One day I was asked that typical work question, "Why did you do that?," referring to something I'd done right at the beginning of the job, which turned out to be the wrong decision. Maybe I'd decided to let some company in China make an Ultraman cupcake on which he was depicted as kind of fat, and the guys in the sales department hated it or something like that. I really can't remember.

Anyway, sometimes there's a practical reason for asking such a question. Someone might want to see if there's some misunderstanding of what the job entails and to try to correct it. But sometimes less practical people just want to give you a hard time, and that's what was happening here. I couldn't answer the question because the "me" who did whatever it was I did was gone. The mind of the past was indeed ungrabbable.

I don't mean that I forgot. I mean that the "me" who made that decision was not the "me" who was now being asked about it. The fact of knowing that it had gone wrong made it impossible to put myself in the position of the person I'd been in the past who thought whatever it was I did was a good idea. I could now only guess at my motivations.

People in situations like this usually just make something up. Most of the time we don't really know what reasons we had in the past for doing something. But we invent an explanation, and then we begin to believe our made-up story. Often we say, "It seemed like a good idea at the time," which is about as close to the truth as we can get without going one step further and just admitting we don't know.

It dawned on me in a kind of a flash that day that I *never* knew my own past. Not really. I just knew what I remembered of it, which was never very much and was always colored by countless reinterpretations of it. As for the future, I may imagine a Brad Warner who will do whatever things I have planned for him next week or next month or whenever. But I don't really know how that stuff will feel or how I'll react when it actually happens.

Okay, then. But we think we at least know the present. Do we, though? To say we know something implies a bit of distance from it. I can't know my own mind here and now because it's too close.

When you first start to come to terms with this it can feel overwhelming. It certainly felt that way to me! It felt like I was adrift in the ocean without a sail or an oar and without any land in sight, even if I did have a way to reach it.

But work with it a little longer, and you begin to see that it is tremendously freeing. Rather than being adrift in the ocean, you feel more like you're floating through the sky. It feels very open and beautiful. This, I believe, is what those Buddhas of the past were trying to tell us.

The phrase "living and dying are coming and going," which Dōgen says should be our answer if someone asks about the ungrabbable mind of the past, present, or future, in the original text is just these four characters: 生死去来 (se*i-shi-ko-rai*). It just means "life/birth, death, past/gone, future/come." Nishijima/Cross translate this as "living and dying, coming and going." Tanahashi has "birth and death come and go." Shasta Abbey's translation says, "It is synonymous with being born and dying, going and coming." As you can see, we're all working with a phrase that is deliberately vague and open-ended. It means all these things, and a few more besides.

The line I've paraphrased as, "Everything in the material world is the Buddha-mind itself" is usually translated something like, "Fences, walls, tiles, and pebbles are the Buddha-mind itself." All the translators are nearly unanimous on this.

What I've paraphrased as "even with no fixed address, the mind arises" is 応無所住而生其心. (This is Chinese, but a Japanese pronunciation would be *omu shoujo jisei kishin*). Nishijima/Cross say, "While having no abode still we should cause the mind to arise." Tanahashi says, "With no place to abide, the mind arises." Shasta Abbey's translation is, "Letting our mind abide nowhere and giving rise to the Mind." They spell *mind* once with a lowercase *m* and once with an uppercase *M*.

Legend has it that Daikan Eno heard this phrase in a marketplace when he was a woodcutter, and it caused him to leave the city to become a monk. Supposedly he was chopping some wood while a monk happened to be chanting the Diamond Sutra nearby. When the monk came to that phrase, Daikan Eno knew it was time to make a big change.

I take this to mean that we usually imagine the mind exists somewhere. Most of us these days imagine it to be in our heads. The ancient Greeks thought that the heart was the organ where thinking and feeling took place. So they must have imagined their thoughts as existing in the center of their chests. But what the sutra says is that even without any location, the mind still arises. It's saying that neither our brains nor our hearts generate what we call consciousness. It arises on its own.

It's a powerful idea. Coming across that idea was one of the things that made me decide to dedicate myself to Buddhist studies. I wanted to know if this radical reorientation of something I thought I understood was just someone's speculative idea or if there could be any truth to it. We know scientifically that the brain is active when thoughts and sensations occur. But to say that the brain *generates* those thoughts and sensations is a whole other matter. The Buddhist answer to this mystery is "mind cannot be grabbed."

Later on we get a bunch of weird phrases about dharmas and the mind that Dōgen created by rearranging a certain set of Chinese characters in different orders so as to mean different things. The phrase "all dharmas are the mind itself" is 万法即心 (*banpou soku shin*). "Triple world is just the mind" is 三界唯心 (*san-gai yui-shin*). "The mind alone is just the mind alone" is 唯心これ唯心 (*yui-shin kore yui-shin*). "The concrete form of Buddha is mind" is 是仏即心 (*zebutsu soku shin*).

"Whether it's self or the external world, don't be mistaken about the mind of Buddha Way" means that mind exists both internally as our subjective sense of mind and self and externally as the world.

My paraphrase is, "In Buddha's truth, the whole Earth is mind. It doesn't change by emerging or vanishing. The whole dharma is mind. We also need to learn the entire mind as the proficiency of wisdom." In the original this is いはゆる仏道には尽地みな心なり、起滅にあらたまらず、尽法みな心なり、尽心を智通とも学すべし (*iwayuru butsu-do ni wa sanchi mina shin nari, ki-metsu no aratamarazu sanbō mina shin nari, sanshin wo chishu tomo manasu beshi*).

My paraphrase is based on Nishijima/Cross. But there's not too much variation among other translations. Tanahashi has, "In the Buddha Way the entire earth is all mind; it does not change by appearing or disappearing. The entire dharma is all mind. Understand entire mind as mastery of wisdom." Shasta Abbey's translation is, "What we call 'in the Way of the Buddhas' means that the whole world is Mind, without Its being changed by anything that arises or disappears. And it means that the whole of the Dharma is Mind. And we also need to experience the whole of Mind as the functioning of spiritually wise discernment."

It's tempting to see this as a kind of idealistic proposition. Phrases such as "the whole Earth is mind" and "it doesn't change by emerging or vanishing" tend to indicate the belief that behind this world of appearances lies an unchanging eternal spiritual something that is being called "mind" here. Christians might call this "God" and Hindus might call it "Brahman."

But Dōgen is not suggesting that this mind stands apart from matter. He is saying that it *is* matter, and vice versa, that matter is mind. In a sense, matter is eternal. In my previous book, *There Is No God and He Is Always with You* (New World Library, 2013), I used a quotation from singer Robyn Hitchcock that explains this so well that I'm gonna use it again:

> Given the existence of the universe, all the molecules in it...have been here for billennia or something. They just keep juggling around. So you've got three of Shakespeare's molecules and you've got two of Himmler's or whatever it is, you know. Part of your fingernail was part of St. Joseph of Aramathea's frontal lobe or something. And you know, large parts of you were once a daffodil in Nova Scotia or something. You know, your feet used to be Winston Churchill. The same things keep getting recycled. It could be that when we pass away our psyches dissolve into lots

of sort of strips of feeling. All the things that comprised us that were held together by our bodies dissolve. You know, hence "I wasn't me to speak of just a thousand ancient feelings" [a lyric in the song he's discussing, called "When I Was Dead"], feelings that have been around since the beginning of human time.

In this sense, then, both mind and matter are eternal and do not change by arising or disappearing. Even if they disappear in one form, they soon reappear in another. There is no reason to think this ever really began at some fixed point in time or that it will ever end in some future time.

When discussing Sanzo's abilities or lack thereof, Dōgen says, "Sanzo's seeing was like not seeing. But that's not it, either." To clarify that weird idea of "seeing that's not like seeing," in his footnote Nishijima says, "Master Dōgen is concerned with the area beyond seeing and not seeing — that is, realization of the practical state." Sounds about right to me.

What I mean by that is that the practical, actual state right now is beyond any definition we can give it with our minds. Oh, sure, you can define it if you want. That's okay. It's just that any definition is different from that which it defines. As Krishnamurti was fond of saying, "the word is not the thing."

Phew! That was a long and intense chapter. Thanks for hanging in there!

24. MONKEYS AND MIRRORS AND STONES

Kokyō

The Eternal Mirror

THIS IS ANOTHER chapter I like a lot. But it's full of obscure Chinese metaphors, and it can be a real struggle just to get through it. Luckily for me, I took a lot of notes when Nishijima Roshi lectured about this. I've referred to those and referenced them in this paraphrasing of the piece. Again, I have taken tremendous liberties with Dōgen's actual words.

This chapter is all about mirrors, but in Dōgen's time in Japan there were no glass mirrors such as we have today. Instead, mirrors were made of polished metal, usually copper. One had to keep one's mirrors highly polished to remove dust and oxidation. Unlike our mirrors, which break and cause seven years of bad luck, these mirrors couldn't shatter, but they could be dented or bent. So when Dōgen talks in this chapter about a mirror being shattered, the image is meant to be much more violent and surreal than what we'd think of today when Henry Rollins punches one and it breaks into little pieces.

The main theme of the chapter is *prajña*, or intuitive wisdom. Dōgen uses the metaphor of a mirror to suggest intuition because an image in a well-kept mirror appears instantaneously and without distortion, but when a mirror is dirty or dented, it doesn't reflect clearly what's put in front of it. Our intuitive sense can be the same.

In this chapter Dōgen makes a lot of references to the "clear mirror" and the "eternal mirror." For the time being, just read the chapter and don't worry too much about what the difference is. The way Dōgen writes this chapter, it's pretty much impossible to tell. I know I never can. I just take them both as symbols for intuition of different kinds. At the end I'll talk about what scholars have said regarding the difference between them.

In fact, since this entire chapter is pretty weird I think the best way to deal with it is to do what I did when I first read it. Just go through it and don't get too worried about whether or not you understand it. Then we'll meet up at the end and talk about it.

The thing all Buddhas and ancestors have transmitted to us is the eternal mirror. When a barbarian shows up, a barbarian is reflected. Even if there are 108,000 of them. When a Chinese guy shows up, a Chinese guy is reflected — for one moment or for ten thousand years. When something old shows up, something old is reflected. When the present shows up, the present is reflected, when a Buddha shows up, a Buddha is reflected, when an ancestor shows up, an ancestor is reflected.

Gayashata was the eighteenth Indian ancestor after Buddha. His mom had a weird dream in which a god was holding up a huge mirror. Then she got pregnant. Seven days later Gayashata was born. From the moment he was born, he smelled good and looked terrific. He was a quiet kid, very different from other children. He had a round mirror[*] with him from the time of his birth. Wherever he went, the mirror went with him.

Gayashata could see all the Buddhist teachings of the past, present, and future in his mirror. Whatever stuff came up, the mirror reflected it perfectly. To look into such a mirror is even better than reading sutras. However, once Gayashata became a monk, the mirror no longer appeared in front of him.

The story of Gayashata and his mirror is very rare, but it does happen sometimes. So it's not like Gayashata was the only example.

---

[*] Throughout this chapter whenever Dōgen talks about mirrors, he's talking about a person's intuitive sense.

One day Gayashata encountered Samghanandi, the seventeenth Buddhist ancestor, who would later be his teacher. Samghanandi said, "That thing in your hands, what is it expressing?" This isn't just a question but kind of a statement — he's saying the thing in Gayashata's hands — the mirror — is expressing "what," or the unnamable aspect of reality.

Gayashata replied, "The big round mirror of the Buddhas has no flaws or blurry bits. You and I see the same stuff; our minds and eyes are identical."

All Buddhas are mirrors like this. It's not wisdom or reason. It's not fundamental nature or attributes. The Buddhas have real wisdom because they're beyond wisdom but we don't consider wisdom to be Buddhas. Remember that preaching about wisdom isn't preaching the ultimate truth. Even if we feel like we have a round mirror of our own, we can't touch it in this life or any other.

As a child, Gayashata didn't learn about the mirror by reading sutras. That's just how he was. He was born with it. Or was it born with him? When he says it has no blurry bits, he means that neither anything inside the mirror nor anything outside it was blurry, either. Because there's no front or back, these two individuals could see the same stuff. That's what happens when a real human being meets a real human being. Subject and object in the here and now are neither self nor other. The eye of the truth is limited only by the eye of the truth.

When Master Daikan Eno was a laborer at his teacher's temple, the cleverest monk there wrote a poem for their teacher and pasted it on the wall:

My body's like the Bodhi Tree[*]
My mind is like a mirror stand
From all dust to keep it free
I wipe it off with a cloth in hand

Daikan Eno thought that was too intellectual, so he came up with his own verse. Then he had someone write it for him, since he couldn't write, and posted it on the wall next to that one:

---

* The tree under which the Buddha got enlightened

In the state of bodhi there is no tree[*]
Nor does a mirror need a stand
We have nothing at all originally
So where could dust possibly land?

We should study these words. Loads of people, including the person who edited the famous ancient collection of koans called the *Blue Cliff Record*, say that Daikan Eno was one of the best. Daikan Eno says we don't originally have anything and asks where dust could land. Since the clear mirror is beyond being in any one place, it doesn't need a stand. In fact, where in the whole universe could there be a speck of dust that's not part of the universal mirror? The universe isn't a place of dust; it's the face of the mirror.

A monk asked Master Nangaku Ejo, "If you melt down a mirror and make it into a statue, where does the reflection go?"

Nangaku Ejo said, "Where did the face you had before you became a monk go?"

The monk said, "After it's been transformed, why doesn't it shine?"

Nagaku Ejo said, "Although it's not shining, it can't delude anybody."

We don't know what the many images[**] that appear in front of us are made from. But here is evidence that they are cast from a mirror. Melting down a mirror and turning it into a statue is the decisive way to study mirrors.

The monk's question isn't just an abstraction. He understands that mirrors can be transformed into other things. The question, "Where did the face you had before you became a monk go?" holds a mirror up to the monk's real face. At that moment, his face might be my face.

The master says, "Although it's not shining it can't delude anybody." That means it doesn't shine and it doesn't deceive. One way to understand this is to think about how if the ocean were to dry up, what

---

[*]   *Bodhi* means "enlightenment."

[**] For the phrase I've paraphrased as "many images" Dōgen uses the word 万像 (*bansho*). This could mean "ten thousand things" but it could also mean "ten thousand statues." Or it could mean "ten thousand images." "Ten thousand things" is a way of saying innumerable things or, in other words, all things in the universe. It's a pun that does not translate.

we would see wouldn't be the bottom of the ocean anymore because it'd be dry land, which is different from an ocean bottom. This moment is a whole bunch of delusions and a whole bunch of shining-mirror reflections.

Master Seppo Gison was talking to his students. He said, "If you want to understand stuff, my concrete state is like the ancient mirror. When a barbarian shows up, a barbarian is reflected. When a Chinese guy shows up, a Chinese guy is reflected."

Master Gensa Shibi stepped out and said, "What if a clear mirror came along?"

Seppo Gison said, "The barbarian and the Chinese turn invisible."

Gensa Shibi said, "I'm not like that."

Seppo Gison said, "So what's your situation?"

Gensa Shibi said, "Please ask me, master."

Seppo Gison said, "Okay. If a clear mirror comes along, then what?"

Gensa Shibi said, "Shattered into little pieces!"

Seppo Gison is talking about the great "what?" — the ineffable, unnamable aspect of the universe. So what about his eternal mirror? When he says he's like one face of the mirror, that means it's beyond being inside or outside. It's constant movement, like a pearl rolling around in a bowl.

"When a barbarian shows up, a barbarian is reflected" refers to Bodhidharma, the Indian master who the Chinese thought of as a barbarian. Seppo says, "When a Chinese guy shows up, a Chinese guy is reflected." The Chinese guy is not "a Chinese guy." He is beyond such characterization. He just shows up and is reflected. He says that they both become invisible when a clear mirror comes along. He might add that the mirror becomes invisible too. Gensa's reply about the mirror being shattered means that he wanted a concrete answer from Seppo but only got back a clear mirror.

In the age of the Yellow Emperor, more than three thousand years ago, there were said to be twelve mirrors. One was supposed to be used for each hour of the day,* one was used for each month of the

---

* The Chinese used to divide the day into twelve hours, as they still did in Japan in Dōgen's time.

year, and one was used for each of the twelve annual sign of the Chinese zodiac. If the twelve hours weren't mirrors, how could we use them to understand the past and present? The past and present are used by the real time we experience right now. It is during that actual time that a Chinese guy shows up.

In the old days in China there was a saying that Tai, the second emperor of the Tang Dynasty (627–650 CE), used people as mirrors and was able to figure out all sorts of problems of harmony and anxiety, sanity and confusion. Some people think that means he used wise advisers to tell him stuff. But that's not the true principle.

Seeing people as mirrors means seeing mirrors as mirrors, and seeing yourself as a mirror, and seeing everything as a mirror. The doings of people can't be traced. They're just real action. Their varying degrees of smartness and dumbness are as mysterious as the weather. They say Emperor Tai understood the universe by understanding people. But that doesn't just refer to asking smart people for advice.

There's an ancient legend that Japan received three sacred mirrors from the gods. Even so, these mirrors, which are in Ise Shrine, Hinokuma Shrine, and the emperors' palace,* are made of physical substance. When something old shows up in front of one of them, something old is reflected. When the present shows up, the present is reflected.

We should learn that showing up and being reflected isn't a matter of recognition or understanding. A barbarian doesn't show up just so he can be reflected. He just shows up for the sake of showing up. He's reflected for the sake of reflecting. That's the real meaning of the eternal mirror.

Gensa asks Seppo what happens when a clear mirror shows up. We should pay attention to this. On what sort of scale is "clear" measured? The clear mirror Gensa is asking about isn't a barbarian or a Chinese guy. There aren't two mirrors. Even though there are not two, the eternal mirror is still the eternal mirror, and the clear mirror is still the clear mirror. Are they the same or different?

Don't imagine that the eternal mirror must be clear. The point is what Daikon Eno meant when he said, "You're like this. I'm like this. All

---

* The last of these is still there today.

the masters of India were like this too." Later on we'll talk about how an ancient Buddhist master said that even the eternal mirror needs polishing. Could that be true of a clear mirror too? What would you say? You gotta learn this stuff!

When Seppo says both the barbarian and the Chinese guy turn invisible he means that in the clear mirror's moment, both are invisible. What's that even supposed to mean? I'll tell you.

The fact that they have both showed up does not get in the way of the eternal mirror. The eternal mirror reflects whatever steps in front of it. But when they're reflected, they're both invisible. So there's a clear mirror and there's an eternal mirror, just as Seppo says. The clear mirror doesn't interrupt the reflection of either the barbarian or the Chinese guy in the eternal mirror.

They don't appear inside the eternal mirror, or on the surface of the eternal mirror, or outside the eternal mirror, or as the exact same thing as the eternal mirror. Pay attention to what Seppo is saying. At the moment when the barbarian and the Chinese guy show up, the eternal mirror is making them show up. If you say that even when the barbarian and the Chinese guy are invisible, the eternal mirror remains, you're just being goofy. Totally goofy.

Seppo Gison asks Gensa Shibi about his situation, and Gensa Shibi replies, "Please ask me, master." Don't miss that little exchange! Master and student are throwing themselves into the moment together like father and son. It's a crucial part of the dialogue. When someone requests that their master ask them a question like this it's because they're already a person who is "it"; they're already a person who is of the ineffable, unnamable *something* of the universe. There's no escaping that kind of question.

Seppo Gison says, "Okay. If a clear mirror comes along, then what?" This question itself is an eternal mirror that father and son work on together.

Gensa says, "Shattered into little pieces!" That's what he calls "the moment when the clear mirror suddenly appears." The clear mirror is the thing that experiences the state of "smashed into little pieces." When the clear mirror expresses itself, "smashed into little pieces" is its expression.

Don't be a dope and think that at one point the mirror was whole and the next moment it was smashed. But does this "smashed into little bits" express the state of the eternal mirror or the clear mirror? I wish I could ask Gensa and Seppo for a few more words. Maybe it's no longer even a question about either one. How is it smashed? The moon hangs in a deep blue sky.

Seppo Gison was taking a walk with Master Sansho Enen (Ch. Sansheng Huiran, dates unknown, successor to Master Rinzai Gigen) when they saw some monkeys. Seppo said, "Each of these monkeys has an eternal mirror on its back."

Sansho said, "How come you call what hasn't been named for ages 'an eternal mirror'"?

Seppo said, "I see a scratch on it."

Sansho said, "What's so darned urgent that you forgot the story?"

Seppo said, "My bad."*

We should study this story. What kind of monkeys did Seppo see? You have to ask this kind of question for a very long time.

Seppo said, "Each one has an eternal mirror on its back." That means even though an eternal mirror is the face of a Buddhist ancestor, an eternal mirror is an eternal mirror and also goes beyond being an eternal mirror.

That they're on the backs of those monkeys doesn't mean there are big mirrors and small mirrors. There is only one eternal mirror. It's as if it's stuck to their backs like you'd stick something to the back of a picture of Buddha. Did they use Elmer's Glue or a Pritt Stick?

Maybe monkeys are backed by the eternal mirror. But is an eternal mirror backed by monkeys? The eternal mirror is backed by the eternal mirror, and monkeys are backed by monkeys.

In Chinese every object has to have a counter, and the counter for mirrors translates as "face." The Chinese phrase Seppo used is like saying, "Each monkey's back has one face of the eternal mirror." That's not an empty teaching. So is it monkeys, or is it eternal mirrors? Heck if I know! Are we originally monkeys? Who are you gonna ask? Whether

---

* He actually says 老僧罪過 *rōsō (no) zakai (nari)*, which means, "It's this old monk's mistake."

or not we're monkeys is beyond our knowledge. Whether we're ourselves or not is something our brains can't grasp.

Sansho said, "How come you call what hasn't been named for ages 'an eternal mirror'?" He's talking about the time before mind or consciousness appeared. Nothing shows its head for eons. "Nameless" describes happy faces and sad faces, and eternal-mirror faces and clear-mirror faces. When what is nameless is truly nameless, ages are not "ages." When ages are not "ages," Sansho's expression can't be true.

Rather, the time before mind or consciousness appeared means today. Don't waste this day. Even though the phrase "nameless for ages" is famous, I don't think it's so brilliant.

Seppo could've said, "The eternal mirror! The eternal mirror!" at this point, but he didn't. Instead he said, "I see a scratch on it." We're likely to think, How could there be a scratch on the eternal mirror? Seppo is probably calling Sansho's phrase about it being "nameless for ages" a flawed statement. Sansho's statement itself is a scratch on the eternal mirror. Sometimes scratches appear on the eternal mirror, and even scratchy mirrors can be the eternal mirror.

Sansho presses on, saying, "What's so darned urgent that you forgot the story?" Is this "darned urgency" about today or tomorrow? Is it about me or you? Is it about the entire universe? Is it about the corner of Silverlake Boulevard and North Vendome in Los Angeles? Pay attention, people!

As for the "story" he's referring to, some stories have never been told, and some have been told too many times. Can we say this story has "realized the truth together with the Earth and all beings," like Buddha said when he got enlightened? It's not something to be fussed over like when you're restringing your bass guitar. It's neither conscious nor nonconscious.

As when the Chinese Emperor Wu met Bodhidharma and said, "I don't know who this guy is," it's like being face-to-face without really seeing each other. In every situation, nonconsciousness is the raw mind and totally clear nonseeing.

Seppo said, "My bad." Usually that would mean "I made a mistake" or "I said something wrong." But when Seppo says "my," he means he is totally himself. Whatever stuff he experiences, he remains just himself. Even if he appears as a Buddha or a Buddhist ancestor at every moment for ten thousand years, what he practices is his own practice of himself.

Both Seppo and Sansho were excellent teachers. We can see from this dialogue that they have maintained the eternal mirror. We ought to try to be like them.

Seppo once preached to his audience, "When the world is ten feet wide, the eternal mirror is ten feet wide. When the world is one foot wide, the eternal mirror is one foot wide."

Gensa pointed at the furnace and said, "How wide is that furnace, then?"

Seppo said, "As wide as the eternal mirror."

Gensa said, "Your feet haven't touched the ground yet."

He names ten feet "the world" and says the world is ten feet. He says one foot is the world and the world is one foot. It's the ten feet of the present moment and the one foot of the present moment, not some abstract ten feet or one foot.

When people talk about this story, they usually imagine the world as being really, gargantuanly huge. But that's like taking a limited view of yourself and pointing over at the next town.

When we look at our own world right where we are, we see it as ten feet wide. That's why Seppo says that when the world is ten feet wide, the eternal mirror is ten feet wide. When we really get this, we're able to concretely see one part of the world.

When you hear about the "eternal mirror" maybe you imagine it like a thin sheet of ice. But it's not like that. The ten feet of the eternal mirror is at one with the ten-foot width of the world. But are they equal to or at one with the gargantuanly huge world? We should really ask ourselves this.

Even though the whole world in all directions is a bright pearl, it can't measure up to the eternal mirror. The eternal mirror is everything that happens in the universe, regardless of what passes in front of it. It is crystal clear both up and down and side to side.

Width means actual width from one side to another, not quantity. It's like measuring in feet and inches. It's one thing that is ten feet wide.

Gensa asks, "How wide is that furnace, then?" This is an unambiguous expression of reality. We should study it for millions of years. Looking into this furnace is looking into the condition of becoming a person who is "who's that guy?" When looking into this furnace, the furnace is not a specific width like seven or eight feet. Gensa doesn't ask this question because he's confused. It's like the words Daikan Eno spoke when Nangaku Ejo joined his order, "What is it that comes like this?" It's not the usual kind of question about how big something is across.

The furnace in Gensa's question is outside all characteristics and proportions. Don't drop this cherry doughnut I'm giving you. Break it open! Make the effort!

Seppo says, "As wide as the eternal mirror." Sit and think about that some. He doesn't want to say the furnace is ten feet wide, so he says this instead. It's not that "ten feet" is right and "as wide as the eternal mirror" is wrong. Lots of people think he was wrong for not saying "ten feet wide." Don't let real action pass you by.

Gensa said, "Your feet haven't touched the ground yet." We should ask where his actual feet really are. We should ask what kind of a thing the ground is. Some people see it as meaning the gates of liberation or as meaning the Buddha's truth. Are feet on the ground the correct situation? Or are feet not being on the ground the correct situation? When the Earth is as it is, words about feet touching or not touching it may be "not yet." Gensa's words express Seppo's real state.

Master Kokutai Koto (Ch. Guotai Hongtao, dates unknown, successor of Gensa Shibi) was asked by a monk, "What's the eternal mirror like before it's polished?"

Kokutai Koto said, "The eternal mirror."

The monk said, "What about after it's polished?"

Kokutai Koto said, "The eternal mirror."

There are times when the eternal mirror isn't yet polished, and there are times after it's polished, but it's always completely the eternal mirror. When you polish it, you polish all of it.

You don't use Turtle Wax or whatever to polish it. You just use the eternal mirror. This isn't polishing the self, and it's not the self polishing something else. It's polishing the eternal mirror.

Before it's polished it isn't dull. Even if some folks say it's black, it's still not dull. It can't be dull. It's the living, eternal mirror! We polish a mirror to transform it into a mirror, we polish a stone to transform it into a mirror, we polish a stone to transform it into a stone, and we polish a mirror to transform it into a stone. Sometimes we polish and polish and get nothing. Then there are times when maybe we could make something but we just can't get it together to polish. This is what the Buddhist ancestors do too.

The story of polishing a stone came from when Baso Doitsu studied with Nangaku Ejo. Baso sat zazen constantly for ten years in his little hut, even in the rain and snow. One day Nangako went to Baso's place and said, "What are you doing these days?"

Baso said, "Nothing but zazen."

Nangaku said, "What's the point of doing zazen?"

Baso said, "To transform yourself into a Buddha!"

Nangaku picked up a stone and started polishing it.

Baso said, "What are you doing?"

Nangaku said, "I'm polishing this stone."

Baso said, "What's the point of polishing a stone?"

Nangaku said, "To transform it into a mirror!"

Baso said, "How can you transform a stone into a mirror by polishing it?"

Nangaku said, "How can you transform yourself into a Buddha by doing zazen?"

People always think that Nangaku was trying to inspire Baso. That's not necessarily so. The actions of a saint are beyond those of regular people. Without the method of polishing a stone, how could the great saints teach us anything? Nangaku used an everyday object to teach a profound lesson. That's the Buddhist way of doing things.

Baso got the lesson right away. That's how direct it was. When polishing a stone transforms it into a mirror, then BLAMO! Baso changes into a Buddha! When Baso changes into a Buddha, he immediately changes into Baso. The very second that Baso changes into Baso, zazen changes into zazen.

That's why the polishing of stones to make them into mirrors is maintained in Buddhist practice. The eternal mirror was made from a stone. Though we polish the mirror, it's actually never been dirty. Stones aren't dirty, but we polish them anyhow. This is the state in which the effort of making a mirror is realized. That's what Buddhist ancestors do.

If polishing a stone doesn't transform it into a mirror, polishing a mirror can't transform it into a mirror, either. Transforming is transforming into a mirror and transforming into a Buddha. Or maybe polishing the eternal mirror makes it into a stone? You can't comprehend the actual state of polishing.

In any case, Nangaku's words are true. In conclusion, polishing a stone really does transform it into a mirror. If stones couldn't become mirrors, regular people couldn't become Buddhas. If we hate stones for being hunks of dirt, you might as well hate people for being hunks of dirt. If people have minds, stones must also have minds. Who can notice that there are mirrors in which stones are reflected? Who can notice that there are mirrors in which mirrors are reflected?

— Preached to the assembly at Kanno-dori-kosho-horin-ji Temple on October 9, 1241

Phew! We got through that! Let's break it down a bit now. In the line I've paraphrased as, "However, once Gayashata became a monk, the mirror no longer appeared in front of him," the bit about the mirror not appearing is 円鏡これより現前せず (*enkyo kore yori genzensezu*). Nishijima/Cross translate this as "the mirror never appeared before him again." According to Nishijima, the implication is that in becoming a monk, one receives the criteria for proper behavior in the form of the precepts. Carl Bielefeldt translates this as "he ceased to shine as a mirror." He believes this means that Gayashata ceased to appear as different or special after he became a monk.

As you've come to expect by now, I tend to favor Nishijima's interpretation. In this case it's because the verb 現前 (*genzen*) means "to appear before." So the reference seems to be about Gayashata using the mirror for himself rather than to his outward special appearance to others. Reading it as the mirror appearing in front of him to display his specialness to others doesn't seem compelling to me. My apologies to Professor Bielefeldt.

In any case, though, the phrase is still weird. I tend to think someone would use their intuitive sense even more after becoming a monk. Although I feel like I understand the bulk of what Dōgen says in *Shōbōgenzō*, there are always small details that don't really work for me. I'm certain that's the way it is for all of us who deal with his texts.

In private conversations with Dōgen fans and experts, I've heard people say things like, "Yup. I don't know what the heck he means there!" fairly often. I think we who write about Dōgen ought to occasionally admit to the world that some of what he says just leaves us scratching our heads.

When that happens to me, I tend to defer to other areas where I'm clear about Dōgen's meaning and read the questionable parts in that light. Here, for example, it doesn't make a lot of sense for Dōgen to say that Gayashata ceased to seem special, since we know he became a revered Buddhist master. Nishijima's idea of his relying on the precepts and on the discipline of the Buddhist order, thus making it unnecessary to check his intuition in ambiguous situations, seems more Dōgen-like to me.

In the original version of this chapter Dōgen doesn't tell the story of Daikan Eno's poetry smackdown with the clever monk the way I have here. Since most of his listeners knew the story, Dōgen just reproduces Daikan Eno's response poem without mentioning the poem he was responding to. But because most English speakers don't know the story, I put the whole thing in here.

The clever monks' poem is 身是菩提樹、心如明鏡臺、時時勤拂拭、勿使惹塵埃。. Since that's Chinese and not Japanese I won't attempt to transliterate the pronunciation. Nishijima/Cross translate it as, "The body is the Bodhi tree / The mind is like the stand of a bright mirror / At every moment we work to wipe and polish it / To keep it free of dust and dirt." Most translations are pretty similar. A few translators try to rhyme it like I did, with similarly sad results.

Daikan Eno's response poem is 菩提木無樹、明鏡赤非台、本来無一物、何処有塵埃. That's also Chinese, so I won't attempt to replicate it in roman letters. Nishijima/Cross translate this as, "In the state of Bodhi there is originally no tree / Neither does the clear mirror need a stand / Originally we do not have a single thing / Where could dust and dirt exist?" Again, other translators say pretty much the same thing, while a few try to rhyme it like I did and make as much of a hash of things as I did.

Nangaku Ejo and the monk's conversation about melting down mirrors and making them into statues is a little different in the translation by Tanahashi from what I've given you here. His version has the monk asking, "When a mirror casts a reflection, where does the light go?" That's a cuter question, and I like it. However, Shasta Abbey, Carl Bielefeldt, and Nishijima/Cross all have the conversation being about melting a disused mirror down to make a statue — sometimes it's specifically a statue of a Buddha, though the story doesn't say that explicitly. When I looked at the original Chinese, the impression I got was of melting a mirror to make a statue.

Bielefeldt explains this story in a footnote that says, "That is, someone whilst still in lay life may exhibit a spontaneous brightness which dissolves after the person begins to train as a monk, as was the case with Kayashata. The monk's question, however, implies a distinction between 'us monks' and 'those lay people.'" Although Bielefeldt and Nishijima Roshi appear to have differing interpretations, maybe they don't. Let me tell you why.

This same story also appears in Dōgen's koan collection *Shinji Shōbōgenzō*, in which it is case 16 of book 2. In his commentary on the koan in his translation of that book, Nishijima says, "Perhaps the monk was asking why he was unable to reflect the truth even though he had become a monk. Master Nangaku said that the statue had its own value as a statue. There was no reason to burden the statue with abstract ideas about reflecting light. The statue just as it was, was fulfilling its function in the universe. In the same way, the monk, just as he was, was living fully in reality." I like that explanation.

Perhaps all of us have a wisdom that shines forth when we're young that gets covered up as we learn more of the ways of the world. As a monk, one tries to return to that childlike state while maintaining one's adult learning. It's a balancing act, for sure!

A bit later we come to a line that says, "This moment is a whole bunch of delusions and a whole bunch of shining-mirror reflections." What Dōgen means is that there's a difference between abstract thinking (delusions) and concrete reality, as reflected by the mirror of intuition. Even so, they both occur at the same time. So we just have to muddle through however we can.

Then there are the lines, "If the twelve hours weren't mirrors, how could we use them to understand the past and present? The past and present are used by the real time we experience right now. It is during that actual time that a Chinese guy shows up." This means that intuitive wisdom happens at just this real, concrete moment. We can see how we use the past and present at this moment.

The line, "We should learn that showing up and being reflected isn't a matter of recognition or understanding" reminds me of the line in "Genjo Koan" about how we may not recognize our own enlightenment. In this case Dōgen is saying that we have intuition — represented in this chapter as a mirror — whether or not we recognize and understand it.

What happens to us doesn't happen so that we can respond to it. It just happens. Similarly, our response is just what it is. It may not have much to do with the event to which we respond. As practitioners of Zen, we try to respond clearly and not out of our accumulated habits and messy emotions. My own practice over the years has often been about this. It's not so easy to do.

Now let's talk about all that clear mirror/eternal mirror stuff. When I was working on this chapter and I reached the part about the eternal mirror and the clear mirror, I got really hung up. I looked through all my notes and commentaries and things, trying to figure out what the difference between the two mirrors was. I came up with nothing. I finally walked away from the computer for a while, and then it dawned on me. The answer was right there in the text itself. Dōgen says right there that there are not two mirrors (二枚なるべからざるなり *ni-mai narubekarazaru nari*)! In other words, there are not two kinds of intuition.

And yet, as Dōgen says, the eternal mirror is still the eternal mirror and the clear mirror is still the clear mirror: ととひ二枚貳あらずといふも、古鏡はこれ古鏡なり、明鏡はこれ明鏡なり (*tatohi ni-mai arazu toiufumo, kokyo wa kore kokyo nari, meikyo kore meikyo nari*). This is a point that Dōgen stresses again and again throughout *Shōbōgenzō*. It all goes back to the question he had when he was a young monk. If we're perfect just as we are, why do we need to practice to realize that? We have intuitive wisdom naturally, and yet we have to work to keep it clear. That's what he means by saying we shouldn't think the eternal mirror must always be a clear mirror. The eternal mirror is our ever-present intuitive sense. The clear mirror is what we get when we work to keep that intuitive sense sharp.

Dōgen says, "At the moment when the barbarian and the Chinese guy show up, the eternal mirror is making them show up. If you say that even when the barbarian and the Chinese guy are invisible the eternal mirror remains, you're just being goofy." The word I'm changing into "goofy" is 錯乱 (*sakuran*) meaning "deranged" or "confused." The words I'm translating as "making them show up" are 現来せしむるなり (*genrai seshimuru nari*). This is an old Japanese phrase often translated as "actualize." But the literal meaning is closer to "cause (something) to come and appear."

This is another of Dōgen's ways of talking about the unity of subject and object, the unity of what we call "ourselves" and what we call the "outside world" or "other people and things." It's not that there is a subject who experiences an object. Subject and object arise together. The mutual relationship between subject and object is what makes the universe exist as it does.

Dōgen says, "The Chinese phrase Seppo used is like saying, 'Each back has one face of the eternal mirror.' That's not an empty teaching."

He's pointing out that Seppo uses the counter 一面 (*ichi-men*), literally "one face," when referring to the mirrors on the monkeys' backs. In Chinese and Japanese different categories of things have different counters, so you can't just say "one mirror"; you have to say something like "one face of mirror." Dōgen is suggesting that each separate thing in the universe has a single reality in common.

Moving right along, I love the phrase "the time before mind or consciousness appeared means today." In the original it's 一念未萌以前というふは今日なり (*ichi-nen mihō izen toiufu ha kyō nari*). All the translations I've seen render this pretty much the same in English as I have paraphrased it.

We imagine that the beginning of the universe was a long, long time ago. And in a sense, that's true. But it's also right now, right this very second. We experience the creation of the universe at every moment of every day. Whether we're sitting on a park bench or stuck in rush-hour traffic or having a terrific time at a summer barbeque or stuck in the most boring office meeting ever conceived, it doesn't matter. *This* is the moment of universal creation. *This* is the most important thing that has ever happened in the history of everything. If you miss it, it's a damned shame.

A little bit after this we come to a line that says, "What's so darned urgent that you forgot the story?" In his footnotes, Nishijima Roshi said, "We should learn whether, in reality, there is anything to be hasty about." I remember being really bothered by that line. My answer at the time would have been, "Damn straight there are things you have to be hasty about!" Lots of things require an urgent response. You can't be carefully considered about every little thing, or you wouldn't ever get anything done!

While I still think you often need to respond immediately without a lot of preplanning, that's very different from acting in haste. Haste is when you're rushing through this thing so you can get to something else. You should never be hasty.

A little while after that there is the line "when Seppo says 'my,' he means he is totally himself." In the original this is 老僧というふこ とは、屋裏の主人翁なり (*rōsō toiufu koto wa okuri no aruji-ō nari*). It more literally means, "As for the old monk, he's the old man who owns this hut." Let me tell you why I paraphrased it so differently.

Remember that what I paraphrased as "my bad" is more commonly translated as, "It's this old monk's mistake." The Nishijima/ Cross translation of the stuff about his being totally himself says, "The old monk means the old man who is master in his house. That is to say, [someone] who solely learns in practice the old monk himself, without learning anything else." The Tanahashi translation adds a parenthetical "of the Buddha" after the word *house* but is otherwise almost the same. I'm not sure why he added that. Carl Bielefeldt turns the second phrase into a command and gives it as, "Do not undertake to study other matters; just examine 'the Old Monk' through your training." That sense doesn't really appear in the original, but it's probably part of what Dōgen is implying.

The object of Zen training, if there can be said to be an object, is to become totally yourself. That may seem odd if you're hung up on ideas of Buddhism being all about "nonself." But nonself refers to a somewhat different sense of the word *self*. It means that the concept of self is far too limiting for what we actually are. However, we can sometimes provisionally call what we actually are a "self," for want of a better word. And in that sense, the object of practice is to become fully and completely what we already actually are.

Moving right along, we come to the phrase, "(The eternal mirror is) one thing that is ten feet wide." This means that the eternal mirror is concrete. It's not just an abstraction. That doesn't mean there's a gigantic eternal mirror out there somewhere floating in space. It means that what Dōgen is calling the "eternal mirror" isn't just a concept. It's a real thing, this intuitive sense.

Dōgen says, "Looking into this furnace is looking into the condition of becoming a person who is 'who's that guy?'" The "who's that guy" part is たれ人 (*tare-hito*), literally "who person." It's one of Dōgen's puns and refers to someone who has lost all traces of self-consciousness and whose state is "beyond words and understanding," to quote Nishijima Roshi's explanation of this passage. Other translators express this as something like, "Who is the one who sees the furnace?" I can see how they got there. But I still think the Nishijima/Cross translation hits the mark a little better. It fits in with Dōgen's standard lines about being a "person who is 'it'" or a "person who is 'what.'"

The part that goes, "We polish a mirror to transform it into a mirror... This is what the Buddhist ancestors do too" sounds a little complicated and weird. But it's not that difficult. It's just that sometimes we try to make whatever we're doing into whatever we imagine its ideal state to be. Sometimes we succeed and sometimes we fail. But in real action we transcend any notion of an idealized state. Even if we carry that idealized idea in our heads, it doesn't matter. We just do what we do. Dōgen reminds us that even the great Buddhist ancestors had the same kinds of stuff to deal with.

All that business about polishing a stone to make it into a mirror is again related to Dōgen's big question when he was a little kid about why we need to do practice if we're already perfect. Even though there is no blemish that needs to be polished away, we polish anyhow.

This is one of the kinds of contradictions in Dōgen's work that always drives people a little nutty. There's no better way to express it than Dōgen already expresses it, because it really is a contradiction. But it's one of those ways in which real life just happens to actually be contradictory.

If you define yourself as deluded or imperfect and imagine a state that is perfect and undeluded, you can make an effort to transform this state into that one. But in doing so, you'd miss out on the perfect thisness of this real state. What we're working on in Zen practice is to notice clearly our own actual condition. In doing so, we subtly transform it. And yet we don't transform anything. As I said, it's impossible to express it without being contradictory.

The great perfection we seek is already here. Yet we need to work on it anyway.

Okay. That was a bear of a chapter and probably a difficult discussion. But take heart! We're almost finished. The next chapter (our final *Shōbōgenzō* chapter) is a little bit easier.

25. CHANTING SUTRAS
Kankin
Reading — or Chanting — Sutras

You MAY RECALL that back in the chapter about "Bendowa" Dōgen said, "From the first time you learn (zazen) from a teacher, you never need to burn incense, do prostrations, recite Buddha's name, or read (chant) sutras anymore. Just sit and get the state that's free of body and mind," and "People who only chant sutras are no better than frogs croaking in a pond." But now he's going to switch it up on us and tell us how to burn incense, do prostrations, recite Buddha's name, and chant sutras.

A lot of people hear these quotes from Dōgen, or hear Bodhidharma's statement about Zen being a "special transmission outside the scriptures," or hear about Zen monks who burn all their books and then imagine that Zen people must be against chanting or indeed even just reading sutras. I often encounter people who are genuinely surprised to hear that Zen monks read stuff or to see Zen monks chanting sutras.

It's not that Zen is a philosophy that forbids or even discourages reading or chanting. It's just that Buddhism is a philosophy of action. Most philosophies exist in the books that are written about them. The books *are* the philosophies. If you understand the books, you understand the philosophy. Buddhism isn't like that. It's a philosophy you *do*.

That doesn't mean reading is worthless. By reading the sutras you can develop an intellectual understanding of Buddhist philosophy, and that's useful. But an intellectual understanding alone is incomplete. It has to be balanced by understanding in action.

Dōgen gets a bit mystical in this chapter. He extends the meaning of the phrase "reading sutras" to include observing nature as a kind of "sutra reading." After all, the sutras were written to try to describe the natural world, of which human beings and the human mind are manifestations. So it makes perfect sense that things like observing the flowing of a stream or looking at the moon are examples of reading sutras. Sitting silently and observing your own mind is also an example of "reading sutras," even if what's in your mind is just images of cartoon characters and food.

Let's see what Dōgen has to say on the subject.

Sometimes the practice and experience of totally righteous enlightenment depends on teachers, and sometimes it depends on sutras. Teachers are Buddhist ancestors who are completely themselves. Sutras are sutras that are completely themselves. It's like this because the real self is completely a Buddhist ancestor and completely a sutra. What we call "self" is not limited to you or me. It's a living eyeball, a living fist.

So there is contemplation of sutras, reading of sutras, chanting of sutras, copying of sutras, and preserving of sutras. That's what the Buddhist ancestors practice and realize. But it's tough to encounter the sutras. You might go millions of places and never even hear just the title of one. Unless you're a Buddhist ancestor you never see, hear, chant, or comprehend the sutras. Even after studying with Buddhist ancestors we can just barely learn sutras in practice.

When you really hear, retain, and receive the sutras, you do it with eyes, ears, nose, tongue, body, and mind, wherever you go and wherever you are. Fame whores* and bullshitters can't practice the sutras because sutras are spread throughout fields and cities and written on rocks and trees. Dirt preaches sutras and so does plain old empty space.

Master Yakusan Igen hadn't given a talk for a long time. The temple

---

* Who can be either male or female, of course.

director tried hinting at him to give a talk by winking broadly and saying, "The monks have been hoping for your instruction for a while."

Yakusan took the clue and said, "Ring the bell!"

The temple director rang the bell, and the monks all trotted down to the lecture hall.

Yakusan plopped himself down in front of them, sat there for a while, and then got up and went back to his room. The temple director bumbled up behind him and said, "How come you agreed to preach but then didn't say anything?"

Yakusan said, "Sutras have sutra teachers. Commentaries have commentary teachers. Why are you concerned about an old fart like me?"

The compassionate teaching of the ancestors is that for fists there are fist teachers and for eyes there are eye teachers. But I'd say to Yakusan, "I don't reject your words, but what are you a teacher of?"

After their poetry smackdown, which I told you about in the chapter "Twirly Flowers Twirl Twirly Flowers," Daikan Eno told Hotatsu, "From now on we'll call you Sutra Reading Monk!" So we ought to know that there are sutra-reading monks. This is Daikan Eno's teaching, and he was awesome sauce. A "Sutra Reading Monk" can't be measured in terms of reading or not reading, or in terms of having ideas or not having ideas. It goes beyond both having and not having. It's never putting down the sutras for millions and millions of years. There is no time when they're not being read. From sutra to sutra there is only the experience of sutras.

The twenty-seventh Patriarch in India, the Utterly Righteous Prajñatara, was invited to do lunch with the king. The king said, "Everybody else recites sutras. How come you don't?"

Prajñatara said, "When I breathe out, I don't follow circumstances. My in-breath doesn't live in the realm of the five aggregates. This way I recite millions of real sutras, not just one or two."

Prajñatara was a badass Buddhist. He understood the truth both concretely and abstractly. When he says his exhalation doesn't follow circumstances, he also means that circumstances don't follow his exhalation. Circumstances might be the brains and eyes as well as the whole body and whole mind. Taking circumstances for a walk and then bringing them back is what he calls "not following" them. "Not following" means totally following. Exhalation is circumstances themselves. But even so, it's not following them.

This is the very moment when circumstances themselves investigate inhaling and exhaling. This moment has never been before, and it won't come back again. It exists only now.

The "realm of the five aggregates" refers to the five *skandhas*, or aggregates that Buddha talked about in his first sermon. There he said that all people are composed of form, feeling, perceptions, impulses, and consciousness. The reason Yakusan Igen says he doesn't live in the realm of the five aggregates is that he is in a world they haven't yet reached. Because he gets this key point, he recites millions of real sutras, not just one or two. This is wisdom without extra baggage. Intelligence and ignorance can't touch this, and neither can smarts or stupidity. It's the essence of the Buddhist ancestors.

The word in Chinese for recite is 転 (*ten*), which can also mean "to rotate." You need to know this in order to get the pun I'm about to make, which doesn't translate into English. Joshu Jushin once got a donation from an old lady, who asked him to recite all the sutras. Joshu got up off his chair, walked around it, and said to the old lady's messenger, "I've finished reciting (rotating) the sutras!"

The messenger reported this to the old lady. She said, "I asked him to recite all the sutras. How come he only recited half of them?"

Evidently the old lady had a certain number of sutras in mind. "I've finished reciting the sutras!" is Joshu's entire sutra. His recitation is as follows. Joshu rotates (which is the same word as *recites* in Chinese) around the chair, the chair rotates around Joshu, Joshu rotates Joshu, and the chair rotates the chair. Everybody gets dizzy. Which isn't to say that reciting sutras is limited to going around chairs or to chairs going around people.

Joshu made a rotation (i.e., recitation). Does the old lady have eyes to see it? Although she griped that he only recited half, she could have said, "I asked him to recite all the sutras. He doesn't need to worry about anything!" Even if she'd said this by mistake I'd have said she really got it.

In the order of Master Tozan Ryokai (Ch. Dongshan Liangjie, 807–869 CE) there was a government official who made lunch for everybody at the temple, offered a donation, and asked Tozan to recite all the sutras. Tozan got down from his chair and bowed to the guy, and he bowed back. Then Tozan led him around the chair and bowed to him again. A couple of minutes later he asked the government guy if he got it. The guy said he didn't. Tozan said, "We just recited (rotated) all the sutras. Why don't you get it?"

"We just recited the sutras" is the easy part. It isn't that reciting sutras is like playing musical chairs or vice versa. And yet Tozan kindly taught us something. So listen up.

My teacher, Tendo Nyojo, quoted this story when a guy from Korea made a donation, asked the monks to recite the sutras, and also asked my teacher to give a lecture. My teacher got up on his seat, made a big circle in the air with his flywhisk, and said, "Now I've recited all the sutras for you." Then he threw the whisk down, just like a rapper dropping the mic, and left the room.

My teacher's words were beyond compare. Maybe you should chant them. Still, did my teacher use a whole eye or half an eye? Do the words he and the ancient ancestors said depend on eyes or tongues, and to what extent? Try to figure that one out!

Master Yakusan Igen didn't usually let people read sutras at his temple. But one day Yakusan himself was spotted reading a sutra. One of his monks asked him, "You don't let us read sutras. How come you're reading one?"

Yakusan said, "I just wanted to shade my eyes."

The monk said, "Is it okay if I do it too?"

Yakusan said, "If you did, you would get so sharp you could pierce ox hide."

The words "I just wanted to shade my eyes" are spoken by shaded eyes themselves. "Shading the eyes" is tossing away eyes and tossing away sutras. It's total shading of the eyes, and eyes being totally shaded. "Shading the eyes" means opening the eyes within the state of being shaded, energizing eyes inside shade, energizing shade inside eyes, adding one more eyelid, using eyes in shade, and eyes using shade themselves. If there weren't sutras for eyes, there could be no shading of eyes.

"You would get so sharp you could pierce ox hide" describes

being too smart for your own good. It's absolute ox-hide and absolute hide for an ox. It's hiding your ox. It's hide-rogen per-ox-hide!* That way, your whole being becomes an ox. When the student copies his master, the ox becomes the eyes, as in "shading the eyes." The eyes become an ox.

Master Yafu Dosen (Ch. Yun-ch'i Chu-hung, c. 1100 CE) said,

> Offerings to Buddhas make you happy and pink
> But reading old teachings is grander
> It might look like just white paper and ink
> But open your eyes, take a gander

Remember that making offerings and reading sutras might be equal sources of happiness and might even go beyond mere happiness. The sutras are just ink and paper, but who can see them that way? We need to work on this problem.

Master Ungo Doyo (Ch. Yunju Daoying, 835–902 CE) once saw a monk sitting in his room, reading a sutra. He said, "Hey, monk! What's that you're reading?"

The monk said, "The Vimalakirti Sutra."

Ungo Doyo said, "I'm not asking you about the Vimalakirti Sutra! *What's* that you're reading?

The monk got it and had a moment of realization.

The master's words can be understood as, "That which you are reading is *what*." They refer to the very act of reading, which itself is part of the ineffable universe. This state is profound and ancient and can't be encompassed by the word *reading*. On the road this monk met a poison serpent (in the form of this question). Being startled, he came to understand his teacher. Yet when we meet as real people, we shouldn't misrepresent things. That's why the monk replies, "The Vimalakirti Sutra."

Reading sutras means reading with the eyes of all the Buddhist ancestors. At that very moment, the ancestors turn into Buddhas, preach the dharma, preach Buddha, and do Buddha stuff. Without this

---

* Actually Dōgen makes a different, less funny pun, "using an ox to become a hide."

moment of sutra reading, there couldn't be any brains, faces, or eyes of Buddhist ancestors.

In Buddhist temples today there are various customs for the recitation of sutras at the request of donors. There are regular group recitations, and sometimes monks just recite them on their own. Also, the entire sangha will chant sutras for a deceased monk.

When a donor makes such a request, the director of the monks' hall puts up a sign that says sutra recitation will take place. After breakfast everybody gets together. They do some prostrations, burn some incense, and ring some bells, according to the established tradition. The donor enters, does prostrations, bows to the abbot, and burns incense. The donor walks around the monks' hall, and then sits cross-legged until the end of the chanting. Sometimes the sutras are chanted aloud, and sometimes they are read silently together.

Sutras are also read on the occasion of the emperor's birthday. If his birthday happens to fall on, say, January 15, the chanting begins on December 15 of the previous year. A few monks each day are selected for this chanting. They get to have snacks before lunch, like maybe noodles or some steamed cakes. The cakes are served in a bowl, and the monks eat them with their hands. You hang a yellow plaque on the wall announcing there's gonna be some chanting for the emperor that day. On the actual day of the emperor's birthday the abbot says a few nice things about the emperor and wishes him a happy b-day. This is a long-established custom.

Yakusan Igen asked the novice Ko (Ch. Gao, dates unknown), "Did you get it from reading sutras or from listening to a teacher?"

Ko said, "I didn't get it from reading sutras or from a teacher."

Yaksuan Igen said, "Lots of people don't read sutras or talk to teachers. How come they don't get it?"

Ko said, "I didn't say they don't get it. But maybe they don't want to directly experience it."

Some in the house of the Buddhas and ancestors experience it directly, and some don't. But reading sutras and listening to teachers are the things we do in our usual lives.

— Preached to the assembly at Kannon-dori-kosho-horin-ji
Temple October 9, 1241

Phew! That was another long one! It was way worse for me than it was for you because the original is about twice as long as what I've given you here. Let me try to walk you through some of the stranger parts.

The lines I've rendered as, "Teachers are Buddhist ancestors who are completely themselves. Sutras are sutras that are completely themselves" are my paraphrasing of the lines 知識というふは全自己の仏祖なり。看経というふは全自己の看経なり (*chishiki toiufu ha ʒen-jiko no buso nari — kankin toiufu ha ʒen-jiko no kankin nari*). Nishijima/Cross and Shasta Abbey interpret this line about the same way as I have. However, Kaz Tanahashi has, "A teacher is a Buddhist ancestor of the entire self. A sutra is a sutra of the entire self." That's also a perfectly reasonable way to translate the lines. In fact, grammatically the Tanahashi translation is closer to the Japanese source material, while Nishijima/Cross and Shasta Abbey take some liberties.

Then we have the line that I've rendered as, "Even after studying with Buddhist ancestors we can just barely learn sutras in practice." In Japanese this is 仏祖参学よりかつかつ看経を参学するなり (*buso sangaku yori katsu-katsu kankin wo sangaku suru nari*). My paraphrasing is close to what Nishijima/Cross have. But Tanahashi has, "Upon studying with a Buddhist ancestor you also study a sutra." No doubt Dōgen would agree with that phrase, but it's not what he says here. The onomatopoeia Dōgen uses here — *katsu-katsu* — indicates something that one is just barely able to do. Shasta Abbey has, "As soon as we have begun to investigate the Buddhas and Ancestors through our training, then, with some considerable difficulty, we begin to explore and train with Scriptural texts." I hate the way they have to capitalize everything like the King James Bible, but I feel they have the meaning right.

A bit later Dōgen says, "Sutras are spread throughout fields and cities and written on rocks and trees. Dirt preaches sutras and so does plain old empty space." He is saying that the actual meaning within the sutras can be found everywhere. The teachers who wrote the sutras were not inventing doctrines. They were perceiving the world as it is and expressing their understanding of it for our benefit.

I'd also add here that the words *Buddhist* and *sutras*, as used by Dōgen, are not limited to any sort of sectarian affiliation. Dōgen never encountered Christianity, Islam, or any Western religion and was probably only vaguely conversant with what we now call Hinduism (a designation that didn't exist in his time). And yet I feel confident saying that there are Christian, Jewish, Hindu, and Islamic scriptures and even atheistic writings that would also be examples of "Buddhist sutras" under his definition, just as there are scriptures regarded by many as Buddhist that would *not* qualify as "Buddhist sutras" in his definition of the term.

Remember that Dōgen was not shy about pointing out elements within what was called Buddhism that he thought were incorrect. What's true is true, regardless of the source. Dōgen famously said that even if a seven-year-old girl says something true, we should honor her just as we'd honor a saint.

The story of Yakusan Igen agreeing to give a lecture and then not saying anything is also found in Dōgen's *Shinji Shōbōgenzō*, as case 79 of part 1. It's wrong to imagine that this was a completely silent teaching, though. Yakusan was trying to teach through real action rather than just words. I would imagine there was a lot going on in that lecture hall that day. Maybe birds were singing outside, and bugs were probably making their bug noises. Maybe the temple director was off to one side fidgeting. And there wasn't just sound. There were all those monks wondering what the hell was going on. Maybe incense was wafting through the air. Maybe it was a little chilly that day. All that precious teaching would have been drowned out if Yakusan Igen had given a lecture. So he just sat and gave everyone a chance to listen to and experience the real world as a sutra.

Dōgen's question to Yakusan Igen, "I don't reject your words, but what are you a teacher of?" could also be rendered as, "Are you a teacher of *what*?" The "what" in question here is 什麼 (*shénme*), a

Chinese word meaning "what." It refers to the ineffable, inexpressible, real nature of the universe.

The line, "A 'Sutra Reading Monk' can't be measured in terms of reading or not reading, or in terms of having ideas or not having ideas" contains the phrase 有念無念 (*unen munen*). This can mean both "reading and not reading" and "having ideas and not having ideas." So I covered my bases by including both interpretations.

Dōgen's commentary on the story about Prajñatara contains the line, " 'Not following (circumstances)' means totally following." This sounds like gibberish, I know. But he is saying that when Prajñatara tries to go against his circumstances, even that action must follow circumstances. The word *circumstances* is tricky. In Dōgen's original, Prajñatara's words are quoted from the Chinese. The Chinese word used is 衆縁 (*shuen*), literally meaning "many connections." Sometimes it's translated as "conditions" or "events."

Prajñatara's attitude might sound fatalistic or deterministic. But Buddhism is neither. In this moment we have free will within the circumstances in which we find ourselves. However, our actions must accord with those circumstances, or they're impossible. This means we have a great deal of choice, but only within our real circumstances. You can choose to throw this book across the room in frustration right now, or keep reading. But if you wanted to ignite it with laser beams from your eyeballs, you couldn't do that. Unless, of course, this book is still being read in the year 5574, when people will be able to shoot laser beams from their eyeballs.*

My favorite lines in the piece come right after this. They are, "This is the very moment circumstances themselves investigate inhaling and exhaling. This moment has never been before, and it won't come back again. It exists only now." The second part needs no explanation. But perhaps the first needs a little. When he says "circumstances themselves

---

* If you are reading this in the year 5574, please note this prediction well. If it comes true, you should build a statue of me.

investigate," he's pointing out that you and I are the three-dimensional, solid, flesh-and-bone manifestations of circumstances. We don't just find ourselves in circumstances. We *are* circumstances.

In the story about a Zen master walking around a chair instead of reciting the sutras, Dōgen says the old lady who made the donation should have said, "I asked him to recite all the sutras. He doesn't need to worry about anything!" My paraphrase is based on how Nishijima Roshi explained this line. The last sentence actually contains the phrase 弄精魂 (*rozekon*), which literally translates as, "play with the soul." So the old lady's complaint may be better translated as, "Why does he just play with his soul?" In other writings Dōgen uses this phrase as a synonym for doing zazen. Since the master obviously did zazen already, Dōgen is suggesting the old lady should have said he didn't need to worry about anything.

A few lines later Dōgen talks about his teacher's words to a Korean donor. When commenting on this story Dōgen asks, "Do the words he and the ancient ancestors said depend on eyes or tongues, and to what extent? Try to figure that out!" I have never come across any Dōgen scholar taking him up on this particular challenge. So how about I take a stab at it? I feel like "depend on eyes" means seeing something and imitating it. "Depend on tongues" would be to say something original of your own. If that's the case, I'd say that Dōgen's teacher did a bit of both.

There are loads of examples of that sort of thing in Dōgen's writing. He values people who are able to come up with unique expressions. But he acknowledges that the mere fact of using a language is an act of imitation and conformity. We use the words and images that our culture provides us. If we tried to speak an entirely unique language, nobody would understand us. Zen also has its unique language. There is a big difference between merely imitating that language and actually using it in a way that makes sense.

When I was learning Japanese there was a phase in which all I could do was make sounds that I didn't really comprehend myself. I'd look up something and then say what was on the page. It was always kind of a thrill when the person I spoke to understood me, because *I* didn't understand me! After a while, though, I started to get the language better. Then when I spoke I actually knew what I was saying. I understood what words like *yoroshiku*, for example, meant when actually used. *Yoroshiku* is an extremely common greeting but has no meaningful English translation. Once I actually got what I was saying, it was a different thing altogether.

Let's keep moving along. When he was asked why he was reading, Yakusan said, "I just wanted to shade my eyes." I think this means that Yakusan is admitting to reading the sutras just for the pleasure of it. He doesn't care if it might get a little in the way of his own intuition. I believe "eyes" here means his eyes of intuition.

The monk asks Yakusan if he can shade his eyes too. Yakusan chides him about becoming too sharp. Normally this is kind of a Zen insult. Being too sharp or too intellectual is seen as something detrimental to Buddhist practice. But, as you saw, Dōgen turned this on its head, as he usually does with pretty much everything.

As for all that stuff about oxes becoming eyes and so forth, I have to admit I sort of get lost there. Nishijima Roshi believed that "becoming a hide" was a symbol of realizing the concrete. The folks at Shasta Abbey have a footnote here that says, "If you were to truly read — that is, to read with the Eye of wise discernment — you would be able to penetrate the Scripture (the hide) and see Buddha Nature (the Ox) in it." The parenthetical stuff is in their original, by the way. They apparently see a reference to the famous Ox Herding Pictures in which the ox is a symbol of enlightenment. And again, they have to Capitalize all Kinds of Things (And if You ask Me, That's just Annoying).

My guess is that Dōgen is saying that to read for pleasure — even if you're reading sutras — is to cast oneself into a man-made imitation of reality. It's easy to get lost there, and it's easy to mistake these man-made imitations of reality for reality itself. In our own era this is even more problematic. Dōgen never saw a movie or TV show, especially the kind we make in America, which attempt to mimic reality with super-realistic special effects and highly polished acting and writing or "reality TV," in which half the lines are scripted and most of the action is preplanned.

I act in fictional films sometimes and have written fiction books, so I obviously don't see them as any kind of evil. Still, I do think our culture has been deeply influenced by a lot of this stuff. Because of this, some of us have highly unrealistic expectations for our actual lives. One of the most obvious examples is how the easy access to pornography has led lots of people to compare their own sex lives to the things they see in porn videos. Of course, no one's sex life is anything like that, not even the sex lives of the people who are in those videos! This is just one easy example. We're confused like this all the time in much subtler ways, and we need to be careful.

I'm not sure if most Dōgen scholars would accept this interpretation. But I haven't seen anyone come up with anything better, so I'm sticking with it!

Dōgen says, "The master's words can be understood as, 'That which you are reading is *what*.' They refer to the very act of reading. This state is profound and ancient and can't be encompassed by the word *reading*." The Chinese word translated as "reading" here is 念底 (*nentei*), which is a combination of two characters, the first of which can also mean "thought" or "attention," and the second of which can mean "basis" or "state." In Japanese this character combination seems weird, but either Dōgen's monks would know what it means in Chinese, or Dōgen would have explained it during his actual talk. He is playing with the odd-seeming Japanese meaning of the character combination here. He's letting his listeners think about the way the word for *reading* can also mean "basis of thought."

Dōgen is having fun with puns again in the line I've rendered as, "At that very moment, the ancestors turn into Buddhas, preach the dharma, preach Buddha, and do Buddha stuff." There's no good way to translate it that gives you a sense of the pun involved, though. The

characters 作仏す (*sabutsu-su*) mean "become Buddha." The characters 説法す (*seppo-su*) mean preach the dharma. Dōgen then mixes the
characters that make up these two words. 説仏す (*setsu-butsu-su*) is
Dōgen's made-up word, meaning "preach Buddha," and 仏作す (*but-
susa-su*) is another made-up word, meaning "do Buddha." What a kid-
der that Dōgen was! The fact that Dōgen uses so many puns tells you a
lot about him and his philosophy, I think.*

As for the last section, the original instructions for chanting the
sutras are far more detailed than those I've given here. I mostly picked
out the parts that were interesting to me, like the stuff about snacks.
This section covers about four pages in some English translations. I've
spared you most of it. You can thank me later.

As intricately detailed as these instructions are, they're also a bit
hard to follow in certain particulars. Different translators solve these
problems in their own ways, as do different native speakers of Japanese. This is probably why every Soto temple I've been to does their
chanting ceremonies slightly differently. However, the general form is
always pretty much the same.

The most significant aspect of this section of the chapter for us
today is that it proves conclusively that group chanting was part of
the practice at the temples Dōgen founded. As I said in the first chapter, sometimes people read his disparaging sounding words about the
chanting of sutras being like the croaking of frogs and assume Dōgen
was against such practices. Yet here we see him setting out the forms for
group chanting in great detail as instructions for his own monks and for
those of future generations.

These days most temples that follow Dōgen's teachings include
some kind of group chanting ritual as part of their regular routine.
Gudo Nishijima was not very fond of these kinds of rituals because
in Japan they have become the most important aspect of temple practice and very few people actually do zazen. He sought to reverse that

---

* And so does my editor, who pointed that out.

by emphasizing zazen and minimizing chanting. Yet even he still did a few chanting things. We always did the regular meal chants during retreats, and we chanted a verse before and after each lecture. Later on, Nishijima started chanting the Heart Sutra regularly with the group at his Zen house in Chiba — I say "house" because it was hardly a temple, just a disused dormitory owned by the company he worked for.

Often Westerners are attracted to Zen because they believe it is completely devoid of anything they consider "religious." These folks are sometimes shocked and dismayed when they encounter ritualized group chanting in Zen temples. I was too, actually, when I first visited San Francisco Zen Center after years of sitting with Nishijima Roshi. They do a pretty extensive chanting service that I found very challenging.

Eventually, though, I learned to like it. I spent a few weeks at Tassajara, their monastery near Big Sur, and during those weeks I went from hating chanting to looking forward to it. I went back again every summer after that.

At first I thought that chanting was just a kind of bonding ritual. It makes a group of people feel more together somehow when you do that kind of thing. I've never really believed it had any mystical significance. I never believed, for instance, that our chants for the prevention of disaster really prevented any disasters. But I do think the togetherness the chanting inspired was a factor in mitigating the worst effects of some of the disasters Tassajara encountered, such as the huge forest fires that have nearly burned the place to the ground several times. Everyone there felt very connected and was therefore committed to helping each other and to helping save their monastery. The chanting and ritual practice played a role in that.

Also, I once read a book called *Lotus in the Fire: The Healing Power of Zen* by Jim Bedard. It's about how Mr. Bedard, a Zen practitioner, survived a very severe bout of cancer with the help of his practice. In that book he writes that while he was in a coma for several days, he was aware of his sangha members chanting for his recovery. While I take this with a grain of salt, it does make me wonder. Bedard is as skeptical of this sort of thing as I would be. Yet he says it really did happen, and who am I to doubt him? So maybe there is something to all that mystical nonsense after all.

If you're ambivalent about chanting the way I was, I'd suggest you try it sometime. It might feel uncomfortable. But you might also start to "learn in practice" — as Dōgen liked to say — what chanting is really all about.

26. DŌGEN'S ZEN
IN THE TWENTY-FIRST CENTURY

AND WITH THAT we come to the end of the first volume of this book. I hope your brain is not too stretched out.

I've gone through a lot of phases of understanding what Zen is. I've changed my mind a number of times. I've often even assumed that I was completely wrong about what Zen is, and that I only understood what it meant to me. In fact, sometimes I wasn't sure I even understood what it meant to me! I just did it.

Lately I've come to the tentative conclusion that what Zen means to me and what Zen actually *is* may not be two different things. No religion, philosophy, or practice will ever mean precisely the same thing even to two people who sit side by side in the same temple for decades, reciting the same verses together and espousing the same doctrines when asked what they believe. Even when two such people might say, for example, "Jesus Christ is the only begotten Son of God," if we probed a bit more deeply we would surely find that the two have different ideas about who Jesus was, who or what God is, what it means to be his "only begotten Son," and so forth.

To me Zen is a communal practice of individual deep inquiry. Let me try to explain what I mean by that. Throughout human history people have been concerned about the deeper meaning of existence. They wanted to understand who and what they actually were and how they fit into the world.

There are many ways to try to figure that stuff out. Some people study human biology and try to understand what they are in terms of the mechanics of the human body, or its evolution. Some people study psychology, trying to define the patterns of the human mind. Some people study by doing things. They write books or poems, or play music or sports. The list could go on, but I think you get my point.

Among those seekers, there is a certain class of people who try to understand the human condition by sitting very quietly and simply observing themselves in action (even sitting still for long periods is a kind of action; try it some time if you have any doubts). By the time the Buddha was born there was already a long tradition of this sort of inquiry in India. It existed elsewhere too, but India was the place where it was most fully developed first.

The Buddha had his great revelation after he split from the group of fellow meditators he'd been wandering with and meditated on his own. After he'd tried a number of meditation styles and found them lacking, he ended up with a group of five guys who'd gotten very deeply into ascetic practices. They were very hard on themselves, going for long stretches without food or shelter, wearing the most basic of clothing, or sometimes just walking around buck naked. The Buddha noticed that this level of austerity really didn't help anything and chose to start wearing clothes and eating decent meals again. This pissed off his companions, who labeled him a sellout and left him to fend for himself.

Our man Mr. Shakyamuni didn't let that stop him. He just kept on meditating, eating in moderation, sleeping in decent-enough places, and so on until he found something profound. After the Buddha had his great awakening he decided to tell those guys about it and maybe teach them how he'd come to the understanding he'd discovered. Although they were still suspicious of him, they chose to listen and they liked what they heard. Those five guys became the world's first "Buddhists," though they did not call themselves that. Everything that has come along since then in the realm of what we now call Buddhism is based on that series of events. I think we ought always to remember how it began.

Buddhism started not when Shakyamuni had his great revelation by himself. Lots of people had done that before. It began when he made his first efforts to transform that into a communal practice. Buddhism, then, is not something you do by yourself. A few years ago several people sent me emails asking for advice about doing solitary retreats. It's odd how this happens. Things like this seem to come in groups, and I never know why. Anyway, four or five people in the span of a month or two came to me with more or less the same questions about how to do solitary retreats.

I remember sort of scratching my head because I really had no idea. None of my teachers ever did that. Dōgen never wrote about it. I couldn't think of anything in the Zen tradition that addressed that question. That's when it occurred to me that this is a communal practice. Although you can — and I think you should — do zazen by yourself, that larger thing we call Zen Buddhism is not something you do by yourself. You can do zazen by yourself. You do Zen Buddhism with other people.

And yet Zen Buddhists have no doctrines and no belief system. That's kind of weird. Every church I've ever visited was all about doctrines and belief systems. As far as I'm aware pretty much all mosques and synagogues are too. The Hindu temples that I know of also spend a lot of time and energy making sure that everyone understands their doctrines and believes the same things. In fact, in many forms of Buddhism they do this too and are very concerned that all members share a common set of beliefs about the universe and can recite the basic doctrines of their form of Buddhism when asked.

But my teachers never cared if I believed what they believed. They never made any effort to get me to memorize any doctrines or creeds. Dōgen in his writings sometimes indicates what he believes about stuff, but he never insists his readers share his beliefs. Noticing this has led me to form a different sort of vision of what we're doing when we participate in this practice.

When we come together to sit on our cushions and stare at the walls, we don't look to anyone else to frame our experience for us. We don't, for example, do guided meditation sessions in which a leader tells us what to focus on or how to breathe. We are totally left to discover for ourselves whatever it is we might discover.

It's just as if we've climbed to the top of a mountain or entered a deep, solitary cave to get away from all distractions and focus on ourselves. But — and this is significant — we are *not* on the top of a mountain or deep in a cave all by ourselves. Instead, we're in a temple or a rented yoga studio or a house or wherever we've found to gather, and we're not alone; we are with a group of others who are similarly interested in this kind of deep inquiry into what it means to be human.

We don't try to impose what we find on each other. Even the person who leads the group does not try to impose what she or he has discovered on anyone else there. We regard every person's unique experience of themselves to be fully and equally valid. Shunryu Suzuki Roshi talked about "beginner's mind," saying that even the most inexperienced Zen practitioner's understanding was just as valid as that of the greatest master. It's different, to be sure. But that does not make it any less valid.

However, in order to establish a space that is somewhat like what one would find if one were to climb to the top of a mountain or enter a deep cave by herself, we have to set up some rules about how to conduct ourselves within the space we have chosen.

Very basically, we have to be quiet and respectful to each other so that everyone involved can get on with the business of studying themselves. In a way, it's like going to the library. People go to libraries to read, but they also go there because reading by yourself at home is kind of lonely and they want to read with other people. Even so, they want to *read*. They don't want to chat or listen to music or listen to you chatting or listening to music. They want to be together, but they want to be quiet.

That, to me, is the ultimate objective of any Zen space — to provide as adequate a place as possible for people to sit quietly together and look deeply into themselves. The people who come to such spaces, we can assume, come because they want two basic things. They want to search within themselves, and they want to do this with others.

One of the ways to do this is to enter a temple and become ordained as a monk. In *Shōbōgenzō*, Dōgen writes a lot about monastic rules. We looked at a couple of those chapters earlier in this book, like the one in which he tells his monks precisely how to clean up after taking a poop and the one in which he tells them how to wear their robes. A huge portion of Dōgen's writings are devoted to this kind of instruction. He was attempting to establish a place that created just the right atmosphere for individual inquiry.

Unlike any other religion I know of, the rules in Zen are strictly about how to conduct ourselves in the spaces in which we gather to work on ourselves. I'm not talking about the Buddhist precepts here, which also include good pieces of advice for how to conduct oneself in society. I'm talking about the specific regulations we come across.

To take what seems to be everyone's favorite example, let's look at the Buddhist ideas about sex. For many Christians, homosexuality is a sin. For Buddhists, at least in the Zen tradition, homosexuality is only addressed in terms of how homosexual *activities* can be disruptive in shared spaces where people come to do deep inquiry of themselves. There are no rules saying that you can't ever have gay sex. There are only rules saying that you can't have gay sex *while undergoing meditation training in a communal setting*, and only because sexual activity of any kind creates all sorts of weird noises and smells, and because it potentially sets up uncomfortable social interactions. Furthermore, it's not just homosexual sex that's disallowed in these settings; all types of sex are against the rules. However, once you leave that setting you can do whatever you like, within the bonds of secular law.

Every other rule that we establish in our communal places of individual deep inquiry is established for the same reason: to make sure everyone involved can focus on what we've all come together to focus on.

So, you may ask, what about chanting old poems, lists of dead people's names, and the rest? Where do those things fit in?

The historical reason we chant the Buddhist sutras is to honor our earliest ancestors in the practice. The first Buddhists didn't trust the written word to be a good carrier of their teachings. So for the first two hundred years or so, the Buddha's teachings were not written down; they were memorized. In order to do this, the monks gathered and recited Buddha's words. We still do that today, even though it's all also available in written form now. This is because we've found that chanting the words together helps us remember them better than just reading them by ourselves.

These activities also have a deeper purpose in helping to build a feeling of community. When people do activities together they feel more kinship with each other. When we chant we do other things like hit a wooden fish to keep time, burn incense, bow, and so forth. This active stuff, with all its movements and coordination, helps bond the group.

This is one of the reasons some people involved in Zen don't like to translate the sutras into English or whatever language they happen to speak. Even in Japan, they chant things like the Heart Sutra, *Enmei Juku Kanon Gyo*, and *Daihi Shin Darani* in very old forms of Japanese that are largely unintelligible to most people these days.

We also chant the names of dead people who were important to the history of Zen. We do this in order to further emphasize that our community is larger than the immediate group of people who happen to show up that day. It extends back thousands of years and will, we hope, extend into the future as well.

For that matter, the hierarchies present in Zen temples that people so struggle with in my country are also intended just to maintain the atmosphere necessary for practice. People get upset when some random guy at the library says *shush* to them, but if the librarian does it we understand that he or she is empowered to shush us. Same deal in a temple.

You may also take the further step of not just chanting with the monks but becoming one yourself. You become a monk because you think there's no better choice for you. No other reason could make any sense. You submit to the censure of other monks because you think it will help you stay on track in your aim to stay true to your commitment. You submit to the authority of your elders and of the temple because it helps you, and not for any other reason. If some among those elders start to actually believe they dominate you when really they serve you, that's their problem. There's no need to be concerned about that.

As groups grow, this gets more complex and jobs are more specialized. Still, I think we should always remember what the bottom line is. And to me, the bottom line is that we are trying to establish a space for personal inquiry.

An interesting thing happens when we do this together. Without ever getting indoctrinated into a common set of beliefs, we find that we start to align with each other, sort of like magnetized pieces of metal do when they're put together in the same space. You begin to discover that all human beings are very, very similar. You discover that your most fondly held belief systems are actually very superficial, no matter how deep they appear to be. You discover that what is truly important is shared with everyone and everything you encounter.

I think Dōgen understood this very clearly and tried to express it in his writing. He did not leave us a set of doctrines and beliefs he thought we should hold. Rather, he left us a body of writings that try to capture what is essential to all human beings, regardless of what they believe or where they come from or what their personal story might be. He asks us to focus on that instead of focusing on things of lesser value and importance.

For us in the twenty-first century, far removed in time and space from Dōgen's environment, this means we too need to work on finding what is truly valuable to us. To be a follower of Dōgen's style of Zen simply means to come together in this spirit and learn how best to allow each other the proper space to find it for ourselves.

BIBLIOGRAPHY

Complete English Translations of *Shōbōgenzō*
(in Order of Personal Preference)

Nishijima, Gudo, and Chodo Cross, *Master Dōgen's Shōbōgenzō*, 4 vols. Guildford, Eng.: Windbell, 2006 (now available as print on demand from Book Surge). This is the translation done by my ordaining teacher and his student Mike Cross (Chodo is his dharma name). It is the closest you'll find in English to a literal translation of the original. Also available for free online.

Tanahashi, Kazuaki, and the San Francisco Zen Center. *Treasury of the True Dharma Eye: Zen Master Dōgen's Shōbō Genzō*, 2 vols. Boston: Shambhala, 2013. Kaz Tanahashi translated *Shōbōgenzō*, with a group of teachers from San Francisco Zen Center acting as cotranslators. A different person worked on each chapter.

Nishiyama, Kosen, and John Stevens. *Shōbōgenzō: The Eye and Treasury of the True Law*, 4 vols. Tokyo: Japan Publications, 1983. This was the standard English edition for a long time but has since gone out of print and can be hard to find. It's more of a paraphrase than a translation but is closer to the original than this book.

Nearman, the Reverend Master Hubert. *Shōbōgenzō: The Treasure House of the Eye of the True Teaching*, 4 vols. Mount Shasta, CA: Shasta Abbey Press, 1996. This is the official edition used by Shasta Abbey, which was founded by Reverend Master Jiyu-Kinnett. It's a reliable translation if you can get past the author's habit of trying to make it sound like the King James Bible. Also available for free online.

Shōbōgenzō in Japanese

Nishijima, Wafu. *Gendaigo-yaku Shōbōgenzō,* 12 vols. Yokohama, Jap.: Kanazawa Bunko, 1978. This is Nishijima Roshi's complete translation of *Shōbōgenzō* into contemporary Japanese, which also contains the entire original thirteenth-century text, based on the 1815 edition compiled by Hangyo Kozen (which was reprinted in 1906, with previously missing chapters added). Wafu is the alternate pronunciation of Nishijima Roshi's given name, Kazuo, and is part of his dharma name. When writing in English he went by Gudo, the other part of his dharma name, meaning "the Way of Stupidity."

There are many other translations of *Shōbōgenzō* into modern Japanese, and the thirteenth-century text in Japanese is pretty easy to find too.

Partial Translations of *Shōbōgenzō*

Cleary, Thomas, trans. *Shōbōgenzō: Zen Essays by Dōgen.* Honolulu: University of Hawaii Press, 1992. Contains thirteen chapters of *Shōbōgenzō.*

Cook, Francis Dojun, with a foreword by Taizen Maezumi. *How to Raise an Ox: Zen Practice as Taught in Master Dōgen's Shōbōgenzō.* Somerville, MA: Wisdom Publications, 1999. Contains ten translated chapters of *Shōbōgenzō,* along with other material.

Soto Zen Text Translation Project. *Shōbōgenzō: Treasury of the True Dharma Eye.* Several translated chapters are available online from Stanford University.

Tanahashi, Kazuaki, ed. *Moon in a Dewdrop: Writings of Zen Master Dōgen.* New York: North Point Press, 1995.

———. *Enlightenment Unfolds: The Essential Teachings of Zen Master Dōgen.* Boston: Shambhala, 2000.

———. *The Essential Dōgen: Writings of the Great Zen Master.* Boston: Shambhala, 2013. The various chapters and excerpts from *Shōbōgenzō* in these books by Tanahashi were gathered into the complete translation listed above.

Waddell, Norman, and Masao Abe, trans. *The Heart of Dōgen's Shōbōgenzō.* Albany: State University of New York Press, 2002. Contains nine chapters.

Books about Dōgen and/or *Shōbōgenzō*

Bein, Steve. *Purifying Zen: Watsuji Tetsuro's Shamon Dōgen.* Honolulu: University of Hawaii Press, 2011.

Bielefeldt, Carl. *Dōgen's Manuals of Zen Meditation.* Berkeley and Los Angeles: University of California Press, 1990.

Bodiford, William. *Soto Zen in Medieval Japan.* Honolulu: University of Hawaii Press, 2008.

Bokusan, Nishiari, Shohaku Okumura, Shunryu Suzuki, and Mel Weitsman. *Dōgen's Genjo Koan: Three Commentaries*. Berkeley, CA: Counterpoint, 2013.

Cook, Francis. *Sounds of Valley Streams: Enlightenment in Dōgen's Zen*. Albany: State University of New York Press, 1989.

Heine, Steven. *Did Dōgen Go to China?: What He Wrote and When He Wrote It*. New York: Oxford University Press, 2006.

————. *Dōgen and Soto Zen*. New York: Oxford University Press, 2015.

————, ed. *Dōgen: Textual and Historical Studies*. New York: Oxford University Press, 2012.

Kim, Hee-Jin. *Eihei Dōgen: Mystical Realist*. Somerville, MA: Wisdom Publications, 2000.

Kodera, Takashi James. *Dōgen's Formative Years in China: An Historical Study and Annotated Translation of the Hōkyō-ki*. Boulder, CO: Routledge & Kegan Paul, 1980.

LeFleur, William R. *Dōgen Studies*. Honolulu: University of Hawaii Press, 1985.

Leighton, Taigen Dan. *Visions of Awakening Space and Time: Dōgen and the Lotus Sutra*. New York: Oxford University Press, 2007.

Nishijima, Gudo Wafu, trans. *Master Dōgen's Shinji Shobogenzo*. Guildford, Eng.: Windbell, 2003.

Okumura, Shohaku, ed. *Dōgen Zen and Its Relevance for Our Time*. San Francisco: Soto Zen Buddhism International Center, 2003.

————. *Realizing Genjokoan: The Key to Dogen's Shobogenzo*. Somerville, MA: Wisdom Publications, 2010.

————. *Living by Vow: A Practical Introduction to Eight Essential Zen Chants and Texts*. Somerville, MA: Wisdom Publications, 2012.

————, trans. *The Wholehearted Way: Translation of Eihei Dōgen's Bendowa, with Commentary by Kōshō Uchiyama Roshi*. North Clarendon, VT: Tuttle, 2011.

Suzuki, Shunryu. *Zen Mind, Beginner's Mind*. Boston: Shambhala, 2011.

Yokoi, Yuho. *Zen Master Dōgen: An Introduction with Selected Writings*. Boston: Weatherhill, 1976.

Special thanks to Charles Pokorny, whose many unpublished papers in the library at Tassajara proved to be very valuable in my research for this book.

ABOUT THE AUTHOR

BRAD WARNER WAS born in Ohio, grew up in Africa, and lived in Japan for eleven years, where he got ordained as a Zen monk. He now resides in the Hipsterville part of Los Angeles. He began sitting zazen when he was eighteen years old under the instruction of Tim McCarthy and was made a dharma heir of Gudo Nishijima Roshi in the futuristic year 2000. He used to work for a company that made movies about giant radioactive lizards eating Tokyo, and now he writes books like this one.

He also travels the world showing people how to sit down and shut up. He has given talks and led Zen meditation retreats in the United States, Canada, England, Scotland, Northern Ireland, Finland, the Netherlands, Germany, France, Poland, Israel, Belgium, Spain, and Japan. His books have been translated into fewer languages than those of anyone you've ever seen on the cover of a meditation magazine, but there are editions in Finnish, Polish, German, and Greek. And supposedly there's one in Hebrew, but he's never seen a copy. Or maybe he has but doesn't know it because he can't read Hebrew. He wishes someone would point it out to him somewhere if the book actually exists.

He plays bass guitar in the hardcore punk band Zero Defex (oDFx).* He has had major roles in several movies, including *Zombie Bounty Hunter M.D.* and *Shoplifting from American Apparel*. He also wrote, produced, and directed his own film, *Cleveland's Screaming*. Plus, he made five albums for Midnight Records under the semifictional band name Dimentia 13.

When he's not doing zazen, Brad can be found at record stores all over the world searching for obscure psychedelia and songs to add to his incredible cheesy seventies playlist. He enjoys bad science fiction movies and cats, though dogs are okay too. He's a vegetarian but tries not to be a total pain in the ass about it.

---

* Did you ever wonder where NOFX got their name? We were around well before them.